Critical Studies in Education and Culture Series

Weaving a Tapestry of Resistance: The Places, Power, and Poetry of a Sustainable Society
Sharon Sutton

Counselor Education for the Twenty-First Century
Susan J. Brotherton

Positioning Subjects: Psychoanalysis and Critical Educational Studies
Stephen Appel

Adult Students "At Risk": Culture Bias in Higher Education
Timothy William Quinnan

Education and the Postmodern Condition
Michael Peters, editor

Restructuring for Integrative Education: Multiple Perspectives, Multiple Contexts
Todd E. Jennings, editor

Postmodern Philosophical Critique and the Pursuit of Knowledge in Higher Education
Roger P. Mourad, Jr.

Naming the Multiple: Poststructuralism and Education
Michael Peters, editor

Literacy in the Library: Negotiating the Spaces Between Order and Desire
Mark Dressman

Thinking Again: Education After Postmodernism
Nigel Blake, Paul Smeyers, Richard Smith, and Paul Standish

Racial Categorization of Multiracial Children in Schools
Jane Ayers Chiong

bell hooks' Engaged Pedagogy: Education for Critical Consciousness
Namulundah Florence

WITTGENSTEIN

WITTGENSTEIN: PHILOSOPHY, POSTMODERNISM, PEDAGOGY

Michael Peters and James Marshall

Critical Studies in Education and Culture
Edited by Henry A. Giroux

BERGIN & GARVEY
Westport, Connecticut • London

Library of Congress Cataloging-in-Publication Data

Peters, Michael, 1948–
    Wittgenstein : philosophy, postmodernism, pedagogy / Michael
Peters and James Marshall.
        p.   cm. — (Critical studies in education and culture series,
ISSN 1064–8615)
    Includes bibliographical references and index.
    ISBN 0–89789–480–4 (alk. paper)
    1. Wittgenstein, Ludwig, 1889–1951. 2. Postmodernism.
3. Education—Philosophy. I. Marshall, James (James D.)
II. Title. III. Series.
B3376.W564P388   1999
192—dc21   98–19216

British Library Cataloguing in Publication Data is available.

Library of Congress Catalog Card Number: 98–19216
ISBN: 0–89789–480–4
ISSN: 1064–8615

First published in 1999

Bergin & Garvey, 88 Post Road West, Westport, CT 06881
An imprint of Greenwood Publishing Group, Inc.

Printed in the United States of America

The paper used in this book complies with the
Permanent Paper Standard issued by the National
Information Standards Organization (Z39.48–1984).

10 9 8 7 6 5 4 3 2 1

To Tina Besley and Bridget Marshall

Contents

Series Foreword

Educational reform has fallen upon hard times. The traditional assumption that schooling is fundamentally tied to the imperatives of citizenship designed to educate students to exercise civic leadership and public service has been eroded. The schools are now the key institution for producing professional, technically trained, credentialized workers for whom the demands of citizenship are subordinated to the vicissitudes of the marketplace and the commercial public sphere. Given the current corporate and right wing assault on public and higher education coupled with the emergence of a moral and political climate that has shifted to a new Social Darwinism, the issues which framed the democratic meaning, purpose, and use to which education might aspire have been displaced by more vocational and narrowly ideological considerations.

The war waged against the possibilities of an education wedded to the precepts of a real democracy is not merely ideological. Against the backdrop of reduced funding for public schooling, the call for privatization, vouchers, cultural uniformity, and choice, there are the often ignored larger social realities of material power and oppression. On the national level, there has been a vast resurgence of racism. This is evident in the passing of anti-immigration laws such as Proposition 187 in California, the dismantling of the welfare state, the demonization of black youth that is taking place in the popular media, and the remarkable attention provided by the media to forms of race talk that argue for the intellectual inferiority of blacks or dismiss calls for racial justice as simply a holdover from the "morally bankrupt" legacy of the 1960s.

Poverty is on the rise among children in the United States, with 20 percent of all children under the age of eighteen living below the poverty line. Unemployment is growing at an alarming rate for poor youth of color, especially in the urban centers. Although black youth are policed and disciplined in and out of the nation's schools, conservative and liberal educators define education through the ethically limp discourses of privatization, national standards, and global competitiveness.

Many writers in the critical education tradition have attempted to challenge the right wing fundamentalism behind educational and social reform in both the United States and abroad while simultaneously providing ethical signposts for a public discourse about education and democracy that is both prophetic and transformative. Eschewing traditional categories, a diverse number of critical theorists and educators have successfully exposed the political and ethical implications of the cynicism and despair that has become endemic to the discourse of schooling and civic life. In its place, such educators strive to provide a language of hope that inextricably links the struggle over schooling to understanding and transforming our present social and cultural dangers.

At the risk of overgeneralizing, both cultural studies theorists and critical educators have emphasized the importance of understanding theory as the grounded basis for "intervening into contexts and power . . . in order to enable people to act more strategically in ways that may change their context for the better."[1] Moreover, theorists in both fields have argued for the primacy of the political by calling for and struggling to produce critical public spaces, regardless of how fleeting they may be, in which "popular cultural resistance is explored as a form of political resistance."[2] Such writers have analyzed the challenges that teachers will have to face in redefining a new mission for education, one that is linked to honoring the experiences, concerns, and diverse histories and languages that give expression to the multiple narratives that engage and challenge the legacy of democracy.

Equally significant is the insight of recent critical educational work that connects the politics of difference with concrete strategies for addressing the crucial relationships between schooling and the economy, and citizenship and the politics of meaning in communities of multicultural, multiracial, and multilingual schools.

Critical Studies in Education and Culture attempts to address and demonstrate how scholars working in the fields of cultural studies and critical pedagogy might join together in a radical project and practice informed by theoretically rigorous discourses that affirm the critical but refuse the cynical, and establish hope as central to a critical pedagogical and political practice but eschew a romantic utopianism. Central to such a project is the issue of how pedagogy might provide cultural studies theorists and educators with an opportunity to engage pedagogical practices that are not only transdisciplinary, transgressive, and oppositional, but also connected to a wider project designed to further racial, economic, and political democracy.[3] By taking seriously the relations between culture and power, we further the possibilities of resistance, struggle, and change.

Critical Studies in Education and Culture is committed to publishing work that opens a narrative space that affirms the contextual and the specific while simultaneously recognizing the ways in which such spaces are shot through with issues of power. The series attempts to continue an important legacy of theoretical work in cultural studies in which related debates on pedagogy are understood and addressed within the larger context of social responsibility, civic courage, and the reconstruction of democratic public life. We must keep in mind Raymond Williams's insight that the "deepest impulse (informing cultural politics) is the desire to make learning part of the process of social change itself."[4] Education as a cultural pedagogical practice takes place across multiple sites, which include not only schools and universities but also the mass media, popular culture, and other public spheres, and signals how within diverse contexts, education makes us both subjects of and subject to relations of power.

This series challenges the current return to the primacy of market values and simultaneous retreat from politics so evident in the recent work of educational theorists, legislators, and policy analysts. Professional relegitimation in a troubled time seems to be the order of the day as an increasing number of academics both refuse to recognize public and higher education as critical public spheres and offer little or no resistance to the onging vocationalization of schooling, the continuing evisceration of the intellectual labor force, and the current assaults on the working poor, the elderly, and women and children.[5]

Emphasizing the centrality of politics, culture, and power, *Critical Studies in Education and Culture* will deal with pedagogical issues that contribute in imaginative and transformative ways to our understanding of how critical knowledge, democratic values, and social practices can provide a basis for teachers, students, and other cultural workers to redefine their role as engaged and public intellectuals. Each volume will attempt to rethink the relationship between language and experience, pedagogy and human agency, and ethics and social responsibility as part of a larger project for engaging and deepening the prospects of democratic schooling in a multiracial and multicultural society. *Critical Studies in Education and Culture* takes on the responsibility of witnessing and addressing the most pressing problems of public schooling and civic life, and engages culture as a crucial site and strategic force for productive social change.

Henry A. Giroux

NOTES

1. Lawrence Grossberg, "Toward a Genealogy of the State of Cultural Studies," in Cary Nelson and Dilip Parameshwar Gaonkar, eds., *Disciplinarity and Dissent in Cultural Studies* (New York: Routledge, 1996), p. 143.

2. David Bailey and Stuart Hall, "The Vertigo of Displacement," *Ten 8* 2:3 (1992), p. 19.

3. My notion of transdisciplinary comes from Mas'ud Zavarzadeh and Donald Morton, "Theory, Pedagogy, Politics: The Crisis of the 'Subject' in the Humanities," in Mas'ud Zavarzadeh and Donald Morton, eds., *Theory Pedagogy Politics: Texts for Change* (Urbana: University of Illinois Press), p. 10. At issue here is neither ignoring the boundaries of discipline-based knowledge nor simply fusing different disciplines, but creating theoretical paradigms, questions, and knowledge that cannot be taken up within the policed boundaries of the existing disciplines.

4. Raymond Williams, "Adult Education and Social Change," in *What I Came to Say* (London: Hutchinson-Radus, 1989), p. 158.

5. The term "professional relegitimation" comes from a personal correspondence with Professor Jeff Williams of East Carolina University.

Preface

Some books are much harder to write than others. This one has been particularly difficult to write because Ludwig Wittgenstein is a difficult philosopher and his writings are not straightforward or easy to understand. We have struggled, together and alone, over a considerable period to come to terms with Wittgenstein's philosophy. The date handwritten on the flyleaf of a copy of *Philosophical Investigations* indicates that one of us started reading this text in 1972. Consistently, over the next 25 or so years we have returned to his work. Over that period each of us independently completed work on the philosophy of Wittgenstein in relation to education. James Marshall has written and published on Wittgenstein in relation to his notion of rule-following, on Wittgenstein's views of mathematics, and on Wittgenstein's view of philosophy; Michael Peters has focused on contemporary interpretations of Wittgenstein by analytic, postanalytic, and poststructuralist philosophers.

Scholarship on Wittgenstein is painstaking. The secondary literature is intimidating in its depth and scope. In writing this book, at different times we felt that Wittgenstein was looking over our shoulders. It is impossible to study Wittgenstein and not be transformed by his writings.

The corpus of his writings — the sheer range of topics he covers and the different styles and philosophical genres he adopts — marks Wittgenstein (despite his own doubts) out as one of the most original philosophers of the twentieth century. To view Wittgenstein against the background of Viennese modernism and in relation to the writings of Schopenhauer, Nietzsche, and Freud is to establish a line of argument that recognizes the significance of the philosophy of the subject (or self) as a tradition in itself and in relation to educational theory. It is also to project an engagement of his thought with the movement of poststructuralism. These themes — these tours through Wittgensteinian country — are the substance of this book.

Acknowledgments

This study could never have been undertaken without the assistance and support of friends and colleagues. We acknowledge in particular the active encouragement and help of Nicholas Burbules (who coauthored Chapter 9) at the University of Illinois at Urbana-Champaign and Paul Smeyers at the University of Leuven. Marshall, in particular, thanks Smeyers for the invitation and his hospitality while he was a visiting scholar at the University of Leuven in the second half of 1997. Peters thanks Barry Hindess at the Research School of Social Sciences at the Australian National University for his kindness and support. Peters also acknowledges the encouragement of Henry Giroux, who has been both generous in his support and tolerant in the acceptance of difference. We also acknowledge our colleagues and students in Cultural and Policy Studies in Education, School of Education, University of Auckland for their encouragement and support. Finally, we thank the University of Auckland for granting us the study leave and for supporting us over the past few years in order that we might complete this book.

Introduction:
Wittgenstein and "After"

Philosophy hasn't made any progress? — If somebody scratches the spot where he has an itch, do we have to see some progress? Isn't it genuine scratching otherwise, or genuine itching? And can't this reaction to an irritation continue in the same way for a long time before a cure for the itching is discovered?

— Wittgenstein, 1980, pp. 86–87e

Ludwig Wittgenstein, the youngest of eight children, was born into a very wealthy family of Jewish extraction and he grew up in the rarefied intellectual milieu of *fin de siècle* Viennese modernism, where artists like Gustav Mahler and Gustav Klimt were regular visitors to the family mansion. In a note he records in 1931 he lists the influences upon his thinking as: Boltzman, Hertz, Schopenhauer, Frege, Russell, Kraus, Loos, Weininger, Spengler, Sraffa (Wittgenstein, 1980, 2:19e). From his Viennese background he inherited a strong skepticism toward traditional philosophy, an attitude of cultural pessimism, the importance of a critique of language and culture, an appreciation of Austrian music and poetry (Bruckner, Grillparzer, Labor, Lenau), his concern for style, a belief in the inexpressible (or mystical), a deep ethical and aesthestic sense, and an ascetic individualism.

The philosophical problems that Wittgenstein was later to pose were engendered in his early years in Vienna. If he initially sought solutions to these problems by studying with Bertrand Russell it would be false to see him as a student or follower of Russell and working on Russell's problems.

Wittgenstein's friend Paul Engelmann encourages us to see him as coming out of pre-World War I Vienna and its intellectual fervor in his *Memoir*. G. H. von Wright says that we must see him first as Viennese and second as an engineer (Janik & Toulmin, 1973, p. 29). In particular, it is very much mistaken to see him as a Cambridge philosopher.

In Vienna at that time there was a great preoccupation with language, not only in the writings of Karl Kraus but also with scientists, architects, writers, thinkers, artists, and musicians. What Kraus so eloquently attacked was: "a society in which all established media, or means of expression — from the language of politics across the board to the principles of architectural design — had seemingly lost touch with their intended 'messages', and had been robbed of all capacity to perform their proper functions" (Janik & Toulmin, 1973, p. 30).

There was little doubt that Wittgenstein was familiar with the ideas of Schopenhauer, Weininger, Kraus, and Freud as a teenager. Equally, there is little doubt that he was very much aware of the turbulent political, social, cultural, and intellectual life that was *fin de siècle* Vienna, where "Gay Vienna" obscured the political unrest, rapid economic change, and the emergence of Nazism, anti-Semitism, and racial problems of the dying Habsburg dynasty. The seeds of his later analysis of philosophical issues were well sown before he left Vienna to study in Berlin.

There he first studied engineering and later at the age of 19, aeronautics at Manchester. His thinking turned to philosophy of mathematics and on the advice of Frege, whom he met briefly in 1911, he went to study the foundations of logic and mathematics with Bertrand Russell at Cambridge. World War I interrupted his work with Russell. He served in the Austrian army and while a prisoner of war he completed his magnum opus, the *Tractatus* (1971), in which he thought that he had solved all of the problems of philosophy. From 1920 to 1926 he worked as a primary schoolteacher, returning to philosophical work under F. R. Ramsey's persuasion and making contact with members of the Vienna Circle, whom he indirectly influenced, before returning to Cambridge in 1929, where he succeeded G. E. Moore as professor of philosophy in 1939. It was during the period 1936 to 1948 that Wittgenstein composed the first part of *Philosophical Investigations* (1953), which was published posthumously. He resigned his chair in 1947, dying of cancer four years later. Wittgenstein's literary *Nachlass* comprises 78 manuscripts, 34 typescripts, and 8 dictations he made to colleagues or pupils. Much of his work has been published in edited collections posthumously. Wittgenstein is certainly one of the greatest philosophers of the twentieth century. His work in philosophy of language, philosophy of logic and mathematics, in philosophical psychology, and on the role of philosophy itself has not only shaped the trajectory of contemporary philosophy but also greatly influenced the intellectual culture of the twentieth century.

One thing that remained constant throughout Wittgenstein's philosophical trajectory was his preoccupation with the limits of language. Clearly his interest in language and with getting clear about language — with how it pictures in the *Tractatus* and with how it is used in the *Investigations* — can be traced to his early formative years in Vienna. Thus, if he is to study with Russell it is not to develop or further the logical work of Russell and the general logicist program but, more likely, to see how logical tools could set the limits for language, for what could be said. Certainly in his introduction to the *Tractatus* Russell saw Wittgenstein as undertaking the former — much to Wittgenstein's chagrin.

The *Tractatus* is comprised of seven major propositions, beginning "The world is all that is the case" and ending "What we cannot speak thereof we must remain silent," arranged in a numbered sequence with subpropositions in an elaborate structure that stylistically and architecturally reinforces and reflects its subject matter. It has the same austere beauty as the mansion Wittgenstein designed for his sister. The *Tractatus* analyzes the logical form of a proposition (or sentence), positing a picture theory of meaning according to which a fact-stating proposition represents the world (truly or falsely) by picturing or mirroring a state of affairs. There is a strict isomorphism between the structure of an atomic proposition and the structure of the state of affairs it depicts. All sentences that are not atomic propositions or truth-functional composites of atomic propositions are consigned to the realm of nonsense, that is, only fact-stating or scientific sentences can be true or false and are therefore meaningful. All other sentences (for example, those in ethics and aesthetics) are, strictly speaking, meaningless or nonsense, including those of the *Tractatus* itself, which Wittgenstein asserts can be shown but not said. In addition to the doctrine of logical form, the *Tractatus* has a mystical, romantic, and ethical side, strongly influenced by Schopenhauer (see Chapter 3). By plotting the limits of (scientific) language Wittgenstein is leaving room for ethics. In the latter part he devotes himself to questions of the I, the subject, the will (*"The limits of my language* mean the limits of my world," 5.6; "The subject does not belong to the world, but is rather a limit of the world," 5.632).

There were considerable problems associated with publishing the *Tractatus*. Wittgenstein needed Russell's introduction in order to publish in the end, but he was so concerned with how Russell had misunderstood the *Tractatus*, as being a continuation of the logicist program as opposed to being a prolegomenon to questions of ethics and aesthetics, that Wittgenstein almost stopped its publication. There seems little doubt that the events of the war, the misunderstandings of his philosophy by Russell and Frege, for example, and the publication problems over the *Tractatus* had scarred him.

Although Wittgenstein had formally given up philosophy after completing the *Tractatus*, in the ensuing period he continued to read philosophy-related works, including those of Freud, although not for the first time. His experience as a school teacher renewed his interest in how children learned language. It was during this period that he came to question his earlier logically pristine conception of language and, in particular, the underlying idea that names refer to objects and that the meaning of propositions is given by the configuration of objects. (From the mid-1930s Wittgenstein also renewed his interest in the foundations of mathematics.) The *Investigations* espouses, by contrast, a pragmatic view of language in which meaning is use and must be learned. Against his earlier view Wittgenstein maintains that there is no common logical form even for descriptive sentences: the fact is that there are many different kinds of sentences (orders, demands, questions, and so forth) that take their meaning from the everyday actions and social activities — "language-games" — comprising a culture or form of life. Language is learned by the child as she or he is initiated into a form of life: that is, it is learned practically. Running through the *Investigations* is also an attack upon Cartesian subjectivity conceived as a doctrine of inner sense and a foundation for language and an attack upon the idea that words have meaning by virtue of naming inner states and that the subject has privileged access to these states. Wittgenstein's famous private language argument indicates that inner states or experiences stand in need of external and public criteria.

Philosophy consists in assembling reminders rather than building a theory; its method is purely descriptive and, as a kind of therapy, it helps us to overcome our bewitchment by language. Wittgenstein's style reflects his interest in promoting a shift in understanding or solving grammatical puzzles (that reflect deep disquietudes in our cultural life): aphorism (after Lichtenberg, Schopenhauer, Nietzsche), metaphor, analogy, little sketches, and diagrams are part of his philosophical style.

Wittgenstein's attacks on academic philosophy were not well received by academic philosophers. If his general approach to philosophy was correct, that academic philosophy asked the wrong kind of questions which, in turn, led to mistaken philosophical theories, then it is hardly surprising that academic philosophers would be opposed to Wittgenstein because their whole raison d'être was under serious question.

PHILOSOPHY "AFTER" WITTGENSTEIN

There is no danger of philosophy's "coming to an end." Religion did not come to an end in the Enlightenment, nor painting in Impressionism. Even if the period from Plato to Nietzsche is encapsulated and "distanced" in the way Heidegger suggests, and even if twentieth-century philosophy comes to seem a stage of awkward transitional backing and filling (as sixteenth-century philosophy now seems to us), there will be something called "philosophy" on the other side of the transition.

— Rorty, 1980, p. 394

Is there life after death? After the intellectual demise of analytic philosophy — of logical positivism and linguistic philosophy — is there still life in the hereafter for philosophy and for philosophy of education? Our answer to this question is unequivocally in the affirmative, and we do not mean to construe our answer in terms of the trivial institutional sense that Rorty (1980, p. 393) grants when he writes "the need for teachers who have read the great dead philosophers is quite enough to insure that there will be philosophy departments as long as there are universities." Rorty's answer does not really impinge on the question of the future of philosophy or the philosopher in a Wittgensteinian sense.[1] He takes for granted the question of the unchanging nature of the university in the postmodern condition where the discourse of excellence is replacing the idea of culture as the organizing center of the story of liberal education.[2] Also, his answer is problematic in its institutional application to philosophy of education, which, as a separate and distinctive academic field within universities in the English-speaking world, has undoubtedly withered since its high point in the early 1970s.[3] Our answer is that there was always life in the sense of a manifold of possibilities; that such life was there from the beginning of the revolution in philosophy of education, dating from Wittgenstein's return to Cambridge, but that it was never seriously contemplated.

One critic, Joseph Margolis (1995), taking a biopsy of recent analytic philosophy, concludes that it is a muddle. Drawing upon the work of recent heirs of the analytic movement — Quine, Davidson, Kim, Rorty, and Churchland — he concludes that the movement can be reduced to three contemporary variants, which he calls naturalism, postmodernism, and physicalism. These variants comprise "the most salient strategies of current analytic philosophy" and together constitute "an explicit generic philosophical policy at the heart of the 'analytic' orientation" (p. 162). Such an enterprise, he suggests, is careless about its larger premises; it speaks only to its own cohort and ignores for the most part any sustained reference to philosophers who challenge its fundamental premises.

What is philosophically interesting about Margolis' claims is that Rorty, who purports to walk in Wittgenstein's shoes, is classified as a postmodernist and yet also is seen as an integral part of the analytic project, demonstrating its inherent weakness. Rorty is a philosopher who champions the "most extreme version of recent analytic 'naturalism,'" which leads to the ultimate repudiation of philosophy.[4] Margolis, in a roundabout way, denies (correctly in our opinion) that Rorty is Wittgensteinian.

Another author, Nicholas Capaldi (1993), who views analytic philosophy as the twentieth-century descendant and voice of the Enlightenment Project, defines it as a product of the doctrines of scientism, Aristotelianism, and an anti-agency view and he maintains its problems result from the interaction of these doctrines. Capaldi argues that neither the strategy of elimination (Russell, Quine) focusing upon syntax, nor the strategy of exploration (Carnap, Kripke, Chomsky, Fodor, Katz) focusing upon semantics, proved theoretically capable of developing a form of analysis that could unambiguously construe the relation of word to object. Forced to admit the role of agency, once it was realized that the question of the role and status of the user of language or the community of users could not be easily evaded, analytic philosophy of language or its successor came to treat the agent as an object of scientific scrutiny (that is, a structure or set of functions of the brain), thus, transforming itself into cognitive psychology.

Significantly, Capaldi (1993, p. 58) identifies a third view of the philosophy of language that does not form part of analytic philosophy: explication. Explication as a strategy focuses upon the pragmatics of language and is best typified, he says, by the Wittgenstein of the *Investigations*, by Heidegger, and by the tradition of pragmatism. Wittgenstein's *Investigations* stands as a repudiation of analytic philosophy. What distinguishes Wittgenstein's explication from Quinean elimination or Kripkean exploration is the belief that there is no theory or scientific background against which we can establish the word-object relation. From a Wittgensteinian view, language is learned as part of a community of practices, that is, it is "not a structure independent of the norms of the users, nor are the norms isolatable from the language" (Capaldi, 1993, p. 81). We take this analysis of Wittgenstein's position to be the reason why, for instance, Rorty (1991) champions the antirepresentationalism of Davidson and Putnam against the representationalism of Dummett, because from Dummett's viewpoint the work of the later Wittgenstein gave us no foundation for the future of analytic philosophy of language, no systematic theory of meaning, and, hence, nothing upon which to build.

What of ordinary language philosophy? On Capaldi's (1993) analysis, ordinary language philosophy originating with Moore's defense of common sense shared Russell's Aristotelian realism but rejected Russell's doctrinaire commitment to scientism and, therefore, also the eliminative strategy. The purpose of analysis was to clarify our common sense beliefs so that we could better understand our fundamental presuppositions on which everything else rested, including science. For Moore, committed to Aristotelian realism, our fundamental presuppositions were objective truths about the world. For Moore and those who followed him — Ryle, Strawson, and Austin — analysis consisted in an Aristotelian exploration of the pretheoretical background of our most basic presuppositions in ordinary language, and philosophical error occurred when we attempted to eliminate them in favor of some speculative hypothesis. Capaldi maintains that Wittgenstein could agree that philosophy is the clarification of presuppositions while insisting that such presuppositions cannot be objective truths about the world independent of human affairs, for the pretheoretical reflects a form of life and cultural action. For Wittgenstein, although the pretheoretical can be explicated, it cannot be conceptualized.

Capaldi (1993, p. 94) explains that *"In ordinary language philosophy, it is alleged that the pre-conceptual can be conceptualized through the exploration of the semantic structure of usage."* This realist commitment of ordinary language analysis as a kind of linguistic phenomenology in large part accounts for Ryle's (1949, p. 10) advertised procedure in *The Concept of Mind* "to determine the logical geography of concepts"; Strawson's (1959, p. 9) claim that "descriptive metaphysics" aims to "lay bare the most general features of our conceptual structure" — an unchanging "massive central core of human thinking" (p. 10); and, perhaps most appropriately, Austin's (1962, p. 3) assertion that a revolution in philosophy occurred, albeit in a piecemeal way, when it was shown "that many traditional philosophical perplexities have arisen through a mistake — the mistake of taking as straightforward statement of fact utterances which are *either* (in interesting non-grammatical ways) nonsensical *or else* intended as something quite different."

ENGLISH-SPEAKING PHILOSOPHY OF EDUCATION

There have been three ways at least of approaching philosophy of education prior to the alleged revolution in philosophy of education. In one approach students were encouraged as prospective educators to have a sound philosophy. Underlying this belief, although not necessarily articulated, can be seen the traditional view that philosophy is foundational for education, that in some way it was able to arbitrate upon questions of truth and values. This foundational position occurs also in the Western European approach to philosophy of education. Sometimes colleagues meant that students should be wise educators drawing upon sound principles to inform their educational practice in classrooms. At its worst this could degenerate into pretentious moralizing with tidbits for teachers. In a second approach, students were introduced to the ideas and works of the great educators; here, for example, they met *The Republic* and *The Emile.* Finally, and especially in the United States, there was a move toward teaching the "-isms" — sometimes called the comparative approach, whereby philosophy and philosophers were divided into types of theoretical position with recognizable theoretical names, such as real-ism, idealism, pragmatism, and the theoretical and practical implications for the practice of education then drawn.

Each approach carried within it the potential for a philosophically respectable approach to education. Yet, as practiced, they were virtually to disappear in the face of what has been called a revolution, and the emergence of a new paradigm of doing philosophy in education — analytic philosophy of education — or APE (as James Walker [1984] was to call it).

THE REVOLUTION IN PHILOSOPHY OF EDUCATION

Histories and critical accounts of philosophy of education have been marked by the historiographic codes of periods, revolutions, ruptures, and paradigms familiar to the history of philosophy proper. Most accounts, for instance, distinguish the earlier phase(s) of philosophy of education from the period, beginning in the late 1950s, when the so-called revolution in analytic philosophy began to shape the destiny of philosophy of education. With some variation these accounts tend to write the history of analytic philosophy of education (APE) in terms of both the revolution of analytic philosophy and APE's institutionalization and dominance in the English-speaking world as the London school, under R. S. Peters and others.[5] They also tend to provide accounts of APE in terms of ordinary language philosophy. This is certainly the considered judgment of both Robin Barrow (1994, p. 4442) and D. C. Phillips (1994, p. 4450), although Barrow cautions us against identifying analytic philosophy with a particular technique or with one of its more recent manifestations as linguistic philosophy and Phillips, in addition to acknowledging the dominance in the United Kingdom of the London school, mentions the work of Scheffler, Green, and McClellan as having "achieved virtual hegemony in the United States."

The revolution in philosophy of education is described succinctly by R. F. Dearden (1982), who was himself a prominent figure in the (British) revolution:

Throughout the 1950s, and in direct response to developments in general philoso-phy, a new conception of philosophy of education was slowly forming and find-ing sporadic expression. But all of this was very far from a state of affairs in which it would become natural to think of educational studies as divided into various disciplines, of which philosophy of education would be one. Yet by 1977, Mary Warnock could uncontroversially open her book *Schools of Thought* by saying that "it cannot any longer be seriously doubted that there is such a thing as the philos-ophy of education." (Dearden, 1982, p. 57)

In this brief paragraph Dearden explicitly characterizes the alleged revolution as being: a transition from a state of affairs in which philosophy of education's status as a legitimate area of study was in question; related to corresponding developments in general philosophy (the analytic and linguistic emphases); and a transition toward a state of affairs in which philosophy of education becomes a legitimate academic area of study (a discipline?). To these characteristics can be added: that philosophy of education was seen as foundational with respect to education, that is, that it was the arbiter or judge on such matters as truth, value, and meaning, and on the correct ways in which human behavior is to be explained.

Dearden concentrates on academic matters, as though analytic philosophy of education evolved on rational grounds, as a result of debate and resolution according to rational criteria. However, this would be to ignore the wider social, institutional, and educational pressures upon philosophy of education. This revolution must be sited in a much wider causal matrix. In the United States two key historical factors for the emergence of philosophy of education as an academic discipline were the formation of the John Dewey Society in 1935 and the Philosophy of Education Society in 1941. The former was established because of what was seen as the pending economic collapse of Western society and the need for a powerful and positive role for the institution of schooling in the reconstruction of American society. The latter was formed in response to the effect on schools of science, industrialization, and the changes in economic and political structures of the previous two decades. In Great Britain the opportunity was offered by the Robbins Report (1962), which made considerable recommendations for the extension of education and the improvement of teacher training. However, Robbins was a response to social pressures of the type already mentioned, of the post–World War II baby boom, and of the increasing demands for education. The London Institute of Education grasped this opportunity, offering courses and training in philosophy of education to meet the demands of the new Bachelor of Education Degrees that Robbins had recommended. At the same time it was to assume and exercise considerable power.

In this list of non-rational factors we must consider also the driving thrust of professionalism. Philosophy of education had to be seen to be an academic discipline capable of respect from colleagues, especially philosophers, and seen to have a coherent research program in which there were clearly identifiable major problems, methodologies for the resolution of problems, and some agreement as to the importance of problems and methodologies. The alleged revolution in philosophy of education should be seen and understood in part as an outcome of this drive for professionalism and not as a rational change, no matter how participants like Dearden saw their role.

This state of affairs did not necessarily require a revolution. Better trained personnel working on these undifferentiated states may well have made them more respectable academically, as in Western Europe. However, they may have remained as fragmented and as lacking a common unifying research program that could have aided professionalism. In the new post–World War II educational world education as an area of study and, thereby, philosophy of education had to be seen as very professional, and APE had the credentials for this political demand.

ANALYTIC PHILOSOPHY OF EDUCATION AND "AFTER"

Abraham Edel (1972, p. 133) was, perhaps, the first to draw attention to the central difficulty in APE construed as ordinary language philosophy— "how to judge what is a correct or adequate analysis": "Analytic philosophy was given a certain cast by the dogmas it inherited from logical positivism. There was a sharp separation of philosophical analysis from empirical inquiry, the sharp separation of the analytic from the normative, and the sharp separation of the analytic from genetic-causal accounts." His diagnosis led him to propose the integration of the empirical, genetic, and normative aspects, yet without fully contemplating what such an integration would do for a method of ordinary language analysis or whether anything resembling analysis in the ordinary language sense was still possible, having disposed of its fundamental assumptions. Some critics, such as R. J. Haack (1976), although not averse to analysis, similarly argued against the sharp distinction between philosophy (conceptual truths) and pedagogy (facts) and advocated a return to traditional philosophy of education. Others, such as David Aspin (1982, pp. 3–4), seeking to defend APE from Kevin Harris' influential attack upon APE as ideology, disputed the alleged hegemony of the London school: "It was never really true that Peters and Hirst were the be-all and end-all in the subject" and even if it was the case in the 1960s and early 1970s, he maintained (writing in the early 1980s), it was no longer true. Aspin goes on to describe both philosophically and sociologically changes that characterized the then complex and diverse nature of a contested philosophy of education.

Although it is probably true to say that Australian Marxism did not, by Kuhnian or sociological criteria, ever really attain the status of a paradigm in philosophy of education, it was to us as New Zealanders, the approach — best epitomized by the work of Kevin Harris (1979, 1980) — that demonstrated the ideological nature of APE.[6]

In all of this commentary and criticism it was seldom recognized that the London school or APE more broadly, although clearly based upon the revolution in philosophy associated with the development of ordinary language analysis, was connected to the thought of the later Wittgenstein in only a tenuous and even contradictory manner.[7] Certainly, R. S. Peters himself only sparingly referred to Wittgenstein directly and not always consistently or in an entirely positive manner. Our argument is that ordinary language philosophy and APE, insofar as they were based upon appeals to the authority of the later Wittgenstein, were, in fact, mistaken in principle and open to serious question on grounds of scholarship, method, and interpretation. Although philosophers who employed the method of conceptual analysis claimed Wittgenstein as their forefather, their interpretation of philosophy and of philosophical method was manifestly anti-Wittgensteinian. It was anti-Wittgensteinian because philosophy as conceptual analysis preserved those essential features from the analytic tradition: its position vis-à-vis other disciplines, its foundational second-order status, its neutral method, and its espoused autonomy. The status and method of philosophy, thus, were not greatly affected by replacing a search for atoms of meaning with a search for essences of meaning.

The work of the later Wittgenstein represents a break with the analytic tradition that is evidenced in Wittgenstein's rejection of both nominalism and the doctrine of external relations, and in Wittgenstein's view of philosophy as an activity — a pursuit separate from science, neither a second-order discipline nor foundational — that is uncharacterizable in terms of a distinctive method. Wittgenstein's liberation of grammar from logic, his rejection of any extra-linguistic justification for language and knowledge, and the semantic holism of the *Investigations* and *On Certainty*, simply collapse and render impossible the set of distinctions (for example, analytic/synthetic, scheme/content) upon which the legitimacy of analytic philosophy depends. For Wittgenstein there is no fundamental cleavage either between propositions that stand fast for us and those that do not, or between logical and empirical propositions. The whole enterprise of modern analytic philosophy rested on the fundamental "Kantian" duality between scheme and content. Rorty (1980, p. 169) has stressed the indispensability of the Kantian framework for modern analytic philosophy when he refers to the way distinctions between what is "given" and what is "added by the mind," or the distinction between the contingent and the necessary are required for a "rational reconstruction" of our knowledge.

Rather than view Wittgenstein solely as a place-holder in the analytic tradition, it is philosophically and historically instructive to position him in terms of his Viennese origins and the general Continental milieu that constituted his immediate intellectual and cultural background. Indeed, this rather obvious insight is, in large part, the basis for our cultural, historical, and literary readings of Wittgenstein and the significance of both the man and his work for education and pedagogy.

THE ORGANIZATION OF THIS BOOK

The subtitle of the book "Philosophy, Postmodernism, Pedagogy" is meant to convey the rough territory we traverse; yet we do so not as surveyors or cartographers but rather as fellow travellers (or even tourists) who walk down familiar streets, recognize famous landmarks, and sometimes get lost only to ask the way from passers-by or native inhabitants. Wittgenstein often talks of doing philosophy in these terms, showing a preference for spatial metaphors. In the preface to the *Investigations*, for instance, he talks of the way in which the natural order of his thought compelled him to travel over a wide field, criss-crossing it in every direction. Later in the *Investigations*, famously Wittgenstein remarks: "Our language can be seen as an ancient city: a maze of little streets and squares, of old and new houses, and of houses with additions from various periods; and this surrounded by a multitude of new boroughs with straight regular streets and uniform houses" (1953, #18).

Our investigations may be likened also to travelling and journey-making. These journeys are not organized group tours; sometimes they indicate a path that arrives at the same destination by a circuitous route rather than by a freeway; sometimes, also we like to get off the main route and spend time in a local township. The word missed from the title of the book is that of self or subject, which provides, so to speak, both the scale and the color key to our travel maps. The self or the subject is both the *philosopheme* and *problematique* that enables us to move from questions of philosophy to those of (post)modernism and pedagogy.

Chapter 1 takes up the suggestion from Terry Eagleton, the Marxist literary critic, that Wittgenstein is the first philosophical modernist. The chapter investigates the meaning of Eagleton's provocative assertion against the background of modernism and postmodernism, exploring Eagleton's work and, in particular, the script he provided for Derek Jarman's film, *Wittgenstein*. Eagleton (1993, p. 5) asks an interesting question in relation to Wittgenstein: "What is it about this man . . . which so fascinates the *artistic* imagination?" Eagleton's approach to Wittgenstein's writings provokes an aesthetic reponse that reveals a strong body of work inspired by Wittgenstein: work in poetry, music, literature, and criticism that somehow has remained separate and independent from the philosophical literature (except, perhaps, for the work of Stanley Cavell). This literary approach that views Wittgenstein in relation to modernism and postmodernism sheds a different perspective on him and his writings.

Viennese modernism, in particular, is the appropriate cultural context within which to understand Wittgenstein and his work. *Fin de siècle* Vienna is strongly influenced by both Schopenhauer and Nietzsche, and in Chapter 2 we show that Nietzsche's work was an influential part of the shared intellectual background against which Wittgenstein crystallized his own ideas. There is clear historical evidence that Wittgenstein read Nietzsche and that he grew up in the company of intellectuals strongly influenced by Nietzsche, including both Gustav Mahler and Gustav Klimt.

In the second part of Chapter 2 we discuss family resemblances between the writings of Wittgenstein and Nietzsche by focussing on two notions: the philosopher as cultural physician and the philosopher of the future. The former shapes Nietzsche's notion of the philosopher of the future whose central responsibility is the project of cultivation and education of humanity as a whole. However, cultural health is not achieved by treating the sick individual, and the malady cannot be cured by reason alone. The philosophers of the future, pace Wittgenstein, must employ all the cultural resources at their disposal to promote what they are capable of becoming. We argue that Wittgenstein ascribes to a similar romantic view of culture as a form of life — one that begins in doing (rather than thinking) — and must be judged in terms similar to the creation of a work of art. There are clear differences with Nietzsche, yet Wittgenstein sees himself as a philosopher of culture and philosophy as a kind of therapy.

In Chapter 3 we begin to look at the notion of the self or subject — a topic of immense philosophical interest recently (see, for example, the writings of Charles Taylor and Michel Foucault). There are a number of questions that can be posed around the notion of the self and these have a history. There are questions such as: what kind of being am I?, on what does my identity depend?, and to what does "I" refer? We will look at the first two questions as they have been posed by earlier philosophers (Descartes, Locke, and Hume) and briefly at more recent logicians (Frege, Russell, Johnson, and Tarski) before turning explicitly to the third question concerning the reference of "I" and the answers of Schopenhauer and Wittgenstein.

Influenced by Schopenhauer, as was Nietzsche and thereby Foucault, on the notion that the self was not an individuated substance, and that "I" did not refer to a substantive self, Wittgenstein does not, however, advance beyond a negative position on the self in his earlier writings. According to Sluga (1996b) for Wittgenstein either "I" referred to the body, which seems to be one interpretation of his comments on the "I," or it referred to nothing, which is the other interpretation. The critical question that we pursue in this chapter is the reference of "I."

Chapter 4 continues issues on the self in the later Wittgenstein, in the writings of Michel Foucault, and in Nietzsche. We also draw upon the work of Elizabeth Anscombe on the first person. The argument in this chapter is that Wittgenstein shifts his questions from "what" questions about the self and questions about the reference of "I" to questions about "how" we use "I" in everyday language, arguing that, similar to his approach to utterances like "I am in pain," Wittgenstein can be interpreted as using an expressivist approach to statements of identity of the form "I am Ludwig Wittgenstein." This is not to be analyzed as a contingent identity statement of the form "a = b," because "I" does not refer, and it is not a description or report of who the "I" is, but expresses identity, who this self or subject is.

We introduce Nietzsche here because he was initially indebted to Schopenhauer, was very influential upon Foucault, and resurrects the body, for example, in *Thus Spake Zarathustra* and *Beyond Good and Evil*. He also introduces the notions of a new philosophy that goes beyond good and evil and the new philosopher who, while grounded in the herd, and who must make sense of what he is saying to the herd, yet can transcend the herd mentality.

Michel Foucault began to pursue questions of the self vigorously from 1979, culminating in the final two volumes of *The History of Sexuality*. For Foucault the self is not an individuated substance, and "I," therefore, not a referring term, but instead a form. There may be several forms that the subject can take and these are said not always to be identical. His concern also is not with "what" questions but with "how" questions — How is the self constituted? and How can I reconstitute my self? In developing the ancient Greek maxim to "care for the self" and emphasizing its priority over "know thyself," Foucault is rejecting the pessimistic Schopenhauerean renunciation of the self and replacing it by a positive affirmation of the self in doing and acting. In such ways the self can take care of itself, according to Foucault.

In Chapters 3 and 4 we have introduced some of Wittgenstein's work on the philosophy of psychology, mainly in relation to first person statements that can be seen as expressions rather than descriptions and reports. In Chapter 5 we look in more detail at Wittgenstein's critique of psychology and his treatment of psychological words like "thinking" and "feeling." We need an outline of his general position on psychology in order to look at Freud. Although Freud claimed to be a psychoanalyst (and to have coined the term), Wittgenstein referred to him usually as a psychologist. We introduce Freud in the latter part of this chapter in preparation for Chapter 6.

Wittgenstein made contradictory remarks about Freud. Sometimes Wittgenstein praised him (although not often), but on other occasions he was dismissed for not being scientific and for advancing speculations in the name of hypotheses. Wittgenstein attempted to separate what was important in Freud, for example, the notion of therapy and the dream was a way of saying something important, from what was not important and merely another story: *une façon de parler*. As Wittgenstein concentrated upon Freud's (1932) analysis of dreams, we concentrate upon *The Interpretation of Dreams*.

First we identify in the *Interpretation* the bones of Freud's position on the analysis of dreams. Then we show how Wittgenstein's attacks on the scientific status of psychology (Chapter 5) are used against Freud. Psychoanalysis was not scientific according to Wittgenstein, and was conceptually confused over reasons and causes. Freud has merely offered a new myth, he says. He also criticizes Freud's view of dreams and offers himself a more positive account of dreaming, arguing that dreams are not repressions of abnormal behavior but are part of normal behavior and can be seen positively, as does Foucault. Freud was criticized for bringing the abnormal to the forefront of human affairs. In the next section of this chapter we generalize the notions of the normal and the abnormal from dreaming to madness, returning to Descartes' *Meditations* and his discussion there of dreaming and madness and his account of rationality. Here, alongside Wittgenstein, we introduce Foucault's approach to these notions.

Finally we take the notion that Freudian theory is just one more way of speaking or telling a story and see how it fits, for example, into writing novels. Our sources here are Thomas Mann and Simone de Beauvoir. Our conclusion is that psychoanalytic theory does not provide a new form of experience but is itself parasitic upon experience. This would seem to be the position of these two novelists and, of course, of Wittgenstein.

Chapter 7 takes us into the realm of nihilism and the end of metaphysics by considering the philosophy of both the later Wittgenstein and Jean-François Lyotard as philosophical responses to European nihilism and the end of metaphysics. Lyotard (1984) locates the problem of the legitimation of knowledge within the general context of the crisis of narratives. He defines postmodernism simply as "incredulity towards metanarratives" and maintains that the rule of consensus that governed Enlightenment narratives has broken down, dispersing the narrative function into many language elements. In one section of *The Postmodern Condition* that investigates the question of delegitimation, Lyotard combines Nietzsche's sense of European nihilism with Wittgenstein's language games in a way that sheds light on both how and what it might mean to philosophize at the close of the twentieth century. By delegitimation Lyotard means the disintegration of contemporary culture and society following the decline of the unifying and legitimating power of the grand narratives of speculation and emancipation. Wittgenstein's (1953) *Philosophical Investigations*, Lyotard argues, provides a way of philosophizing in face of this disintegration, which leads in new ethicopolitical directions and self-consciously to his own philosophy of the *differend* (Lyotard, 1988) as a philosophical response to European nihilism and cultural pessimism, an attempt to outline a kind of legitimation not based upon the performativity of the system as a whole.

Rorty has emerged as one of the foremost contemporary American philosophers. David Hollinger (1995) takes Rorty's position to be definitive of a kind of postethnic liberal politics he advocates for America; a paradigm epitomizing the shift from an ethnocentrism (in the mid-1980s) to developing a more inclusive notion of the *ethnos* in the 1990s. In Chapter 8 we trace the trajectory of Rorty's thought and examine his "postmodernist bourgeois liberalism" in terms of what he calls "the politics of the *ethnos*." We argue that Rorty's position, fortified by a reading of Wittgenstein, falls down in its approach to the question of other cultures exactly to the extent that it has deviated from a Wittgensteinian view. We also examine some of these points of tension or deviation to argue that Rorty's current position provides a dangerous description for liberal politics in the postmodern condition.

Chapter 9 was written with our friend and colleague Nicholas Burbules from the University of Illinois at Urbana-Champaign when he was on leave for a semester at the University of Auckland in 1996. Its purpose is to explore the importance of style to philosophy through a study of Wittgenstein's writings. We highlight the fact that the question of style remained an obsession of Wittgenstein's throughout his career, and we argue that it is inseparable from his practice of philosophy. Finally, we suggest, in terms more fully explored in Chapter 10, that Wittgenstein's style is, in a crucial sense, pedagogical. By this we mean that appreciating his style is essential to understanding the purpose and intent of his philosophy, especially his later philosophy. In the context of the culture of Viennese modernism, we interpret Wittgenstein's philosophical style as related to his double crisis of identity concerning his Jewish origins and his sexuality, both inseparable from his concern for ethics and aesthetics and from his personal life. We explore how these concerns are manifested in his work and his way of doing philosophy and, finally, we try to show how Wittgenstein's style may be seen as deeply pedagogical.

In Chapter 10 we again focus on Wittgenstein's styles as a way of legitimating both the importance of Wittgenstein the person and the significance of his (auto)biography in a way that analytic philosophers might find hard to accept. We argue that Wittgenstein's contribution to education is not as a philosopher who provides a method for analyzing educational concepts but rather as one who approaches philosophical questions from a pedagogical point of view, that is, Wittgenstein's style of doing philosophy is pedagogical. We argue that Wittgenstein's styles are essentially pedagogical and can be seen in the repertoire of non-argumentational discursive forms that are designed both to shift our thinking and to help us escape the picture that holds us captive. We argue that it is this notion of philosophy as pedagogy that is a characteristic feature of Wittgenstein's later thought.

The final chapter revisits earlier themes to provide in outline arguments for a pedagogy of self. Such a notion symbolizes a shift from a philosophy of self, with its search for unity and essences, for transcendental viewpoints or a priori grounds, to a pedagogy of self. The adoption of the term pedagogy is meant to indicate not only the extent to which formal educational institutions play a crucial role in the (post)modern world in shaping our subjectivities (and, therefore, must be the permanent object of critique) but also the complex ways in which we learn to become subjects or selves, thus, drawing attention to a continual process of becoming that might be advertised as pedagogical.

NOTES

1.   In this respect, Wittgenstein's (1980a, p. 61e) remark speaks loudly: "Am *I* the only one who cannot found a school or can a philosopher never do this? I cannot found a school because I do not really want to be imitated. Not at any rate by those who publish articles in philosophical journals."

2.   See Readings' (1995b) excellent essay "The University without Culture?" and his related earlier essays "From Emancipation to Obligation: Sketch for a Heteronomous Politics of Education" and "For a Heteronomous Cultural Politics: The University, Culture, and the State" (Readings, 1993b, 1995a). See also essays by Peters (1989; 1992).

3.   D. C. Phillips (1994, p. 4455) regards the situation in the 1990s as "complex, and relatively healthy" in the sense that "philosophers are working with a variety of approaches, in a variety of fields and the discipline is marked by an eclecticism perhaps unrivaled in previous periods." This postmodern eclecticism in philosophy of education after Wittgenstein, perhaps, reflects a new understanding that "a universal rule of judgement between heterogeneous genres is lacking in general," to use Lyotard's (1988, p. xi) expression.

4.   Margolis (1995, p. 177) characterizes Rorty's position in terms of: "True" has no explanatory uses. We understand all there is to know about the relation of beliefs to the world when we understand their causal relations with the world; our knowledge of how to apply terms such as "about" and "true of" is fall-out from a naturalistic account of linguistic behavior. There are no relations of being made true that hold between beliefs and the world. There is no point to debates between realism and antirealism, because such debates presuppose the empty and misleading idea of beliefs being made true.

5.   Maloney (1985) is unusual in this respect. Although she categorizes philosophy of education in the United States in terms of periods — comparative, 1942–53; transitional, 1954–57; analytic, 1958–67; prospective, 1968–82 — she does not acknowledge the influence of the London school in the United States.

6.   Harris acknowledges his concerns over the troubling notion of ideology and attempts to deal with these in Harris (1982). See also Jim Walker's (1984) "The Evolution of the APE: Analytic Philosophy of Education in Retrospect" and the local historiographic war that broke out between James Kaminsky (1986, 1988a, 1988b) and Kevin Harris (1988). See also Kaminsky (1993).

7.   The exceptions to this generalization are: Gilroy (1982, p. 79), who makes plain that Wittgenstein in rejecting reductive analysis rejected also both conceptual analysis and linguistic analysis per se; Marshall (1985), who disputes the Wittgensteinian interpretation of human behavior as rule-governed, which is adopted by R. S. Peters (among others) to underwrite the analysis of concept of authority (and discipline); and Rizvi (1987, p. 34), who in a pivotal paper first tracks out the espoused indebtedness of analytic philosophers of education to the work of the later Wittgenstein and, second, shows how "Wittgenstein's anti-essentialism would seem to render the philosophical suppositions of conceptual analysis without any theoretical justification." Marshall (1987) in a later publication spells out an alternative to APE by reference to the philosophy of the later Wittgenstein.

1

Terry Eagleton: Wittgenstein as Philosophical Modernist (and Postmodernist)

> Philosophy is merely what binds us to the fact that everything is just the way it is. Everything is open to view, nothing is concealed. No ground, no essences, no first principles (p. 18).
>
> "We search for what's hidden," Wittgenstein went on, "dupes that we are of a dream of depth. Anything to avoid the unbearable presence of reality. If we could register that for one moment in our mind we'd be free. Or perhaps we would go mad" (pp. 20–21).
>
> Wittgenstein spoke up suddenly in his high voice, startling Bloom a little. "You speak of languages as though they were garments to be put on and off at will. There are limits to such cosmopolitanism. In the end, we speak as we do because of *what* we do. *Wenn ein Löwe sprechen könnte, würden wir ihn nicht verstehen*" [If a lion could speak, we would not be able to understand him] (p. 132).
>
> — Eagleton, 1987

Why begin a book on Wittgenstein with a chapter discussing Terry Eagleton's interpretation? Eagleton is not exactly a Wittgensteinian scholar; he is more a literary critic than a philosopher and his interests as an academic Marxist hardly qualify him as one who might approach Wittgenstein in sympathetic terms. The answer is bound up with the approach and style of this book; an emphasis on literary, cultural, and (auto)biographical readings of Wittgenstein's works, their intertextuality, the expression of the spirit of European (Viennese) modernism in the *Tractatus,* and the anticipation of certain postmodern themes in his later works which, on the one hand, cast him in close philosophical proximity to Schopenhauer,

Nietzsche, and Heidegger and, on the other, project his writings into an interesting engagement with poststructuralist thought. This chapter begins with a discussion of Eagleton's script for the film by Derek Jarman, *Wittgenstein*. It examines Eagleton's thesis that Wittgenstein is the first philosophical modernist — that the true coordinates for Wittgenstein's writings are Joyce, Picasso, and Schönberg, rather than Frege, Russell, and logical empiricism. In the second part of the chapter, we follow Eagleton (1982) in viewing Wittgenstein's later works as displaying deep affinities with poststructuralist thought and with a body of thought that shaped poststructuralism.

WITTGENSTEIN AS MODERNIST PHILOSOPHER

Colin MacCabe (1993, p. 1), in the Preface to *Wittgenstein* observing the changes that Jarman and Ken Butler brought to the original Eagleton screenplay of *Wittgenstein*, suggests: "Eagleton sees the substitution of a figure of English eccentricity for his European philosophical modernist." Indeed, Wittgenstein as philosophical modernist — perhaps the last (rather than the first) great European philosophical modernist — is the major theme that runs through Eagleton's "Introduction to Wittgenstein." Eagleton (1993, p. 5) begins his introduction by drawing our attention to the impact that Wittgenstein has had upon contemporary artists. He asks "What is it about this man . . . which so fascinates the *artistic* imagination?" As he says: "Frege is a philosopher's philosopher, Bertrand Russell every shopkeeper's image of the sage, and Sartre the media's idea of an intellectual; but Wittgenstein is the philosopher of poets and composers, playwrights and novelists, and snatches of his mighty *Tractatus* have even been set to music." If Eagleton is unkind to Russell (and to shopkeepers), he is certainly correct about Wittgenstein — at least the Wittgenstein of the *Tractatus*. In the period since Wittgenstein's death at 62, on April 28, 1951 — less than 50 years ago — there has been a burgeoning of artistic and fictional works about him or inspired by him, the Jarman-Eagleton film and script *Wittgenstein* being only one of the the latest contributions.

Indeed, soon after his death Wittgenstein became a fictional character in Iris Murdoch's *Under the Net* (1957). This was followed by a stream of fictions and poetry written as Wittgensteiniana, to use Charles Bernstein's (1990) word. Bernstein lists among his examples Bruce Duffy's novel *The World As I Found It* and a range of poetic works: Alan Davies's *Signage*, Steve McCaffery's *Evoba*, Tom Mandel's *Realism*, Ron Silliman's "The Chinese Notebook" in *The Age of Huts*, Keith Waldrop's *Water Marks*, and Rosmarie Waldrop's *The Reproduction of Profiles*. In relation to Bernstein's list, Marjorie Perloff (1992, p. 193) remarks:

But these are only a handful of works recently written under the sign of Wittgenstein. From novels like Ingeborg Bachmann's *Malina* (1971, English translation 1990), Thomas Bernhard's *Wittgenstein's Nephew* (1986), and Terry Eagleton's *Saints and Scholars* (1988), to poetry collections like Michael Palmer's *Notes for Echo Lake* (1981), Joan Reallack's *Circumstantial Evidence* (1985), Jan Zwicky's *Wittgenstein Elegies* (1986), and Charles Bernstein's own *The Sophist* (1987), to performance pieces like David Antin's "The Idea of Poetry and the Poetry of Ideas" (1985), John Cage's Charles Eliot Norton Lectures *I-VI* (1989), and Laurie Anderson's "Language is a Virus from Outer Space" (1985), to artist's books like Johanna Drucker's *Through Light and the Alphabet* (1986) and hybrid critical/poetic texts like Guy Davenport's *Geography of the Imagination* (1981) and Louis Zukofsky's *Bottom* (1963, but out of print until 1987), poems and fictions have declared themselves as manifestly Wittgensteinian.

Perloff (1992, 1996) is perhaps too quick to proclaim a Wittgensteinian poetics or at least to proclaim it at the expense of other aspects of Wittgenstein's work. In addition to the works that Perloff cites, we could add musical works inspired by him or based upon his work (for example, Elizabeth Luyten's motet based upon the *Tractatus*), or readings of Wittgenstein's architecture (Wijdeveld, 1994). We might also add artists (in the sense of visual arts) per se.

Joseph Kosuth curated an exhibition called "The Play of the Unsayable: Wittgenstein and the Art of the Twentieth-Century," first shown in Vienna on the centenary of Wittgenstein's birth (at the Wiener Secession, September 13–October 29, 1989) and later, in an expanded version in Brussels (at the Palais des Beaux-Arts de Bruxelles, December 17, 1989–January 28, 1990), and at the Brooklyn Museum. The exhibition assembled the works of contemporary artists and photographers,[1] noting family resemblances or morphological similarities among them, using large chunks of text from Wittgenstein (along with excerpts from Derrida, Kristeva, Barthes, Foucault, Englemann, and others) to frame the exhibition or installation and to raise afresh the question concerning the collective concept of what we call art.

Wittgenstein's significance and impact on contemporary visual arts is not restricted to the movement known as conceptual art as practiced by Kosuth; indeed, his work has been of considerable importance to the Art & Language group, centering around the British artists Terry Atkinson (whose early writing drew upon a combination of Wittgenstein and Trotsky), David Bainbridge, Michael Baldwin, and Harold Hurrell. Perloff's Wittgensteinian poetics, insightful as it is, tends to obscure and minimize the other perspectives, aesthetic and otherwise, from which one can choose to view Wittgenstein's works: Wittgenstein once said (in a tone of high seriousness) he would like to write a book of philosophy composed entirely of jokes.

Ray Monk (1991, p. xvii) begins his brilliant biography also by noting that "Ludwig Wittgenstein exerts a very special fascination that is not wholly explained by the enormous influence he has had on the development of philosophy this century."[2] He explains that there is a gulf "between those who study his work in isolation from his life and those who find his life fascinating but his work unintelligible." What the many introductions to his work do not explain, Monk (1991, p. xviii) argues, is "what his work has to do with *him* — what the connections are between the spiritual and ethical preoccupations that dominate his life, and the seemingly remote philosophical questions that dominate his work." His aim is to rectify this situation by "describing the life and work in one narrative" and to show "the unity of his philosophical concerns with his emotional and spiritual life." The narrative that Monk tells provides a kind of dramatization of his philosophy, bringing it to life.[3]

Certainly, as evidenced by the range of works cited, Eagleton's opening assertion is not far off the mark: Wittgenstein has fascinated and excited the artistic imagination in a way few philosophers have. Why? Eagleton (1993, p. 1) acknowledges the personal mythology surrounding the man, even in his own lifetime, and the "fairy tale quality about his rags-to-riches career" that tends to "lend itself easily to literary or dramatic representation." However, he suggests, there is something more than the personal legend with its depth of anguish and self-reflection that accounts for Wittgenstein's artistic significance. There is a clear set of connections that mark out the *Tractatus* as the exemplar, in the philosophical realm, of a modernist work of art that locates it squarely within the coordinates of cultural modernity.

Eagleton (1993, p. 5) comments:

The *Tractatus*, one might claim, is the first great work of philosophical modernism — not a theoretical reflection on that avant-garde cultural experiment, but an example of it in its own right, the point where the modernist impulse migrates out of film and poetry and sculpture and comes to occupy philosophy itself from the inside. Its true coordinates are not Frege or Russell or logical positivism but Joyce, Schönberg, Picasso. Like many a modernist work of art, the *Tractatus* secretes a self-destruct device within itself: he who understands these propositions, Wittgenstein remarks abruptly at its conclusion, will recognise that they are nonsense. For the *Tractatus*, absurdly, strives to articulate what it itself has placed under the censorship of silence — the relation of language to the world.

The doctrine of showing and saying, as Wittgenstein says in the preface to the *Tractatus* — of drawing a limit to the expression of thought — is central to Eagleton's reading of Wittgenstein as modernist. The ladder-like propositions of the *Tractatus* perform an impossible task of manifesting the structure of language and its relation to the structure of reality. The same modernist irony that characterizes the self-undercutting and self-canceling gesture of the *Tractatus*, Eagleton maintains, is to be found in modernist art as a whole: the attempt to express the inexpressible. Wittgenstein says, "There are, indeed, things that cannot be put into words. They *make themselves manifest*. They are what is mystical" (Wittgenstein, 1971, 6.522). The *Tractatus* repeats the modernist refrain typical of "the great experimental art of the early twentieth century": the world is all that is the case, but its value and meaning lie elsewhere ("It is not *how* things are in the world that is mystical, but *that* it exists" [6.44].) The *Tractatus* as a modernist work displays the same obsessive self-reflection on its own form and medium that characterizes modernism as a movement: "the *Tractatus* is the place where philosophy begins to bend back on itself and interrogate its own medium, which is of course language itself" (Eagleton, 1993, p. 7).

Clement Greenberg defined modernism as the historical tendency of an art practice toward complete self-referential autonomy. He writes in the now famous essay on modernist painting:

I identify Modernism with the intensification, almost the exacerbation, of this self-critical tendency that began with the philosopher Kant. Because he was the first to criticise the means itself of criticism, I conceive of Kant as the first real Modernist. The essence of Modernism lies, as I see it, in the use of the characteristic methods of a discipline to criticise itself — not in order to subvert it, but to entrench it more firmly in its area of competence. Kant used logic to establish the limits of logic, and while he withdrew much from its old jurisdiction, logic was left in all the more secure possession of what remained to it. (Greenberg, 1973, p. 66)

A reading of Wittgenstein's *Tractatus* in terms of Greenberg's definition seems to lend weight to Eagleton's thesis. The *Tractatus* is certainly about the limiting conditions of philosophy, of language and its power to represent the world. In this Kantian sense Wittgenstein is a philosophical modernist but coming after Kant he is not the first. Eagleton's claim is that Wittgenstein is the first philosophical modernist in the sense that he artistically demonstrates such limits. Wittgenstein does not simply "criticise the means of criticism," he shows his readers the central significance of such limits in the ladder-like propositions of the *Tractatus*. In this sense, then, he is considered by Eagleton to be the first philosophical modernist.

M. H. Abrams (1981) suggests that modernism involves a self-conscious and radical break with the traditional bases of Western culture and Western art and that the precursors of this break are artists and thinkers who questioned our cultural certainties, including Western conceptions of the human self. Calinescu (1987, p. 3) also suggests that the term "modernism" is "to convey an increasingly sharp sense of historical relativism. This relativism is in itself a form of criticism of tradition." Tradition is illegitimate; it can no longer offer examples to imitate.

Modernism is symbolic of that huge cultural shift from "a time-honoured aesthetics of permanence, based on a belief in an unchanging and transcendent ideal of beauty, to an aesthetics of transitoriness and immanence, whose central values are change and novelty" (p. 3). The nature of modernism centers around the notion of the autonomy of art: the "idea that the core of modernism is the reflective examination of the nature of the artistic medium, with purity as an ideal" (p. 3). Eagleton (1986, p. 139) himself expresses a similar thought this way:

A sense of one's particular historical conjuncture as being somehow peculiarly pregnant with crisis and change. . . . A portentous, confused yet curiously heightened self-consciousness of one's own historical moment, at once self-doubting and self-congratulatory, anxious and triumphalistic together. . . . At one and the same time an arresting and denial of history in the violent shock of the immediate present, from which vantage point all previous developments may be complacently consigned to the ashcan of "tradition."

There are clear echoes of this description of modernism in Wittgenstein's self-conscious break with traditional philosophy and ways of doing it. As he says in the preface: "the *truth* of the thoughts that are here communicated seems to me unassailable and definitive. I therefore believe myself to have found, on all essential points, the final solution of the problems." The *Tractatus* is like a temple, beautiful in its logical austerity, that shelters the nonsensical and deep contradictions of philosophy and the truths of language in relation to the world, at the same time making room for ethics and asethetics, as falling outside the domain of fact-stating discourse.

Eagleton's insights have their performative extension in the work of conceptual artists like Joseph Kosuth who utilizes Wittgenstein to articulate "art after philosophy."[4] As an American experimental artist in the mid-1960s Kosuth was influential in establishing conceptual art. He cited the "ready-mades" of Marcel Duchamp as constituting the dramatic shift from appearance to concept and, therefore, the beginning of modern art and he enunciated the formal principle that the work of art is a tautology, implying that artistic activities are self-verifying. For Kosuth the desire to understand cultural formation and, in particular, art in relation to language is the basis to operationalize a Wittgensteinian insight: the production of a language whose function it is to show rather than say. "Art, it can be argued, *describes* reality. But, unlike language, artworks — it can also be argued — simultaneously describe *how* they describe it. Granted, art can be seen here as self-referential, but importantly, not *meaninglessly* self-referential. What art shows in such a manifestation is, indeed, *how* it functions" (Kosuth, 1991, p. 247).

Wittgenstein's *Tractatus* can be understood in terms of the aesthetic concept of modernity with its roots in Romanticism and its rejection of bourgeois modernity based upon a confident belief in progress, science, and technology. In this sense, Wittgenstein's doctrine of saying and show-ing is one of the central modernist devices to the resolution of thinking the unthought and expressing the inexpressible. Such a view coheres with the ultimate principle of aesthetic modernity: the attempt "to present the unpresentable," as Jean-François Lyotard (1984) argues, basing his argu-ment on an analysis of the Kantian sublime (see also Lyotard, 1993).

Lyotard's view here is worthy of further consideration, because he provides an interpretation of Wittgenstein's later work in relation both to (post)modernism and to Nietzsche and the question of European nihilism. Although we deal with these themes more fully in Chapters 2 and 5, it is important to foreshadow them briefly here also, because they impinge upon Greenberg's definition and give the question of modernism a different kind of Kantian twist. Lyotard sets up the discussion in terms of Habermas's assertion that if modernity has failed, it has done so by allowing culture as the totality of life to become splintered into narrow and separate specialities that are the province of experts. In other words, culture has become separated from the problems of existence. Only when aesthetic experience no longer issues judgments of taste, when it is no longer part of the language game of aesthetic criticism but takes part in cognitive processes and normative orientations, is there the prospect of a re-integration of culture. In short, Habermas looks to the arts to provide the basis for a unity of experience, bridging the gap between the cogni-tive, the ethical, and the political. Yet Lyotard inquires as to the sort of unity Habermas has in mind: "Is the aim of the project of modernity the constitution of sociocultural unity within which all the elements of daily life and of thought take their places as in an organic whole? Or does the passage that has to be charted between heterogeneous language games — those of cognition, of ethics, of politics — belong to a different order from that?" (Lyotard, 1984, pp. 72–73). The first option, which Lyotard identi-fies with Hegel (and Habermas), does not challenge the notion of a dialec-tically totalizing experience; the second, he suggests, approximates Kant's *Critique of Judgment*, "but must be submitted . . . to that severe reexamina-tion which postmodernity imposes on the thought of the Enlightenment, on the idea of a unitary end of history and of the subject" (p. 73). Both Wittgenstein and Adorno, Lyotard argues, were the first to initiate this critique.

Lyotard uses the term "delegitimation" to explain the result of the splintering of culture into different language games or discourses; there is no universal metalanguage that can knit together the diverse and prolifer-ating threads of discourse into one transparent language. Science plays its own game and is incapable of legitimating itself, let alone all other language games. This disintegration of culture and, above all, of the impossibility of legitimation of knowledge through a metalanguage, is what Lyotard dubs one of Nietzsche's primary concerns in his investigation of the question of European nihilism. As he argues, *fin de siècle* Vienna was weaned on the pessimism accompanying this cultural disintegration. Artists and philosophers — Musil, Kraus, Hofmannsthal, Loos, Schönberg, Broch, Wittgenstein, and Mach — "carried awareness of and theoretical and artistic responsibility for delegitimation as far as it could be taken" (Lyotard, 1984, p. 41). Wittgenstein's strength was that he did not succumb to the logical empiricism developed by the Vienna Circle, but "oulined in his investigation of language games a kind of legitimation not based on performativity" (p. 41). Wittgenstein's later philosophy, then, is seen as providing a positive response to the question of European nihilism; a way forward. There is no overarching metalanguage or master narrative into which the competing claims of different discourses can be mediated and resolved; the linguistic turn provides no meta-resolution. There are only language games, in the plural, each with its body of irreducible rules, and although there are family resemblances — a notion that smacks of genealogy and suggests unity in diversity — these are purely contingent, cultural links. Legitimation can only spring from our own linguistic practices.

Lyotard (1984, p. 77) detects in the Kantian sublime an earlier modulation of Nietzschean perspectivism and "it is in the aesthetic of the sublime that modern art (including literature) finds its impetus and the logic of avant-gardes finds its maxims." In the *Critique of Judgment* Kant (1987) attempts to determine what justification is possible for aesethetic judgments or judgments of taste (that is, judgments about the beautiful in nature and in art). The central difficulty is how is it possible to judge something as beautiful on the basis of a feeling of pleasure (that is, something very subjective) and yet still demand universal assent? Lyotard explains that Kant answers this question within the tradition of the subject he uncritically inherits from St. Augustine and Descartes. The subject possesses different faculties: a faculty to conceive and a faculty to present. "Knowledge exists if, first, the statement is intelligible, and second, if 'cases' can be derived from the experience which 'corresponds' to it. Beauty exists if a certain 'case' (the work of art), given first by the sensibility without conceptual determination, the sentiment of pleasure independent of any interest the work may elicit, appeals to the principle of a universal consensus (which may never be attained)" (Lyotard, 1984, p. 77). Judgments of taste involve an agreement between the capacity to conceive and the capacity to present an object corresponding to the concept. This agreement is made without rules, giving rise to what Kant calls a reflective judgment, which may be experienced as pleasure.

The sublime, on the contrary, is a different sentiment entirely. It occurs "when the imagination fails to present an object which might, if only in prinicple, come to match a concept" (Lyotard, 1984, p. 78). The idea of the world as "the totality of what is" and the idea of the simple as that which cannot be broken down further, are ideas of which no presentation is possible; they are unpresentable. Lyotard suggests that modern art is the attempt to present the unpresentable. Wittgenstein's *Tractatus* conforms to Lyotard's definition precisely. He attempts to present the unpresentable, both the idea of the world as the totality (of facts) and the idea of the simple, upon which correspondence of language (propositions) with the world rests. Wittgenstein shows us the unpresentable in the ladder-like propositions of the *Tractatus*, which are in a strict sense nonsensical, but, nevertheless, contain a deep truth that cannot be said.

One of the central and most seductive ideas of aesthetic modernity — as a current of thought countering the concept of modernity — is the idea that something lies hidden from us, yet guides our thought and behavior. The various experimental analytical methods developed by Freud, Nietzsche, and Marx were expressions of this deep desire to uncover that which remains hidden in language, self, culture, and economy. Wittgenstein's early thought is also an expression of this desire: to lay bare the limits of the sayable and thus, in romantic fashion, to protect and make room for ethics and aesthetics. They belong to the realm of the unsayable. By plotting the limits of language, focussing upon the general form of the proposition, Wittgenstein could, thereby, provide an account of the logical structure governing language and its representative power of denotation. The world is made up of states of affairs that are logical pictures of facts embodied in propositions. Only such fact-stating propositions have sense, and complex propositions are truth-functions of elementary propositions. This doctrine and analytical method provide intellectual resources to the Vienna Circle. Moritz Schlick's formulation turns the doctrine into a method of verification for the meaning of sentences. Where for the Vienna Circle Schlick's manifesto "The meaning of a sentence is its method of verification" becomes a mantra for the final defeat of metaphysics and the legitimation of science, for Wittgenstein the doctrine, which later became "logical atomism" in the hands of Russell, was a means to preserve the status of ethics and aesthetics, not their demise: "What we cannot speak about we must pass over in silence."

Wittgenstein's later thought is radically postmodern in the sense that it dispenses with this central and comforting trope of aesthetic modernity. It no longer clings to the seductiveness of the idea that something remains hidden — a crystalline, pure, logical essence — that directs our thought, language, and culture, and that can be revealed through a form of analysis. Instead, Wittgenstein embraces the thought that everything already lies in plain view before us; that there is no one method of analysis that reveals a hidden structure.

WITTGENSTEIN AS PHILOSOPHICAL POSTMODERNIST

Eagleton has pursued Wittgenstein on other occasions. In terms of his own question of why Wittgenstein so fascinates the artist's imagination he writes a novel that seeks to bring Wittgenstein's ideas and class position out into the open by putting Wittgenstein in dialogue with three other characters. In the novel of ideas *Saints and Scholars* (1987) Eagleton investigates in a literary form Wittgenstein's philosophy and temperament in relation to the political context of revolutionary Europe and a meeting with a number of not-so-improbable people. The year is 1916. Wittgenstein has left Cambridge for the solitude of the west coast of Ireland. He meets with Nikolai Bakhtin, brother of the famous Marxist aesthetician, and they become travelling companions. Finally, together they run into both James Connolly, on the run and injured after the Easter Rising, and Leopold Bloom. In this novel of ideas the four main characters, holed up in a little cottage, begin to argue with each other over the radical possibilities facing Europe.

In the novel Eagleton describes Wittgenstein's quest for a kind of logical purity in the *Tractatus* with the city of Vienna: "Habsburg Vienna had lost the meaning of truth, a city of kitsch and self-delusion. . . . Vienna was smothered in a jungle of styles, scrolls, arabesques, cultural graffitti, smelling of polychrome and polished leather" (1987, p. 35). Speaking of Wittgenstein's early conception of language, Eagleton describes the picture theory of meaning and its logical relation to the structure of the world in terms of a counterpoint with Vienna. "There was a place where all the rules governing the inner structures of things came together, and this was mathematics. Mathematics was the mother tongue of the human race, into which the whole world could be translated. It was a kind of monastery, chaste, disciplined and entirely true. It was everything that Vienna was not" (p. 38). The novel is somewhat static and even lifeless, yet it serves for Eagleton as a kind of literary praxis for his criticism (embodying it, anchoring critical ideas in conversation and dialogue) and foreshadows the script he writes for the Jarman film. Although Eagleton's novel is less successful than the script, it, nevertheless, captures quite well the moment of insight that motivates Wittgenstein to change the direction of his thinking:

One day a friend took his photograph on the steps of the Senate House and Wittgenstein asked him where he was to stand. "Oh, roughly there," the friend replied, casually indicating a spot. Wittgenstein went back to his room, lay on the floor and writhed in excitement. *Roughly there*. The phrase had opened a world to him. Not "two inches to the left of that stone," but "roughly there." Human life was a matter of roughness, not of precise measurement. Why had he not understood this? He had tried to purge language of its ambiguities. . . . Looseness and ambiguitity were not imperfections, they were what made things work. (Eagleton, 1987, p.42)

Here the biographical interrupts the philosophical. It is a theme he returns to in "Introduction to Wittgenstein" making the connection between "looseness and ambiguity" of language and the invention of new forms of writing.

If the early work holds one kind of attraction for the artist, the later writings manifest another. For they belong to that heretical subcurrent of philosophy which works by joke, anecdote, aphorism, by the striking image or gnomic saying, distilling a whole complex argument in some earthy dictum or sudden epiphany. One thinks of the various jokers in the philosophical pack, from Kierkegaard and Nietzsche to Adorno and Derrida, those thinkers who could only say what they meant by inventing a whole new form of writing. The *Tractatus* may have the shimmering purity of an Imagist poem or Suprematist canvas; but the *Investigations* read more like an assemblage of ironic fables or fragments of a novel, deceptively lucid in their language but teasingly enigmatic in their thought. (Eagleton, 1993, pp. 8–9)

Eagleton is surely correct to mention Wittgenstein in the company of Kierkegaard, Nietzsche, and Derrida. He likens Wittgenstein to the Freudian analyst engaged in the work of demystification to teach us to see differently through the adoption of a new style of thinking and of doing philosophy. It is a style that makes uses of the variety of language that exists in our culture, which exploits all its various forms to show us what lies on the surface in front of us, so to speak — the familiar and the ordinary. Just as there cannot be a private language, so, too, there cannot be a self so deep that it "eludes the reach-me-down categories of our social existence" (Eagleton, 1993, p. 10). Wittgenstein in his later work deconstructs the romantic myth of self as a unique and private essence, unified, and at once the source of our inspiration and genius — a self that can be made transparent and accessible to ourselves through analysis. It is this bourgeois notion of inwardness and inner experience that buttresses Western ideological individualism and sanctions a view of society comprised only of individuals — rational, autonomous, and self-interested.

At this point Eagleton resists the temptation to construe Wittgenstein as philosophical postmodernist, instead casting him in terms of resemblance to "the great artistic modernists" (1993, p. 11). It is, we think, more fruitful to see Wittgenstein in his later work as more radically postmodernist and, thus, closer to Nietzsche and French poststructuralism than to modernism (or, at least, in a critical tension with his early modernist self).

As someone who displays close affinities to Schopenhauer, Nietzsche, and Heidegger and the body of thought that shaped poststructuralism, Wittgenstein pits himself against a Hegelian cultural modernity.

This is, perhaps not unsurprisingly, an interpretation Eagleton (1982) makes himself much earlier in his career. He writes that Wittgenstein considered using a quotation from *King Lear* — "I'll teach you differences" — as an epigraph for the *Investigations* and quotes from Rush Rhees's personal recollections that Wittgenstein made the suggestion at one time to a friend that although Hegel wanted to make things that looked different the same, he wanted to show how things that looked the same were different (Eagleton, 1982, p. 64). Starting from this observation, Eagleton goes on to show the parallels between Wittgenstein and Derrida. For Eagleton,

Wittgenstein and Derrida are alike in suspecting all philosophy of immediacy, all grounding of discourse in the experience of the subject. The sign for Wittgenstein is not the mark of an inward sensation (intending, for example, is not an experience); meaning is an effect of the signifier, which must always already be in play, traced through with its history of heterogenous uses, for the meaning of the subject to emerge at all. For Wittgenstein, as for post-structuralism, the subject is "written" from the outset, an effect of the play of the signifier. . . . Difference and identity are equally effects of discourse. (1982, p. 66)

Eagleton (1982, p. 65) is concerned that the British Wittgenstein — the "Wittgenstein of Geach and Strawson" — has lost its distinctively European timbre. He interprets Wittgenstein, like Derrida, as engaged in a process to unseat metaphysics and to replace it with the everyday. The private sign is a metaphysical chimera, argues Eagleton, "an instance of that philosophy of phenomenological self-presence," that is fractured by language-games and by the recognition that difference and identity alike are effects of discourse. There is no metalanguage into which claims made in ordinary language can be transparently parsed. Above all philosophy is not a privileged language that can resolve first-order disputes. There is only language, and concepts take their force from their loc on within practical forms of life: "what has to be accepted, the given, is   so one could say — *forms of life*" (Wittgenstein, 1953, #226). Eagleton's purpose is, however, to make the comparison between a Nietzschean Wittgenstein and Derrida, who leave everything as it is and a conception of language as carnival that he attributes to Mikhail Bakhtin.

Aware that the death of God has left metaphysics securely in place, Wittgenstein and Derrida seek to complete the task which Nietzsche began, and in doing so risk moving into an alternative form of religion. The strength and weakness of deconstruction is that it seeks to position itself at the extreme limit of the thinkable. This rocks the foundations of metaphysical knowledge to the precise extent that, posed at the extreme edge as it is, it threatens like Wittgenstein to leave everything exactly as it was. (Eagleton, 1982, p. 74)

Eagleton's overall intention is to demonstrate the superiority of main-stream Marxist aesthetics that admits a notion of ideology, provides strategies of de-reification and de-fetishization, and explains the historical conditions of metaphysics.

Our strategy here is not to debate the superiority of one tradition of aesthetics over another, or even to assess Eagleton's argument, but rather to take up his suggestions of a reading that, first, places Wittgenstein in relation to modernism, providing an aesthetic reading of his work, and, second, construes Wittgenstein in his later work as someone who has strong affinities both with a European counter-Enlightenment tradition in philosophy exemplified by Nietzsche and with the movement of post-structuralist thought. These are themes that we deal with explicitly in subsequent chapters.

NOTES

1.   One passage, for example, included the works of Gerhard Richter, Jeff Wall, Clegg and Gutman, Michael Zumpt, Andy Warhol, Richard Prince, Francis Picabia, Sarah Charlesworth, Günter Förg, and Christopher Williams. Another sequence begins with Peter Weibel's *Gem-ein-sam* and includes Barbara Bloom's pair of portraits from *The Reign of Narcissism*, Dan Graham's video *Yesterday/Today*, which televises the viewer's entry into the gallery space, Franz West's *Psyche*, a mirrored vanity table, two Cindy Sherman self-protraits, Michelangelo Pistoletto's pair of arched mirrors, *La Tavole della Legge*, Jan van Oost's twin monumental mirrored coffins, Magritte's *Perspective* (*Le balcon de Manet II*), and Marcel Broodthaers' *La Salon Noir*, which has portrait mugs in an open coffin.

2.   Monk (1991, p. xvii) notes that "there have been at least five television programmes made about him and countless memoirs of him written, often by people who knew him only very slightly." There was a British Broadcasting Corporation film of interviews and other material about Wittgenstein made by Christopher Sykes Productions in 1988. The Derek Jarman film had its origin in 1990 when Tariq Ali was asked by the commissioning editor, education, at Chan-nel 4 to develop an idea for a series on philosophy. Ali suggested a set of 12 one-hour dramas based on a set of philosophers from Ancient Greece to modern times and four scripts were commissioned (*Socrates* by Howard Brenton, *Spinoza* by Ali, *Locke* by David Edgar, and *Wittgenstein* by Eagleton). As Jarman (1993, p. 65) comments: "I had thought of making a film of Ludwig some years ago. 'Loony Ludwig in the Green Valleys of Silliness.' Then Tariq rang. We had a ten-day shoot for fifty minutes on TV. A week or so into pre-production, the BFI [British Film Institute] threw down a challenge. Some more cash for a seventy-two minute film."

3. It is extraordinary that analytic philosophy rules out of court the question of philosophical style, of philosophical genres and, specifically, of the relevance of narrative and narratology to philosophy not only in the obvious sense of separating questions of form and content or life and works (and, therefore of auto/biography and philosophy) but also in terms of narrative as a form of philosophy — the fable, the parable, the homily are genres of philosophical discourse.

4. See Kosuth's famous essay "Art After Philosophy," first published in *Studio International, 178*(195) (October 1969): 134–37; *916* (November): 160–61; *917* (December): 212–13.

2

Nietzsche and Wittgenstein:
Philosophers of the Future

I am still waiting for a philosophical *physician* in the exceptional sense
of that word — one who has to pursue the problem of the whole
health of a people, time race, or of humanity — to muster the courage
to push my suspicion to its limits and to risk the proposition: what
was at stake in all philosophy hitherto was not at all "truth" but something else — let us say, health, future, growth, power, life.

— Nietzsche, 1974, p. 35

[There is no being] behind the doing, acting, becoming . . . the doing is
everything.

— Nietzsche, 1992, p. 179

The problems arising through a misinterpretation of our forms of
language have the character of depth. They are deep disquietudes;
their roots are as deep in us as the forms of our language, and their
significance is as great as the importance of our language.

— Wittgenstein, 1953, #111

It is not surprising that in Anglo-American philosophy there have been
very few attempts to link Nietzsche and Wittgenstein or to examine the
philosophy of one in terms of the other. Philosophers in the analytic tradition who read Wittgenstein have not been inclined to read Nietzsche (this
is certainly the case until recent reception of Nietzsche in Anglo-American philosophy); and those who read Nietzsche sympathetically tended
not to view Wittgenstein as an analytic philosopher.

There are a number of reasons for the absence of this link in Anglo-
American philosophy. Nietzsche's initial reception in the English-speaking world took place during the period 1896–1915, from the period
immediately following his death through until the outbreak of World
War I. The reception was both literary (Bridgwater, 1972) and philosophical, although there was little apparent connection between them. A philosophical revival of his work, driven by an interest in his ethics and
especially its connection to evolutionary theory and positivism, took
place in Anglo-American philosophy in the period immediately following his death, even though it was not always flattering.[1] Nietzsche's
philosophical reception on the Continent began in earnest in the late
1920s with Karl Jaspers, E. F. Podach, and Julian Benda.[2] The "nazifica-
tion" of Nietzsche dated from the same period. The contemporary philosophical reception of his work occured mainly in Germany and France
during the post-war period with the most influential interpretations being
those of Martin Heidegger (1961), Georges Bataille (1945), Gilles Deleuze
(1962), and Jacques Derrida (1972).[3] Although it was primarily Walter
Kaufmann (1950) who, in the post-war period, introduced Nietzsche to
Anglo-American philosophy, and, later, Arthur Danto (1965), the new
Nietzsche that has emerged from literature departments in the United
States has been more a product of the influence of Continental readings.[4]
A serious revival of his work in the English-speaking world, motivated
once again by an interest in his ethics, did not occur again until the 1980s.[5]

Taubeneck (1991, p. 160) maintains "Kaufmann's interpretation shaped
the reception in English from 1950 to at least 1974, or for nearly quarter of
the century." Kaufmann (1974, p. v) in the preface to the 1968 edition of
Nietzsche: Philosopher, Psychologist, Antichrist provides a snapshot of the
English philosophical bias against Nietzsche that prevailed until recently:
"In 1952 when I visited C. D. Broad at Trinity College, Cambridge, he
mentioned a man called Salter. I asked whether he was the Salter who had
written a book on Nietzsche, to which Broad replied: 'Dear no; he did not
deal with crackpot subjects like that; he wrote about psychical research.'"
It is only in the 1980s, and partly as a result of the impact of German and
French receptions of Nietzsche, that the study of Nietzsche's philosophy
has become acceptable in the English-speaking world. Strangely, neither
Bernd Magnus and Kathleen Higgins (1996) nor Ernst Behler (1996) see fit
to comment upon the relative absence of Nietzsche in the Anglo-American philosophical literature and curriculum prior to the 1980s. Given this
absence of Nietzsche it is no wonder that there have been few attempts to
link Nietzsche and Wittgenstein (at least in the analytic tradition). There
are, of course, some exceptions to this generalization.[6]

This chapter aims to make a modest start in rectifying this situation. It
has two main parts: the first section presents a historico-cultural reading
of Wittgenstein interpreted within the context of Viennese modernism, an

intellectual context strongly shaped by Nietzsche. This section is designed to show that Nietzsche's work was, in effect, part of the shared intellectual background against which Wittgenstein crystallized his own ideas. We invoke the French concept of an *energetics* to explain a pervasive and background cultural influence of Nietzsche upon Wittgenstein. There is also clear historical evidence that Wittgenstein read Nietzsche and that he grew up in the company of intellectuals strongly influenced by Nietzsche, including the musician Gustav Mahler and the painter Gustav Klimt, both of whom were regular visitors to the Wittgenstein family mansion. In a more indirect historical sense, Wittgenstein was influenced by the Nietzschean, Oswald Spengler, and both Nietzsche and Wittgenstein (perhaps more so than any other two modern philosophers) were strongly influenced by Schopenhauer.

The second part of the chapter is more directly philosophical in that it discusses aspects of Wittgenstein's philosophy, especially his later philosophy, which exhibits clear family resemblances with aspects of Nietzsche's work. We discuss these resemblances by focussing, first, on the notion of the philosopher as cultural physician — a phrase that appears in Nietzsche's notes of the early 1870s and that he had used at one stage as a title for a book considered a companion to *The Birth of Tragedy* — and, second, on the philosopher of the future, a phrase that Nietzsche used consistently in his later works. The earlier notion of cultural physician informs and shapes Nietzsche's notion of the philosopher of the future, whose principal concern is the health of culture. The central responsibility of the philosopher of the future is the project of cultivation and education of humanity as a whole. The philosopher-physician does not create cultural health by treating the sick individual, by, for instance, enhancing his or her rational autonomy. The cultural malady is not primarily a cognitive disorder that, thus, can be cured by reason alone. The philosopher of the future employs all the cultural resources at his or her disposal to promote what we are capable of becoming.

Wittgenstein ascribes to a similar romantic view of culture as a form of life; culture as an expressive and natural force, one that begins in doing (rather than thinking), and can be judged in terms similar to the creation of a work of art. Wittgenstein also sees himself as a philosopher of culture and philosophy as a kind of therapy.

WITTGENSTEIN, NIETZSCHE, AND VIENNESE MODERNISM

Janik and Toulmin's (1973) *Wittgenstein's Vienna* was the first to demonstrate the significance of a historico-cultural approach to understanding Wittgenstein and the importance of the Viennese cultural milieu to understanding his work. Adopting a Kantian interpretation of the early

Wittgenstein, they argued he was addressing the problem of representation, a problem that arose in the culture of Viennese modernism. Janik and Toulmin argued that Wittgenstein was extending in his own way the critique of language and culture initiated by Karl Kraus (and Fritz Mauthner) and they emphasized a romantic and ethical interpretation of the *Tractatus* where, as they assert, "Only art can express moral truth, and only the artist can teach the things that matter most in life" (Janik & Toulmin, 1973, p. 197).

In retrospect, there is a notable absence in Janik and Toulmin's interpretation: it neither mentions nor makes anything of Nietzsche's influence on *fin de siècle* Vienna or upon many of Wittgenstein's intellectual contemporaries and forbears. Allan Janik (1981, p. 85) identifies Wittgenstein with the spirit of the Austrian counter-enlightenment characterized by a focus upon the limits of reason, in the tradition of Lichtenberg, Kraus, Schopenhauer, Kierkegaard, Weininger, and Nietzsche. Also, von Wright (1982), in an influential essay, argues that Wittgenstein displays a Spenglerian attitude to his times: Wittgenstein understood himself to be living in "an age without culture," an age where modern philosophy was no longer able to provide the metalanguage that united the family resemblances of culture's various manifestations. Although von Wright (1982) attributes Wittgenstein's notion of family resemblance to Spengler's *ursymbol* he does not go further to discuss the direct influence of Nietzsche upon Spengler or the way Nietzsche's influence upon Wittgenstein is mediated through Spengler.[7]

In a similar manner, Stanley Cavell (1988) views Wittgenstein as a "philosopher of culture" and provides a reading of the *Investigations* as a depiction of our times, agreeing with von Wright's assessment of Wittgenstein's attitude as Spenglerian, suggesting that Spengler's vision of culture as a kind of nature is shared in a modified form in the *Investigations*. Cavell (1988, pp. 261–62) argues that the *Investigations* "diurnalizes Spengler's vision of the destiny toward exhausted forms," toward the loss of culture and community; Cavell draws our attention to the way Wittgenstein's uniqueness as a philosopher of culture comes from "the sense that he is joining the fate of philosophy as such with that of the philosophy of culture or criticism of culture." By doing so, he argues, Wittgenstein is calling into question philosophy's claim to a privileged perspective on culture that could be called the perspective of reason.

It is worth investigating Spengler's influence a little further. Wittgenstein refers to Spengler a number of times in his notes during the 1930s. In 1931 in the context of a discussion of his own Jewishness as a thinker, that is, one who merely reproduces rather than invents a line of thinking (which, he considers, is the mark of a true genius), he lists Spengler among those (including Boltzmann, Hertz, Schopenhauer, Frege,

Russell, Kraus, Loos, Weininger, and Sraffa) who influenced him most (Wittgenstein, 1980a, p. 19e).

The irony of Wittgenstein's remark is that Spengler owed much to Nietzsche. *The Decline of the West* was an imaginative reception of Nietzsche's ideas and, as he himself commented in a letter written in 1921, "today it is not possible to express anything which hasn't already been touched upon in Nietzsche's posthumous works" (cited in Farrenkopf, 1992–93, p. 166). There is no doubt that Wittgenstein's cultural pessimism and despair — his rejection of technoscientific civilization, his distrust of progress, his sense of cultural dissolution and decay — were inherited, in part, from Spengler and in a mediated fashion, from Nietzsche, but also directly from Schopenhauer.

As Christopher Janaway (1994, p. 104) remarks, Nietzsche and Wittgenstein are to date the only philosophers to have been strongly influenced by Schopenhauer. Wittgenstein started reading Schopenhauer as an adolescent not in an academic setting but "as part of the stock of ideas with which Viennese high society was furnished" (p. 104). Weiner (1992, p. 9) suggests that since the groundbreaking work of Janik (1966), the connection between the two thinkers, and the early Wittgenstein's intellectual debt to Schopenhauer, has gradually come to light. The young Wittgenstein seized upon Schopenhauer's *The World as Will and Representation*, believing it to be fundamentally right, although in need of some clarification; while Wittgenstein in his maturity came to see a certain shallowness in his thinking. The *Tractatus* — its conceptual structure, its mysticism, its language of ethics and aesthetics — is unmistakably Schopenhauerian. The connection to Schopenhauer helps explain the ethical point of the *Tractatus* and an enduring cultural pessimism.

McGuinness (1982, p. 40) suggests a direct historical relationship between Wittgenstein and Nietzsche over the question of nihilism: "Wittgenstein thought that nothing was to be hoped for from by about 1850. The only hope lay in Russia where everything had been destroyed. . . . Hence his kinship with Nietzsche is very evident." In his biography of the young Ludwig, McGuinness (1988, p. 36), discussing Grillparzer's opposition to nationalism, radicalism, and progress, suggests that such a view was not peculiarly Austrian but was rather a part of a wider German counternarrative shared by both Schopenhauer and Nietzsche. McGuinness (1988, p. 225) indicates that the young Wittgenstein brought a copy of volume eight of Nietzsche's collected works (which contained *The Anti-Christ*) and that Wittgenstein responded to Nietzsche's "hostility to Christianity" in a diary entry dated December 8, 1914. McGuinness (1988, p. 225) says, "Nietzsche seemed important for Wittgenstein because Nietzsche's starting point was the same as his own."

This reading of Wittgenstein is given additional credibility by Jacques Le Rider's (1990, 1993) interpretation of Viennese modernism. Le Rider

(1990) argues that the Viennese moderns, by whom he means Loos, Kraus, Schönberg, Klimt, Mahler, and Hofmannsthal, among others, were "less aggressive" than their counterparts in other European capitals. Viennese modernism, he suggests, "was not a triumphant movement. . . . Without exception, they were marked by Nietzsche's contempt for such 'modern' ideas as democracy, historicism, scientism or progress" (p. 2). He argues that *fin de siècle* Vienna prefigured certain central themes of postmodernism and lists "the triumph and crisis of individualism," "the quest for mythologies capable of regenerating modern culture," and "the questioning of scientific and technical rationality." The Schopenhauerian-Nietzschean ethos that tempered Viennese modernism helps explain both Wittgenstein's skepticism toward modernism — whether in the sciences and technology or in literature and the arts — and his final dissociation with the logical empiricism of the Vienna Circle, built as it was on a new-found faith in science and of extending the scientific method into philosophy itself.

Le Rider (1991) sees Nietzsche as the common starting point for most Viennese modernists, arguing that "The crisis of the individual, experienced as an identity crisis, is at the heart of all questions we find in literature and the humane sciences" (p. 1) and remarks that "Viennese modernism can be interpreted as an anticipation of certain important 'postmodern' themes" (p. 6). He has in mind, for instance, the way in which Wittgenstein's philosophy of language "deconstructs the subject as author and judge of his own semantic intentions" (p. 28). He remarks in terms of the crisis of identity how Wittgenstein, "like all assimilated Jewish intellectuals, found his Jewish identity a problem" and the problem of his Jewish identity was coupled with a crisis of sexual identity, when at least at some periods of his life he sought refuge from his homosexual tendencies in a kind of Tolstoyan asceticism (p. 295). He suggests:

Wittgenstein, who . . . looked back nostalgically on a well-ordered world where everyone had his place, found modernity uncultured because it had lost its power to integrate, and left individuals in a state of confusion. The only ones who can keep their balance and personal creativity are those whom Nietzsche calls the strong men, that is the most moderate, who need neither convictions nor religion, who are able not only to endure, but to accept a fair amount of chance and absurdity, and are capable of thinking in a broadly disillusioned and negative way without feeling either diminished or discouraged. (p. 296)

Le Rider (1991) argues that the consequences of this double crisis of identity, much more than is commonly accepted, are intimately tied up with the fundamentals of his thought and with a number of his intellectual preoccupations: "his interest in Weininger and in psychoanalysis, his mystical tendencies, but also his reflections on genius, on the self, and on ethics" (p. 296). The importance that Le Rider places upon Nietzsche as part of the cultural fabric of Viennese modernism exercised upon a young Wittgenstein is borne out by other scholars of *fin de siècle* Vienna.

McGrath (1974, p. 2) traces the intellectual biography of the Telyn Society ("Pernerstorfer circle") in Vienna during the late nineteenth and early twentieth centuries. This group, which was named after Engelbert Pernerstorfer, included among its members Gustav Mahler, Victor Adler, and Sigfried Lipiner (the boy genius).

In response to the political and cultural crises of the brief liberal era, the members of the circle were drawn with increasing force to the ideas of three great thinkers whose works expressed profound alienation from liberal ideals: Schopenhauer, Wagner, and Nietzsche. Although it has been frequently argued that Nietzsche's influence began to be felt significantly only in the 1890s, the history of the circle shows that as early as the 1870s this philosopher attracted an intensely loyal following among the student population of Vienna.

The Telyn group, prepared well during their student years, carried on their crusade for cultural renewal within the variety of professional activities in their adult years. As McGrath (1974, p. 83) indicates: "Nietzsche provided them with the ingredients for an all embracing outlook based on a belief in the coherence of the arts and cultural unity of art and society."

The Telynen explicitly accepted Nietzsche as their educator and pledged themselves to a life of self-overcoming on the model set forth by Nietzsche in *Schopenhauer as Educator*, in which Nietzsche calls for members of the cultural community "to further the production of the philosopher, of the artist, and of the saint within us and outside us" (1983, p. 56). They lived the teaching of Nietzsche: "Everyone who possesses culture is, in fact, saying 'I see something higher and more human than myself above me. Help me, all of you, to reach it, as I will help every person who recognizes the same thing'" (p. 61).

Aschheim (1992, p. 14) notes that Nietzsche had dwelled upon a *fin de siècle* theme that was to become a defining feature of the new consciousness that Carl Schorske (1980, p. xix) calls "post-Nietzschean culture": "the perception of pervasive decadence and degeneration and the accompanying search for new sources of physical and mental health."

PHILOSOPHERS OF THE FUTURE

> If mankind is not to destroy itself . . . it must first of all attain to a hitherto altogether unprecedented *knowledge of the preconditions of culture* as a scientific standard for ecumenical goals. Herein lies the tremendous task for the great spirits of the coming century.
>
> — Nietzsche, 1996, #25, p. 25

Major proposition: He [the philosopher] is able to create no culture; but he can prepare it and remove restraints on it. . . . He acts as a *solvent* and a *destroyer* regarding all that is positive in a culture or religion (even when he seeks to be a *founder*).

— Nietzsche, 1990, #170, p. 71

I was thinking about my philosophical work and saying to myself: "I destroy, I destroy, I destroy."

— Wittgenstein, 1980a, p. 21e

Wittgenstein and Nietzsche

One of the earliest attempts to link the two philosophers comes in an essay called simply "Wittgenstein and Nietzsche" written by Erich Heller (1988) on the occasion of the appearance of Wittgenstein's *The Blue and the Brown Books* in 1958, originally published in *Encounter* in 1959, and later published in *The Artists Journey into the Interior and Other Essays* (1965). He suggests that Wittgenstein resembled Nietzsche:

In his homelessness, his restless wanderings, his perpetual search for exactly the right conditions in which to work, his loneliness, his asceticism, his need for affection and his shyness in giving it, his intellectual extremism, which drove thought to the borders of insanity, the elasticity of his style, and . . . in one philosophically most important respect, like Nietzsche he knew that philosophical opinion was not merely a matter of logically demonstrable right or wrong . . . it was above all a matter of authenticity. (Heller, 1988, pp. 143–44)

Heller first notes the family resemblances between Wittgenstein and the major figures of Viennese modernism (he mentions Weininger, Loos, Kraus, Musil, Schönberg) and goes on to suggest that the break between the *Tractatus* and the *Investigations* is of the same kind as that between Nietzsche's *Birth of Tragedy* and *Human, All Too Human*, in the sense that in both cases the break is attributable to a disenchantment with metaphysics and a loss of faith of any formal or logical correspondence between language and thought, and reality (1988, p. 149). In the turn away from a correspondence version of truth Heller believes that Nietzsche and Wittgenstein share a similar nihilism that "one day will be seen as an integral part of the tragically self-destructive design of European thought" (p. 145) in that their work is both "inseparable from the critique of its medium" and embodied in the doubt of its own possibility (p. 157). Although Heller recognizes differences between the two thinkers in "the scope and object, the approach and humour, the key and tempo of their thought," he maintains they share an all-important "creative distrust of all those categorical certainities that . . . have been allowed to determine the body of traditional thought" (p. 150). Heller concludes that Wittgenstein's statement

"What is the aim in philosophy? — To show the fly the way out of the fly-bottle" masks a kind of nihilism. In Heller's interpretation there is no way out, only more and more fly-bottles. Our interpretation runs against Heller's in that we do not consider Wittgenstein, or for that matter Nietzsche, to be nihilists. We see them both as offering positive responses to the question of nihilism.

It also runs against that of Meredith Williams (1988, p. 403), who argues that while "there is overlap in project, method, and style . . . there are equally striking differences." She argues:

Though both adopt the aphoristic style, the tone and affect of each is quite different. . . . Though both adopt diagnosis as their distinctive way of dealing with problems, Nietzsche's method of genealogy is psychological and historical, whereas Wittgenstein's method is grammatical and conceptual. Finally, though both seek to overcome the philosophic tradition, their attitudes towards what both hold to be overcome are by no means identical . . . for Nietzsche, the problem is social and cultural — contemporary society is diseased, is decadent. . . . For Wittgenstein, the problem is personal — the individual is in the grip of an illness.

We disagree with Williams both in terms of the comparison of method and problems to be overcome. Williams overestimates the differences in terms of method: Nietzsche's method is also grammatical and conceptual, and Wittgenstein's method inclines him toward accepting a description of our language games as a form of natural history. As will become clear later in this chapter, although philosophy for Wittgenstein is intensely personal, we believe his later philosophy clearly addresses problems and disquietudes in our language and culture.

Gordon Bearn (1997, p. xv) starts from and accepts Heller's position that Nietzsche and Wittgenstein share a similar philosophical break and development but he does not read them as Heller does, as contributing to the nihilism of contemporary culture. Rather he interprets them, following Stanley Cavell, as providing us with a rest from a kind of nihilistic anxiety aimed at easing our existential cares and "waking us to the wonder of existence." Although we agree with Bearn against Heller's nihilistic interpretation of both Nietzsche and Wittgenstein, our argument is, rather, that Wittgenstein can be usefully seen, in Nietzsche's sense, as a physician of culture and as a philosopher of the future. If we adopt Nietzsche's notion of the philosopher as cultural physician and use it to understand both Wittgenstein's view of the role of philosophy and his style of philosophizing, we will come to see Wittgenstein's later work as offering a philosophical response to nihilism. To embrace such an interpretation has several advantages: most broadly, it provides a reading consistent with the influence of *fin de siècle* Vienna upon Wittgenstein's thought (and, more specifically, makes sense of the influence of

Schopenhauer, Spengler, Kraus, Mauthner); it also helps us to understand both how the question of culture was central to Wittgenstein's thought and the role he ascribed to philosophy; finally, it elucidates what it means to philosophize at the end of the twentieth century, after our loss of faith in what Jean-François Lyotard (1984) has called metanarratives. Our strategy in the remainder of the chapter will be to identify Nietzsche's concept of culture and the cultural significance of philosophy and to use these ideas as a framework to interpret Wittgenstein's philosophy of the future.

Nietzsche's Philosopher as Cultural Physician

During the period 1872–75 Nietzsche started working on a major project that was to provide a sequel or companion to *The Birth of Tragedy*. He variously titled this proposed work *The Last Philosophy*, *Philosophy in the Tragic Age of the Greeks*, and *The Philosopher as Cultural Physician*. The notion of culture runs through these notes, as it does through the corpus of Nietzsche's works: not only was he concerned to understand what it is and to develop knowledge of the conditions for its renewal in the age of science, he wished to define the cultural significance of the philosopher, and above all, to signal the importance of the philosopher as a physician of culture, as one who could prepare the ground of culture, and in the figure of the future philosopher-artist, create new values. In order to do so the philosopher must first turn his life into a work of art, because the philosopher's product is his life, before his works.

The prospect of a purely scientific culture, for Nietzsche, was an impossibility: "because science lacks the ability to determine value and command obedience which characterizes genuine cultural force; because it opposes human needs and values; and because it stands in opposition to itself" (Breazeale, 1979, p. xxvii). Scientific knowing based upon a correspondence theory of knowledge and a mirroring of an independent reality could not in itself legitimate itself or determine the meaning or value of the truth it sought. Investigating the natural antagonist to the ascetic ideal in *The Genealogy*, Nietzsche (1956, p. 289) says "Science is too dependent for that, it always requires a normative value outside itself in order to operate securely." To make philosophy scientific, to turn it into a science, is "to throw in the towel" (#55, p. 111).

In the notes he compiled for "The Philosopher as Cultural Physician" (1873) Nietzsche outlines what he sees as the value of philosophy in clearing up superstitions, eliminating the theory of the soul, and dismantling the fixed value of ethical concepts. Against the ascetic ideals that rule traditional philosophy, Nietzsche's philosophy does not oppose the sensuousness of the body. His philosophy of the future has essentially a destructive task: to destroy dogmatism in all its forms — in religion and in science — and what he calls blind secularism. As such, "Philosophy is *not something for the people*; thus it is *not the basis of a culture* but merely the tool of culture" (#174, p. 74). In this role it serves as the tribunal of education in an age without culture: schools must follow philosophy in destroying secularization and subduing the barbarizing effects of the knowledge drive: *"Philosophy reveals its highest worth when it concentrates the unlimited knowledge drives and subdues it to unity"* (#30, p. 9). During this early period Nietzsche felt that modern education showed all the symptoms of decay. As part of a secularization and with the promotion of a scientific world view it had lost its ability to confer unifying values. Above all: "Education contradicts a man's nature" (#41, p. 104). The so-called educated classes only hindered the cultural physician and Nietzsche placed his hope in the education of the lower classes.

Philosophy, in terms of its own self-critique, must overturn naive realism of science to undermine it from within by mastering the knowledge drive, but it must also move beyond the purely negative moment of skepticism, if philosophy were to become an affirmative cultural force and philosophers were to become cultural legislators in the form of the philosopher-artist. Philosophy can pave the way or clear the ground for culture by showing the anthropomorphic character of all knowledge and by recognizing the power and necessity of illusion.

Culture emanates from the central significance of great art that makes self-conscious use of illusion. By accepting the ultimacy of illusion and by recognizing illusions for what they are, art can deal creatively with them: "truths are illusions which we have forgotten are illusions; they are metaphors that become worn out and have been drained of sensuous force" ("On Truth and Lies in a Nonmoral Sense," Nietzsche, 1979, p. 80). The new philosopher will disentangle the nets of language, realizing that words cannot establish an unambiguous relation to the world.

David Breazeale (1979, p. xxvii), in his introduction to the early notebooks of the 1870s, describes the notion of culture underlying Nietzsche's view: "Nietzsche's fundamental idea of culture is the Goethean one of harmonious manifoldness or unity in diversity. Culture is not an artificial homogeneity imposed by external restraints or ascetic self-denial, but an organic unity *cultivated* on the very soil of discord and difference. . . . One of Nietzsche's most important discoveries was the unifying function of values and goals and his interpretation of them as essential instruments for the creation and the preservation of culture." Nietzsche states his aim is "to comprehend *the internal coherence and necessity of every true culture*" (#33, p. 10) and he interprets the goal of culture as the production of great works that unify by mastering the drives of the people. Culture is "the unity of artistic style in every expression of the life of a people" (Nietzsche, 1983, p. 4).

The central task of the philosopher-artist is to create new values capable of guiding us in the future, values that will shape our institutions, particularly our schools, and help us to evaluate our past. It is a prominent theme in Nietzsche's later writings. His early view of the philosopher as cultural physician shapes Nietzsche's notion of the philosopher of the future. The fundamental concern of the philosopher of the future, like the cultural physician, is the health of culture. Nietzsche never abandons his early view that philosophy might effect a cultural regeneration. Nietzsche speaks of "a new species of philosophers" (Nietzsche, 1989, #2, p. 11) for whom the falseness of a judgment is not necessarily an objection against it: "The question is to what extent is it life-promoting, life-preserving, species-preserving, perhaps even species-cultivating" (#4, p. 11). Only a philosophy that risks recognizing "untruth as a condition of life" places itself beyond good and evil and, thereby, can accomplish the task of the re-evaluation of all values. Such a philosopher of the future will be free from "the seduction of words" (#16, p. 23) and will understand that what we take to be the truth of beliefs is often only the result of grammatical habits (see, in particular, Nietzsche's discussion of the will, which he suggests "is a unit only as a word" [#19, p. 25]). Although Nietzsche insists that he is the first psychologist — one interested in an explanation of belief rather than its truth — he is speaking of a depth of psychology that would enable him to understand the development of the will to power, morphologically, in short, a genealogy of values. The philosopher of the future is "the man of the most comprehensive responsibility who has the conscience for the over-all development of man — this philosopher will make use of religions for his project of cultivation and education just as he will make use of whatever political and economic states are at hand" (#61, p. 72). Nietzsche talks of "genuine philosophers" in contrast to "philosophical laborers": "*Genuine philosophers, however, are commanders and legislators*: they say, '*thus* it *shall be!*' . . . Their 'knowing' is *creating*, their creating is a legislation, their will to truth is — *will to power*" (#211, p. 136).

Wittgenstein and the Romantic View of Culture

> In the beginning was the deed.
>
>   —Wittgenstein, 1980a, p. 3.

Wittgenstein, like Nietzsche, holds a Romantic view of culture. Romanticism is that countermovement of thought that sought to redeem the spirit of man in relation to culture and nature. In this sense, it can be interpreted as a movement that provides a counterpoint to the Enlightenment view that construed the essence of man as consisting in the possession of reason. Against this image of man that subjects both man and culture to the ultimate tribunal of reason, the Romantic view emphasized man as a cultural being where human life was seen as emerging through culture as both an expressive and natural force. As Yuval Lurie (1992, p. 195) argues:

From a Romantic point of view, the life pursued and achieved by human beings in a culture was judged similar in kind to the creation of a work of art. Culture, on this view, was seen to provide the necessary aesthetic framework for thus expressing the life of man. It was seen as a joint communal effort to produce a "great work of art." Within such an effort, individual human beings affiliate themselves by learning to express themselves within its refined practices and cherished customs. In so doing, they contribute to a given cultural tradition, draw sustenance from it, and, thereby, give deeper meaning to their lives.

Lurie (1992) suggests that Wittgenstein sought to redeem the idea of man as a cultural being in two different literary contexts: in the remarks Wittgenstein makes about what he calls "the natural history of man" and in a series of remarks he makes about art, religion, and ritual. The first set describe rule following activities through the processes of initiation into certain basic linguistic practices (language games), centering around topics such as naming, meaning, intending, knowing, and the like. The second set, referring directly to aesthetics, describes religious, artistic, and ritualistic behavior as manifestations of "the spirit of man." Lurie (1992, p. 196) maintains: "Ultimately the goal is to bridge the gap created in philosophical thinking between culture and nature by offering both *a naturalized view of the spirit of man* and a *cultural view of the nature of human beings* and their doings."

Human life begins in doing rather than thinking, and Wittgenstein naturalizes our conception of culture and human beings by placing an "emphasis on actions rather than thoughts, on responses rather than reasons, on descriptions rather than explanations, on attitudes and skills rather than on opinions and justifications" (Lurie, 1992, p. 197). By stressing a mode of being that is grounded in actions Wittgenstein seeks to restrict the roles of reason and intellect and to dispel their philosophical importance by returning them to their natural origins. Concept formation comes about through an extension of human beings in their ability to learn to react in culturally determined ways to different things being the same: "It is the ability of a group of human beings to adopt shared responses and to develop common judgements (as to what counts as the 'same') which brings about the formation of concepts" (p. 198). Rule following, on Wittgenstein's account, is "formulated abstractions of certain *cultural practices*" (p. 199). As Lurie (p. 199) explains further:

Linguistic practices do not come into being as a result of rules formulated and interpreted in the realm of reason and then pursued to their logical conclusions in understanding and speech. Rules are not the metaphysical basis for the emergence of language games. It is the other way round. Language games are the basis in action for the emergence of what is referred to as "reason." And it is on the basis of such practices that rules are later derived and articulated by means of abstract reasoning. Rules are merely the abstract expressions of socially administered and refined deeds.

Culture on Wittgenstein's view, then, offers human beings a spiritual home in the sense that they can devote themselves to its observance through tradition or invent new cultural forms. Language is the "foremost *cultural* creation of man" (Lurie, 1992, p. 203) because it provides "a cultural and hence also a spiritual expression of refined, natural (forms of) life" (pp. 202–3).

It is against this background that Lurie (1992) interprets Wittgenstein's remarks that the spiritual (forms of) life that we refer to as culture no longer exists. We now live, Wittgenstein argues using Spengler's term, in an age of "civilization," where natural forces that once found their expression in the creation of cultural practices have been replaced by reason alone. Civilization is an age of spiritual decline, where culture disappears.

It is this view of culture, which Wittgenstein embraces, that brings him into close proximity to Nietzsche. Jacques Bouveresse (1992, p. 29) discusses Wittgenstein's view of the epic of the disappearance of his own culture where "the dissolution of traditional organic relations consecrates the triumph of individualism." He suggests "Just like Nietzsche, Wittgenstein saw in the disappearance of the will to tradition and the triumph of disorganisation principles for the essential characteristics of the modern age."

Building upon this view, we are particularly struck by a number of thematically related remarks Wittgenstein makes on contemporary Western culture and the scientific world view in the context of remarks made in 1929 and the early 1930s. He talks of "my cultural ideal" (1980a, p. 2e), wondering whether it derives from Schumann's time though continuing that ideal instinctively and in a different way. He distinguishes technical refinement in modern film-making with the formation of a style, where spirit plays a role (p. 3e). In the context of examining a remark made to him by Engelmann, who looks at what he has written and finds it splendid, Wittgenstein says "he is seeing his life as a work of art created by God" (p. 4e). Quoting himself, he says: "The earlier culture will become a heap of rubble and finally a heap of ashes, but spirits will hover over the ashes" (p. 3e). In the sketch for a foreword to *Philosophical Remarks* Wittgenstein is, perhaps, most explicit about his sympathies. "This book is written for those who are in sympathy with the spirit in which it is written. This is not, I believe, the spirit of the main current of European and American civilization. The spirit of this civilization makes itself manifest in the industry, architecture and music of our time, in its fascism and socialism, and it is alien and uncongenial to the author" (p. 6e).

In an age of civilization the arts disappear (as does culture), yet their disappearance does not imply a judgement about those individuals who make up civilization. The strong simply turn their attention to other things. This passage has the unmistakable ring of Nietzsche about it in terms not only of the conception of culture it presages but also in the concern for the audience or reader and the idea that the work will be understood only by those "fellow citizens" who share a similar ideal and form his "cultural milieu" (Wittgenstein, 1980a, p. 10). Wittgenstein continues: "A culture is like a big organization which assigns each of its members a place where he can work in the spirit of the whole; and it is perfectly fair for his power to be measured by the contribution he succeeds in making to the whole enterprise. In an age without culture, on the other hand, forces become fragmented and the power of an individual man is used up overcoming opposing forces" (p. 6e). Our age, Wittgenstein suggests, is not that where men work toward the same end in the formation of a great cultural work but rather one of an "unimpressive spectacle of a crowd" where the best work for purely private ends. Still this is not to deny that the energy exists: "I realize then that the disappearance of a culture does not signify the disappearance of human value" (p. 6e).

Wittgenstein suggests that the typical Western scientist will not understand the spirit in which he writes because the scientist belongs to a civilization characterized by progress and dedicated to constructing an ever more complicated structure. For such scientists clarity is only a means to an end. By contrast, for Wittgenstein clarity is an end in itself. By way of distinguishing his way of thinking from that of the typical scientist he says: "I am not interested in constructing a building, so much as in having a perspicuous view of the foundations of possible buildings" (1980a, p. 6e). Wittgenstein sharply distinguishes between science and philosophy. As Hans Sluga (1996, p. 25) observes, Wittgenstein stands in opposition "to those movements in the twentieth century that have sought to reconstruct philosophy in a scientific manner," and he refers to Wittgenstein's ironic remark in the *Blue Book* (1958, p. 18) that the philosophical tendency to ask and answer questions in the manner of science is the real source of metaphysics. Wittgenstein elaborates why he considers this to be the case in the following lucid remark made in 1947: "The truly apocalyptic view of the world is that things do not repeat themselves. It isn't absurd, e.g., to believe that the age of science and technology is the beginning of the end for humanity; that the idea of great progress is a delusion, along with the idea that the truth will ultimately be known; that there is nothing good or desirable about scientific knowledge and that mankind, in seeking it, is falling into a trap. It is by no means obvious that this is not how things are" (1980a, p. 56e). Although he finds scientific questions interesting, they never really grip him as philosophical problems do (p. 79). The problem of culture is a philosophical problem that cannot be resolved through science or through adopting a scientific method because scientific civilization is part of the problem.

In a wistful passage written in 1931, Wittgenstein reflects upon his work.

There are problems I never get anywhere near. . . . Problems of the intellectual world of the West that Beethoven (and perhaps Goethe to a certain extent) tackled and wrestled with, but which no philosopher has ever confronted (perhaps Nietzsche passed them by). And perhaps they are lost as far as western philosophy is concerned, i.e. no one will be there capable of experiencing, and hence describing, the progress of this culture as an epic. Or more precisely, it just no longer is an epic, or is so only for someone looking at it from outside, which is perhaps what Beethoven did with prevision (as Spengler hints somewhere). (1980a, p. 9e)

Only in the language of prophecy in which the great poets speak is it possible to provide an epic description of this culture as a whole because the end can only be foreseen. Its signs are subtle and obscure and the description is comprehensible only to the few. Yet Wittgenstein holds open the possibility that "Perhaps one day this civilisation will produce a culture" (p. 64e).

Wittgenstein and Philosophy as Therapy

If Wittgenstein shares a similar notion of culture to Nietzsche, it is also the case that he, like Nietzsche, speaks of a new way of philosophizing (Wittgenstein, 1980a, p. 1e) — a new style of philosophy or of thinking (see chapters 9 and 10) — that is therapeutic (Wittgenstein, 1953, #133) and designed to resolve puzzles that arise in our language through grammatical investigations. Both Nietzsche and Wittgenstein emphasize the importance of language — its powers to mystify us — and philosophy as the means by which we can undertake grammatical investigations to demystify metaphysical problems. Nietzsche (1989, #16, p. 23), for instance, writes in relation to the "I think" or the "I will": "I shall repeat a hundred times; we really ought to free ourselves from the seduction of words!" The "old philologist" (Nietzsche's self-description) tells us we must become aware of and overcome grammatical habits (p. 24). He talks of the awkwardness of language and investigates, as does Wittgenstein, the misleading grammatical forms that produce a metaphysical illness: "Formerly, one believed in 'the soul' as one believed in the grammar and the grammatical subject: one said, 'I' is the condition, 'think' is the predicate and conditioned — thinking is an activity to which thought *must* supply a subject as cause. Then one tried with admirable perseverance and cunning to get out of this net" (#54, p. 67).

For Wittgenstein, too, philosophy can be likened to the "treatment of an illness" (1953, #254) and, in terms similar to Nietzsche, he suggests that metaphysical problems arise when we attempt to use scientific methods to investigate philosophical problems. He asserts "We are engaged in a struggle with language" (1980a, p. 11e) and suggests "Philosophy is a battle against the bewitchment of our intelligence by means of language" (1953, #109). There are significant differences in Wittgenstein's views between, say, the *Tractatus* and the *Investigations*. As P.M.S Hacker (1996, p. 110) notes, although "the *Tractatus* programme for future philosophy formally propounded a cognitive conception of philosophy," neverthe-less, analysis was seen to "reveal the logical forms of reality." By contrast: "The *Investigations* delineates a purified non-cognitive conception of philosophy. It is indeed the case that there are no philosophical truths; what appear as such are grammatical propositions which are familiar rules for the use of words in the misleading guise of statements. They neither say nor show anything about the logical form of phenomena" (Hacker, 1996, p. 110). Hacker (p. 111) maintains that there are two primary aspects to Wittgenstein's later conception of philosophy: the first emphasizes philosophy as "a quest for a surveyable representation of the grammar of a given problematic domain, which will enable us to find our way around when we encounter philosophical difficulties"; the second emphasizes philosophy as "a cure for diseases of the understanding." In both these aspects Wittgenstein's conception may be favorably compared to Nietzsche's: the first corresponds to Nietzsche's own grammatical and philological investigations; the second to Nietzsche's notion of the philosopher as cultural physician. Both aspects point fruitfully to paral-lels in Nietzsche's and Wittgenstein's conception of future philosophy, although there are also strong differences within these broad parameters.

Broadly speaking, both Wittgenstein and Nietzsche argue that philo-sophical illnesses (or what Hacker calls "pathologies of the intellect") have corresponding physiology given by the representation of expres-sions that are philosophically problematic. Philosophical problems that arise from misinterpretations of the forms of our language "are deep disquietudes; their roots are as deep in us as the forms of our language, and their significance is as great as the importance of our language" (Wittgenstein, 1953, #110). These are primarily questions of cultural health. They concern deep problems that often arise when the practical engagement with human life has been ignored. As Wittgenstein writes: "The way to solve the problem you see in your life is to live in a way that will make what is problematic disappear" (1980a, p. 27e). Insofar as we are still preoccupied with the same philosophical problems as the Greeks and have made no "progress," it is "because our language has remained the same and keeps seducing us into asking the same questions" (p. 15e).

There are also striking differences between Nietzsche and Wittgen-stein. Nietzsche would not agree that philosophy "leaves everything as it is" (Wittgenstein, 1953, #124) or that it is concerned only with "establishing an order in our knowledge of the use of language" (#132). For him "new philosophers" — "philosophers of the future" — are those who go beyond good and evil to legislate new values and "to teach man the future of man as his *will*" (Nietzsche, 1989, #203, p. 117). "*Genuine philosophers*," Nietzsche says, "*are commanders and legislators*: they say, '*thus* it shall be!'" (#211, p. 136).

NOTES

1. Leiber (1997, p. 250, n1) provides a sample of papers written in the early 1900s. He quotes one source (Herbert Stewart in 1909) as commenting that "nothing . . . quite so worthless as 'Thus Spake Zarathrustra' or 'Beyond Good and Evil' has ever attracted so much attention from serious students of the philosophy of morals."

2. Steven Ascheim's (1992) *The Nietzsche Legacy in Germany, 1890–1990* is perhaps the most comprehensive cultural history of Nietzsche's reception and influence in Germany. His account provides a reading of the complex and "changing relations between Nietzsche and German politics and culture" (p. 15). His interpretation avoids reducing the significance of Nietzsche's work to a single authentic and authoritative meaning. His account centers on the "complex and interconnected modalities of irrationalism and modernism and Nietzsche's definitive complicity in both" (p. 16), and he argues,

These two dispositions, so central to twentieth-century consciousness, were never simply destructive and reactionary nor emancipatory and progressive. The dangers and positive possibilities could never be neatly severed. Germany's leading irrationalist and modernist, the inveterate Nietzschean Gottfried Benn, captured this in his 1933 remark that the "irrational means close to creation, and capable of creation."
Nietzsche was foundational to this specific consciousness of creation as radical and experimental freedom; in later discourse he became the central symbol of the post-christian, postrationalist, nihilist predicament and its correlated, profoundly destructive, and liberating possibilities. The capacity for symbolically incarnating fundamental issues marked Nietzsche's reception throughout its history. (p. 16)

3. For recent overviews of Nietzsche's reception see Behler (1996), Schrift (1995, 1996), and Large (1993).

4. See, for example, Allison (1977), De Man (1979), and Nehamas (1985).

5. Leiber (1997, p. 251) provides the following survey of the new appreciation of Nietzsche's ethics in the English-speaking world:

For Alasdair MacIntyre . . . Nietzsche is the first to diagnose the failure of the project of post-Enlightenment moral theory. . . . For Annette Baier, he is one of those "great moral philosophers" who show us an alternative to the dominant traditions in modern moral theory in which we "reflect on the actual phenomenon of morality, see what it is, how it is transmitted, what difference it makes." For Susan Wolf, he represents an "approach to moral philosophy" in which the sphere of the "moral" comes to encompass those personal excellencies that Utilitarian and Kantian moral theories seem to preclude. For other recent writers, he figures as the exemplar of a philosophical approach to morality that these writers either endorse (e.g., Philippa Foot) or reject (e.g., Thomas Nagel, Michael Slote). Indeed, in looking at the claim common to critics of morality like Slote, Foot, Wolf, and Bernand Williams — that "moral considerations are not always the most important considerations" — Robert Louden has recently asked, "Have Nietzsche's 'new philosophers' finally arrived on the scene?"

The essence of Leiber's (p. 252) position, one that is consistent with the theme of this chapter, is that Nietzsche is "a genuine critic of *morality* as a real cultural phenomenon, while recent Anglo-American writers are only critics of particular *philosophical theories of morality.*"

    6.   See, for example, Heller (1959), Williams (1988), Janaway (1989), and, most recently, Bearn (1997).

    7.   Baker and Hacker (1980, p. 32) note that family resemblance appears in Nietzsche's (1989) *Beyond Good and Evil*. It occurs at #20 (p. 27) in the section entitled "On the Prejudices of Philosophers" where Nietzsche is explaining how philosophical concepts do not just suddenly appear in the history of thought or evolve autonomously but grow up in relationship with each other in a linguistic system. The section, because of its resonances with Wittgenstein's own views, is worth repeating:

That individual philosophical concepts are not anything capricious or autonomously evolving, but grow up in connection and relationship with each other; that, however suddenly and arbitarily they seem to appear in the history of thought, they neverthelesss belong just as much to a system as all the members of a fauna to a continent — is betrayed in the end also by the fact that the most diverse philosophers keep filling in a definite fundamental scheme of possible philosophies. Under an invisible spell, they always revolve once more in the same orbit; however independent of each other they may feel themselves with their critical or systematic wills, something within them leads them, something impels them in a definite order, one after the other — to wit, the innate systematic structure and relationship of their concepts. (Nietzsche, 1989, p. 27)

It also clear that Wittgenstein read Nietzsche's *Human, All Too Human*, because he refers to it in a note in 1947: "Nietzsche writes somewhere that even the best poets and thinkers have written stuff that is mediocre and bad, but have separated off the good material" (1980a, p. 59e).

3

Schopenhauer and Wittgenstein: The Reference of "I"

The I, the I is what is deeply mysterious.
— Wittgenstein, 1961, 80e

Wittgenstein was an enigmatic character: or should one say, person, or self, or subject? Or should one take a more modern approach to these philosophical problems and talk of subjectivity? He designed houses and many of their mechanistic requirements with a holistic technological and aesthetic approach. In a letter to Bertrand Russell he referred to Mozart and Beethoven as "the actual sons of God." He watched cowboy films and read thrillers among many other things. In these respects he was, perhaps, a postmodern version of the Renaissance man. Yet, in spite of his obvious enjoyment of many aspects of contemporary culture he remained deeply suspicious, if not deeply critical and pessimistic, of its effects or outcomes for human beings. We have discussed these general issues above. In relation to identity, the self, or subjectivity, these general issues on culture and pessimism strike hard at the traditional liberal notions of the self, particularly those based upon personal autonomy.

In recent years there has been an increased interest in the notion of the self, for example, in the writings of Michel Foucault and Charles Taylor (1989), to select two writers from vastly different philosophical traditions. There are a number of questions that can be posed around the notion of the self and these have a history. There are questions such as: What kind of being am I?, On what does my identity depend?, and To what does "I" refer? We will look at the first two questions as they have been posed by earlier philosophers before turning explicitly to the third question concerning the reference of "I" and the answers of Schopenhauer and Wittgenstein. In the next chapter we will turn to Foucault's account of the self.

Influenced by Schopenhauer, as was Nietzsche and thereby Foucault, on the notion that the self was not an individuated substance and that "I" did not refer to a substantive self, Wittgenstein does not, however, advance beyond a negative position on the self. According to Sluga (1996b) for Wittgenstein either "I" referred to the body, which seems to be one interpretation of his comments on the "I," or it referred to nothing, which is the other interpretation. From Wittgenstein's general pessimistic view this means at the least that if "I" refers to the body it is totally open to cultural, social, and historical influences because it is an object in the world, or that if there is nothing in the world of objects that is referred to by "I," nothing can be done from cultural, social, and historical influences, essentially in the world of objects, to a "nothing" not in the world of objects. This latter position on the self would permit a disengagement from a society seen as in an irreversible state of decay. This is a very dark reading of Schopenhauer's theoretical (but not personal and practical) position on the self. Wittgenstein's own position was deeply pessimistic also. However, this pessimism was not adapted by Foucault. He argued consistently that something could be done by the self to the self. Those issues need considerable unpacking in a tour through a city that includes Schopenhauer, Nietzsche, Wittgenstein, and Foucault, but a city that can be traversed in various "vehicles," and that one can track by various routes. In other and more analytical words, we are not arguing that there are direct and explicit uses of, say Schopenhauer by Wittgenstein (although there are some), or of Nietzsche by Foucault, but that there is a certain communality of views based upon the notion that the self is not an individuated self, substance, or object. It must be added, however, that although Wittgenstein knows his Schopenhauer and Foucault his Nietzsche, neither engaged explicitly with the philosophical traditions, and made few references to early influences upon them or to their sources in their major published works.

INTRODUCING WITTGENSTEIN ON THE SELF

Let us start from this 1950 comment by Wittgenstein (1980a, p. 84e): "There is nothing outrageous in saying that a man's character may be influenced by the world outside him (Weininger). Because that only means that, as we know from experience, men change with circumstances. If it is asked: How *could* a man, the ethical in a man, be *coerced* by his environment? — the answer is that even then he may say 'No human being has to give way to compulsion,' yet under such circumstances he *will* as a matter of fact act in such and such a way." It is interesting here that, as late as 1950, Wittgenstein is still referring to Weininger, who was certainly a formative influence upon him (Janik & Toulmin, 1973) (and might have been dismissed as merely that). The points we would note here are that first, Weininger was himself influenced by Schopenhauer and second, that of the continuity of thought in Wittgenstein with his *fin de siècle* Vienna.

Wittgenstein says "men change with circumstances." By this he means that in spite of what a person professes to think certain circumstances can change his actions and thereby the person's character. What is changed: the body with its actions, decisions, verbal behavior, thinking or "the ethical in a man?" This opens up the possibility that as the actions change, and that is the change in character noted by Wittgenstein, that the ethical self has not changed. Normally we would expect the self, the ethical, to have changed and not merely the observed behavior of a self, but Wittgenstein does not say this. Because it is left open, the possibility exists that there is either no self at all, or that there is merely a set of bodily characteristics, which is referred to by Wittgenstein's use of "man." Either the self refers to the body or it refers to nothing. This is a paradox and dilemma in both Wittgenstein's earlier and later works. Thus, in a section clearly influenced by Schopenhauer (Wittgenstein, 1961, p. 80e): "The thinking subject is surely mere illusion. But the willing subject exists . . . The I, the I is what is deeply mysterious. The I is not an object. I objectively confront every object. But not the I" and "'I' is not the name of a person, nor 'here' of a place, and 'this' is not a name. But they are connected with names. Names are *explained* by means of them" (Wittenstein, 1953, #410, emphasis added).

It would appear that "I" does not refer to what we normally think of as a self, soul, subject, or person, given that to name is to refer. The I is a mystery, but it is certainly not an object. Indeed, there is a hostility in Wittgenstein's writings to any notion of a substantive and individuated self. Yet late in his life he is to say: "But it is still false to say . . . I is a different person from LW" (Wittgenstein, 1982, (II):88). These two quotations open up a possible paradox of the self in Wittgenstein's writings, because how can "I" not refer to a self, but not be a different person from LW? This is the paradox that will be explored below, before turning to Wittgenstein's notion that names are explained by the use of "I."

He says also that "I" explains a name (Wittgenstein, 1953, #410). To understand this we must consider the conditions under which "I" is learned and how "I" is taught to children, because it can be argued from a broadly Wittgensteinean position that there is a kind of logical connection between the meaning of some concepts and the conditions under which they are taught and learned (Macmillan, 1985; McCarty & McCarty, 1995). Wittgenstein's position is not that there are causal relations between a concept and the actual events or processes of teaching and learning, but rather between the concepts that are learned and the concepts of teaching and learning. Thus, certain general facts constitute a background situation against which particular concepts are learned. Thus, in *On Certainty* he talks about certainty and doubt, and correct judgments and mistakes, noting, for example, (1969, p. 156): "In order to make a mistake, a man must always judge with certainty" and (1969, p. 160): "The child learns by believing the adult. Doubt comes after belief." We will argue that the use of "I" needs to be understood against the logical background in which we acquire meaning for "I" and that this has further bearing upon how we use "I" in utterances such as "I am LW."

Wittgenstein returned often to the topic of the self in his discussions of mind, mental states, and actions. According to Hans Sluga (1996b): "To trace Wittgenstein's discussion of the self, means . . . to trace the complex web of connections between questions of mind and language." This is the path that we will take also.

THE SELF AND LANGUAGE

In relation to language and philosophy Wittgenstein said (1953, #109): "Philosophical problems . . . are not empirical problems: they are solved, rather, by looking into the workings of our language, and that in such a way as to make us recognise those workings: in spite of an urge to misunderstand them. The problems are solved, not by giving new information, but by arranging what we have always known. Philosophy is a battle against the bewitchment of our intelligence by means of language." And slightly later (1953, #126): "Philosophy simply puts everything before us, and neither explains nor deduces anything. Since everything lies open there is nothing to explain. For what is hidden, for example, is of no use to us."

Wittgenstein is not saying in the last sentence that all that is hidden is of no use, and that everything is clearly open, becaue what is of use and important to resolving philosophical puzzles may be obscured, difficult to see, and hidden in that sense. We may have an orientation toward viewing the world, like a pair of glasses that can distort our vision or prevent us seeing something (1953, #103). A proper function of philosophy is not to change to different glasses (academic philosophy), but to take these glasses off, so that we can view various uses of language more appropriately. Another possibility is that something is so familiar that it has become hidden, and philosophical perplexity has arisen because that which is so familiar has been ignored. The work of philosophy, therefore, "consists in assembling reminders" (#127) about our language. Thus, "the results of philosophy are the uncovering of one or another piece of plain nonsense and of bumps that the understanding has got by running its head up against the limits of language" (#119). Philosophy in Wittgenstein's sense is to smooth out these bumps by destroying what is nothing but houses of cards so that we come to "command a clear view of the use of our words" (# 121). One such bump or house of cards is the notion of the self, but in order to understand the position he takes we need to look at earlier notions of the self or personal identity.

PERSONAL IDENTITY

Descartes is arguably responsible for initiating a quagmire in his discussion of the nature of the self. In the well-known *Meditations* (1967) he argued from the awareness of his thoughts that he existed as a substance named or signified by "I," and that this substance was immaterial and entirely distinct from the body. This was the outcome of determining what "this 'I' was." Even so it is not obvious how "this 'I'" refers at all, for the uses of terms like "this," "that," "here," and "now" need disambiguating for their reference to be made clear. As Wittgenstein points out they do not operate like proper names or referring expressions.

In his *Essay on Human Understanding* (II, XXVII, 3–10) Locke (1964) discusses several notions of identity beginning his discussion by categorizing four types of identity. These he says are: identity of matter, identity of organized biological matter such as vegetables, identity of animals, and personal identity. Locke is not merely showing that identity has several meanings, but rather that attention must be paid to the things to which it is attributed. Thus, identity is said by Locke to be different in the four categories that he considers. In the case of matter identity depends upon there being the same atoms, but for persons it is different: "it being the same consciousness . . . personal identity depends on that only."

However, on the nature of the self Locke differed from Descartes: he did not think that the self was a thinking substance but that at best was annexed to a substance, and that being the same self depended only upon the same consciousness and not upon the same substance. Thus, Locke concludes his discussion of personal identity by asserting that if I who was Socrates am now the present Mayor of Queenborough, then I am. Thus, the self is identified with consciousness, and the identity of the self depends upon the same consciousness, that is, an identity statement asserting the same consciousness over a time interval.

In what are a number of confusing sections a major point of Locke's is that in order to say that I who am doing something now had certain experiences in the past then I do not have to ascertain that I am the same substance (stuff, body, and so forth) as the person who had earlier experiences (Hacker, 1990, p. 473). In Locke the self rests as something quite mysterious.

Hume says that identity is a relation that a thing has to itself, thus commencing with the logically pure schema a = a, as properly representing identity. However, he does have doubts about this notion, saying: "We cannot in any propriety of speech, say, that an object is the same with itself, unless we mean, that the object existent at one time is the same with itself existent at another" (Hume, 1964, I, IV, ii, p. 201). Hence what we are trying to express is a proposition of form a = b. A proposition of this contingent form does not have the logical purity of the proposition a = a. However, because we cannot *reason* from a = a to a = b or vice versa, we cannot be certain of identity.

We also cannot establish this from observation. If it were thought that at least continuous observation between time t_1 and time t_2 would establish a contingent identity statement, Hume's response is that far from establishing a relation of identity this would only establish unity (1964, I, IV, ii, p. 200). Thus, Hume is led to conclude in typical skeptical fashion that identity "can never arise from reason, but must arise from the imagination" (p. 209).

In relation to the self Hume says (1964, I, IV, vi) there is no constant invariable impression that would give rise to the notion of a self as a simple continuant or unity — we cannot have an impression from constant observation of any such unity. When I examine the notion of the self, Hume says, I can only find a particular perception — "I can never catch myself at any time without a perception, and can never observe anything but the perception" (p. 252). He ends by asserting that the self is merely a series or collection of perceptions in a constant flux with no real connections between these distinct perceptions and with no substantial underpinning entity to provide any unity. As the notion of identity as a relation arises from the imagination, we cannot therefore be certain about identity statements.

This philosophical bump started from Descartes's emphasis on cognition in the famous dictum *"cogito, ergo sum"* from which he inferred that insofar as I exist I am a thinking substance or being. Thereby we have a dualism between mind and body. Now this presents a fundamental philosophical puzzle that if my very self depends upon consciousness, and my identity depends upon memory, and I am in no way logically dependent upon my body, then perhaps I could change bodies. This possibility is pursued extensively by Shoemaker (1963). He talks of a mind-body operation in which two minds are removed from their accompanying bodies and inserted in the other body. It seems from the premises provided in the tradition that such an operation is logically possible and although this might be of considerable interest to neoliberal neurosurgeons, such notions were dismissed by Wittgenstein somewhat scathingly (1975, #60–66). Certainly such thinking was indicative of people who did not know their way about (1953, #23).

IDENTITY STATEMENTS

In Locke and Hume we can identify a relation of identity expressed in
identity statements that seem to be either of the form a = a or a = b. The
former is analytic and the latter contingent, it is normally said. We will
start with two propositions that can be thought to exhibit the logical form
of a contingent identity statement, a = b; (1) "The president of the United
States is Bill Clinton" and (2) "I am Ludwig Wittgenstein." The normal
interpretation is that these all exhibit the same form (or can be analyzed in
ways that permit them to be considered as contingent propositions of
identity). In the two propositions we have a mixture of names, definite
descriptions, and the first person pronoun, or "I," and these can be treated
as the same, as being potential substitution instances for "a" and "b" in
the proposition a = b.

First within the Anglo-American philosophical tradition contingent
identity statements of form a = b are usually considered to be logically
inferior to a proposition of form a = a. This second proposition is sometimes said to represent pure identity, to which at best contingent propositions like a = b approximate or aspire from their position of inferior
contingency toward the logical purity of a = a.

As we have seen this is to be found in Hume's *Treatise*. It was to be
repeated by Bertrand Russell who, arguing from the logical purity of
"Everything is identical with itself," that is, given any particular a, then a
= a is analytically true, then proceeded to use the denial of this proposition to define the null set, that is, the set of all things not identical with
themselves, and this became the base for his approach to reducing mathematics to set theory. (There is a difficulty here because strictly speaking
the denial of a = a would appear to be meaningless and, therefore, its use
to define the null set seems questionable.)

W. E. Johnson (1923) in his discussion of identity says that the most
trivial and apparently insignificant use of the relation of identity occurs
with the use of the formula x = x, where "what is primarily meant is that
in repeated occurrences of the word x . . . the word shall mean in any later
occurrence what it meant in an earlier occurrence" (1923, p. 186). Thus, for
Johnson the relation of identity is not to be construed so that "an object is
identical with itself" has some kind of logical priority, as in Hume. In
Alfred Tarski's logic (1946, pp. 54–56) identity theory is not seen as part of
the fundamental core of logic, but is introduced as follows: "x = y if, and
only if, x has every property which y has, and y has every property which
x has." As x can be a substitution for y then x = x is only provable within
the system and only after x = y has been introduced into the system.

Wittgenstein (1971) also holds that identity is not necessary in logic
because a name cannot refer to more than one individual. However,
names can be symbolized in more than one way. Thus, for Wittgenstein a

contingent identity statement a = b is to be understood as "a" = "b," that is, it is a relation that exists between names of objects but not between the objects themselves. This possibility was supported by Frege (1960, p. 56), and Wittgenstein seems to have adopted this position from Frege, whose "logical work is constantly presupposed in Wittgenstein's writings" (Kenny, 1973, p. 26). For Wittgenstein the notion that an object is identical with itself says "nothing at all."

How does Wittgenstein deal with these puzzles about identity? How does he get a clear command of a view of self or a perspicuous representation that provides an understanding that destroys the bump constructed above by doing philosophy? The short answer is that he does not get a clear idea of a self, if by self is meant getting command of a clear idea of the self as an entity, referred to by "I." For Wittgenstein this is to confuse the meaning of "I," to assume that it operates referentially in the language and that propositions of the form "I am LW" are of the same logical form as a contingent identity statement: a = b. Our grammar confuses us. Instead "I" is used to explain a name (Wittgenstein, 1953, #410) — this point is developed below.

"I AM LW"

Does the analysis of contingent identity statements above apply to "I am LW"? Here the grammar of the two propositions that were provided as potential examples of contingent identity statements is misleading, because it suggests that they have the same logical form. Because we think this to be the case, that a = b represents the real form of the proposition "I am Ludwig Wittgenstein," this presents a feeling or character of intellectual depth into our inquiry into identity, but the depth is really a "deep disquietude" (Wittgenstein, 1953, #111), because the grammar has led us astray.

Wittgenstein distinguished between the real and the apparent form of a proposition. He had done this early, in the *Tractatus* (1971, 4.002). "Language disguises thought. So much so, that from the outward form of the clothing it is impossible to infer the form of the thought beneath it." To treat these propositions as having the same logical structure is to work from the outward clothing. Later he is to claim in similar fashion (1971, 5.41) that "modern theory of knowledge" actually takes the superficial appearance of these propositions to display their real logical form. Admittedly Wittgenstein was talking in those sources about different kinds of propositions, but the point must still be valid for propositions concerning personal identity. However, they are not valid because they fall under some general position on language or from any general theory of language which, it has been argued, Wittgenstein held. Whether the latter is correct, Wittgenstein certainly held that this position between true and apparent logical form held when philosophical inquiry from the alleged form of a proposition led to "the bewitchment of our intelligence by means of language." As we have seen earlier the mind-body transplant problem is one such bewitchment. It almost seems that bewitchment (or philosophical complexity and perplexity) is to be taken as a sign of mistaking the apparent logical grammar for the true logical grammar, though not an infallible sign.

There are three main reasons why propositions like "I am LW" do not have the traditional logical form of contingent identity statements, that is, a = b. These are concerned with: the difficulties in understanding traditional accounts of contingent identity statements, which have been introduced earlier; the differences from a = b of "I am LW," and the peculiar referential status of "I" in "I am LW." Not surprisingly these reasons are deeply embedded in academic or Anglo-American philosophy. Because enough has been said on understanding identity statements in general, we will turn to the second two reasons. Of necessity discussion of these two reasons must be run together because it hinges on the referential status of "I" to a self.

Wittgenstein had expressed early concerns in the *Tractatus* against a Cartesian conception of the self. Yet a Cartesian interpretation can be given for his picture theory of meaning. Thus, Harré and Gillett (1994, p. 18):

His [Wittgenstein's] early philosophy was entirely congenial with the understanding of the mind as a Cartesian realm in which subjects built up a picture of the world from their contact with it. The mind, so conceived, had direct relations to primitive features of reality, read off pictures of structured combinations of those features from states of affairs in the actual world, and performed logical operations on the resulting (pictured) combinations of those features. In his later philosophy, he rejected this picture theory in its entirety.

There is textual evidence in *Tractatus* (1971, 5.54ff), however, that he had begun to reject the Cartesian notion of the self quite early in his philosophical journey (Sluga, 1996b, p. 323).

Wittgenstein says that modern theory of knowledge is tainted by a philosophical flaw arising from our failure to distinguish between the real and apparent logical grammar of propositions (1971, 5.541; compare 1975, #1). Wittgenstein is quite explicit that he is referring to Russell and Moore (1971, 5.541; 5.5422). (Sluga makes the point that this is an odd criticism by Wittgenstein to make of a philosopher who had used just such a distinction in his logic, for example, in his famous analysis of propositions such as "The King of France is bald." Elsewhere in *Tractatus* Wittgenstein is acutely aware of this. The resolution that Sluga adopts is that Wittgenstein in the passages quoted is referring only to a draft of a book by Russell that, because of Wittgenstein's criticisms, was never completed.)

Russell had used a (broadly) Cartesian position on the self in which he held that there is a real self that is logically simple and that is capable of thought and perception (Sluga 1996b, p. 351). Russell held there that a proposition was more than the sum of its parts; it was a unity, and this unity was conferred by the self, a thinking subject who was able to confer this unity. He also held that "I" was a "proper name referring to this 'unity,'" although later he was to see it as a definite description. Thus, for Russell in this source (Sluga 1996b, p. 324): "The unity of the proposition was grounded in the unity of the thinking subject. . . . A broadly Cartesian conception of the mind, thus, appeared to be prerequisite for a satisfactory theory of meaning."

Wittgenstein's criticisms of Russell here, based upon the general claim about the misunderstanding of the logic of propositions, should not just be interpreted in terms of a general hostility toward Cartesianism and a notion of a self that was logically simple. What he is also attacking is the notion that (academic) philosophy, starting from its misunderstanding of the real logical grammar of a proposition, plunges into a philosophical mire of moves toward theory — in this case a theory of mind and a theory of language. Thus, Wittgenstein's position is that Russell's puzzle over the unity of a proposition, starting from the fact that a proposition was more than the sum of its parts, turns us in a certain direction toward something more deeply hidden and perhaps not yet articulated and formulated theory.

His points (Wittgenstein, 1971, 5.54ff) were not merely directed against theory construction per se, however, but also, and ultimately, against a self that was logically simple, transparent to reason, and one that could judge or think about perceptions and propositions. He was also stating here that understanding was "not essentially a Cartesian or inner set of processes but a range of moves or techniques defined against a background of human activity and governed by informal rules" (Harré & Gillett, 1994, p. 19).

The crux of Wittgenstein's objections to Russell's Cartesian position is that a proposition has a unity in itself and has no need for a thinking subject. His argument, which we take from Sluga (1996b, p. 325), is to the effect that "A believes that p" and "A says p" are really of the form "'p' says p." Now in order for A to say or believe p, A must be able to represent the content of the proposition "p" to its self. That means that the self must be able to represent the proposition "p" and must, therefore, be of the same logical complexity as "p." It cannot, therefore, be simple. The view of a Cartesian self, therefore, is incoherent and must be abandoned. This is not, of course, to demand that the self as such be abandoned. So for Wittgenstein the self cannot be Cartesian in that it is logically simple and capable of thinking, believing, judging, and so forth.

Rousseau had made similar objections to this notion of the self. He is arguably the first writer to bring a clearly defined notion of self, an ordinary self, and that of a largely atomistic and autonomous self, above the threshold of visibility in Western thinking (Gutman 1988, compare Taylor, 1989, chap. 20, who places Rousseau in a longer theoretical tradition). However, as Rousseau was concerned to draw limits to the domain of reason and its overevaluation, in his atomistic self it is the emotions that provide the basis for individuality or the self. Rousseau could not accept that what we need to become better as individual human beings is more reason and more rationally based learning, because that would presuppose some Cartesian notion of a self sufficiently transparent to be both made fully transparent by reason and also to be made better by reason. Instead of rationality laying bare the nature of the self by excluding through a harsh application of binary logic by Rousseau of all that belonged to the social, the self does not become transparent for Rousseau and rests as a muddle and a puzzle. It is certainly not logically simple. By rational standards it is, therefore, incomprehensible. Reason cannot penetrate this confusion and muddle. If muddle and confusion are not amenable to being penetrated and made clear by reason then it is difficult to see how the self can be made better by reason, for what aspects of the self could be identified in such muddle and confusion sufficiently well, if at all, in order for them to be made better?

Thus, early in *The Confessions of Jean-Jacques Rousseau* (1925), Rousseau says: "I felt before I thought." This is not merely a rejection of the metaphysics of rationality being definitive of the self as is inherent in Descartes's, "I think, therefore I am," or a rejection of arid rationalism, especially materialistic and mechanistic interpretations of human being, but instead an affirmative expression of the emotive life as the basis for the self (compare the metaphysics of the self in Simone de Beauvoir's early novels, *She Came to Stay* and *The Blood of Others*).

Wittgenstein's anti-Cartesianism was hardly original, because there were well-rehearsed objections to the Cartesian position available (Sluga 1996b, p. 327). It is most likely that Wittgenstein was made aware, and perhaps first made aware of these objections, in his early reading of Schopenhauer. Unfortunately Wittgenstein seldom acknowledges his intellectual debts. Objections to the Cartesian notion of the self are also to be found in Nietzsche and these were probably as influential upon Foucault as the antihumanist thrust of structuralism. As Schopenhauer also influenced Nietzsche (see next chapter) we will turn now to his account of the self.

SCHOPENHAUER

According to Russell (1946, p. 781) what is most striking about Schopenhauer's philosophy is that he is a pessimist, and this, Russell believes, is inconsistent with a considerable optimism in philosophy. Although Schopenhauer paraphrased his philosophy in the words, the world is the self-knowledge of the Will, this was a will that was essentially evil and the source of endless suffering. This suffering is not alleviated by the advancement of knowledge, because this brings more suffering. Because there can be no happiness, we can only pursue our futile purposes awaiting death. According to Russell (p. 784): "All this is very sad."

The limited way out (which Schopenhauer draws from Indian philosophy) is not to exercise the will, as the less we exercise the will the less we suffer. This means that man must turn away from the world of which phenomenal existence is an expression, and practice such things as chastity, voluntary poverty, fasting, and self torture. Janaway (1989, p. 26) suggests that his views here, particularly his views on suffering, were influenced by his wide travelling as a young man before he studied philosophy systematically. Because the will is the key to Schopenhauer's philosophy, it is in need of some exposition. Furthermore, the will is part of Schopenhauer's account of the self that influenced Wittgenstein's early account of the self (for example, 1971, 5.632–5.641, compare 1961, p. 82e).

The early influences upon Schopenhauer's philosophy were Kantian (Coppleston, 1965, p. 28). These are clear in Schopenhauer's doctoral dissertation, which leads onto his major work *The World as Will and Idea* (1923). Important here are the preservation of the Kantian notion of thing-in-itself and the notion that although space and time are a priori conditions of the perception of the external world they can also be included in the world as object, as presented to a subject (compare Wittgenstein, 1961, p. 83e). Schopenhauer also attempted to bypass the subject-object dichotomy because he believed that starting from either the subject or the object led to problems that were not able to be solved (1923, p. 44): "We start neither from the object nor from the subject, but from the *idea*, as the first fact of consciousness. Its first essential fundamental form is the antithesis of subject and object." This was Schopenhauer's answer to the Kantian dichotomy. The problems that he wished to bypass from the subject-object dichotomy were (p. 44): "We see then that the system which starts from the subject contains the same fallacy as the system . . . which starts from the object: it begins by assuming what it proposes to deduce, the necessary correlative of its starting point."

In Schopenhauer the idea unified the subject and the object in an "inseparable and reciprocal dependence" (1923, p. 40). For him the world is entirely idea (p. 38) but only insofar as the basis of all knowledge involves the dependence of subject upon object and vice versa. This means that the idea is the external phenomenal world, a world that exists only for knowledge, but this is not the only side of the world, because "it has an entirely different side — the side of its inmost nature, its kernel — the thing in itself . . . will" (p. 39).

Schopenhauer believed that metaphysics was possible. Here he parts company with Kant arguing that the claim that experience can never be a source of metaphysics was unfounded (Schopenhauer, 1968, vol. 1, p. 427): "The world and our own existence present themselves to us necessarily as a riddle. But now it is simply assumed that the solution to this riddle could not proceed from the thorough understanding of the world itself, but must be sought in something entirely distinct from the world (for that is the meaning of 'beyond the possibility of all experience')."

Metaphysics for Schopenhauer then is not restricted to a priori knowledge. Thus, his philosophy is not a mere bookish academic reaction to Kant but is related to reality, to ordinary experience as well as scientific knowledge. For Schopenhauer we are not passive disembodied spectators of a world of objects. Instead we are essentially embodied and active. The world for Schopenhauer is my representation. By this he means that the world is only that which appears to the representing subject, that is, a world of objects, and the world is exhausted in its perceptability. The world of objects of which we have knowledge is a world of appearance, but for there to be objects there must also be subjects. Now the nature of the subject is crucially important if, for example, charges of solipsism are to be avoided (for example, passages such as those referred to above in the *Tractatus* and the *Notebooks* are seen by Hacker [1986] as being influenced by Schopenhauer, and inclining Wittgenstein to solipsism). Janaway (1989) denies that Schopenhauer and Wittgenstein were solipsists.

In Schopenhauer's account of the self the subject is never an object and therefore cannot be an appearance for the subject, yet a subject is necessary for there to be objects. Thus, the subject is not in space and time, but is like an eye, which cannot see itself, yet which mirrors the world. However, the eye that is not seen constitutes limits on what is seen and on the world. It would be mistaken to argue from the fact that the subject does not exist in the objective world that it did not exist or was illusory or a mere nothing. The point made by the eye image of the "I" is merely that the subject is not something that is to be found in the world of objects. As Janaway says (1989, p. 328): "No one with a Schopenhauerean background would think that the non-objective status of the subject entailed its illusoriness."

So far the self is something of a mystery in Schopenhauer. First, the self is not merely a representer of the world. Then, starting with the self and self knowledge, he turns to the will. He distinguishes knowledge of objects from knowledge of our willed actions. The will for Schopenhauer is not to be distinguished or separated from action. We do not will and cause an action, nor do we make inferences from our observed actions to our willing those actions. Will is action. Instead of some mental act of willing issuing in some bodily movement, my will is expressed in action. My will is thus embodied. As I have knowledge of my will, in a form of immediate knowledge, I have access to the self, not provided to the "I" of the eye of representation. Willing thus has priority over the intellect in Schopenhauer's thought.

Schopenhauer uses the priority of the will over the intellect to launch an attack upon the rational and transparent self of Descartes. The body is a manifestation of will but in Schopenhauer's thought will comes to signify any end-directed process, whether conscious or not. Finally he presents us with a picture of the whole world springing into objecthood because of an all-pervading essence that he calls will. The will in us is also the will to life, an urge to live and to go on living.

For Schopenhauer the "I" is not merely will but a fusion of will and intellect with the will in primacy. Even so it is dependent upon the development of an organism's brain and nervous system. Schopenhauer now takes the pessimistic turn that Russell has identified. He argues, because of the dictates of the will, that we are bound to be in an almost continual state of anguish and despair, tormented if not driven by desires and unseen forces that we can never fully comprehend, control, or satisfy. Schopenhauer as metaphysician does not present us with anything optimistic about either the human condition or the possibilities for the human condition (for example, emancipation). Rather, all such hope is misplaced.

The minimal solution to this state of affairs is to restrict as far as possible the operation of the will through such things as fasting and celibacy. There are ways in which we can escape from the will according to Schopenhauer. One such way is through aesthetic experience, because we can be so involved in contemplation of the object that we cease to evaluate it in terms of our needs and desires and cease to will. In an aesthetic experience the subject ceases to be a subject of will and becomes a passive receptor of objective experience. Thus, one regards the world without imposing conceptual categories upon it and without regarding oneself as separate from the world. In such experiences one merges with what is experienced. However, in this interest free merging with experienced objects there is a change also in the object, which becomes more real itself. It becomes, according to Schopenhauer, an idea in almost a Platonic sense. Thus, Schopenhauer sees us as becoming closest to reality through aesthetic experiences. This awareness cannot be communicated, however, and all that philosophy can do is bring us to the brink of such comprehension. As Schopenhauer says (1968, vol. 2, pp. 611–12): "Philosophy's theme must restrict itself to the world; pronouncing in all respects what the world is, what it is in its innermost nature, is all that it can honestly achieve. . . . Here is precisely the point where the mystic proceeds positively, and from here on nothing remains but mysticism."

Thus, the only way to salvation in this world is to deny the will, to desist from seeking such things as possessions, power, and pleasure. Even if we tend to think this way, and in a highly individualistic manner, this is the source of immorality, according to Schopenhauer. Rather than being an individual experiencing subject, as subjects of experiences, we are manifestations of the world will. Once we realize this we are no longer likely to drive a wedge between a self and the rest of the world. If we are part of the world then we must impose our will as little as possible against that world or against other individuals.

Morality for Schopenhauer is not, therefore, concerned with moral principles, especially of the rational kind (Kant), because concepts are as inappropriate in ethics as they are in aesthetics. Ethics is a matter of the self taking a proper stance to the world as a whole and viewing the relationship between the self and the world correctly. Ethics is certainly not concerned with knowledge. Little can be said, therefore, about what seems to be a mystical account of the world and, given the illusory notion of the individual self, what must be a mystical account of the self and its relationship to the world.

WITTGENSTEIN AND SCHOPENHAUER

There are a number of similarities that can be identified between Wittgenstein and Schopenhauer. The earlier quotation on the respective role of philosophy and mysticism might be said to set the form or structure of the *Tractatus*. It certainly provides some explanation for the cryptic comments in the *Tractatus* from 6.4 to 6.54. To a certain extent these remarks are divorced in the *Tractatus* from the earlier remarks on logic and the world. Those later remarks have taken us to the Schopenhauerean brink, where mysticism is to take over. However, there are other explicit similarities in the text of the *Tractatus*: for example, on ethics and aesthetics (1971, 6.421), the mystical and inexpressible (1971, 6.45; 6.522), the world as a whole (1971, 6.45), and the "I" (1971, 5.6410). His indebtedness to Schopenhauer is clearer in the *Notebooks*. Some examples: "It would be possible to say (à la Schopenhauer)"; "It is not the world of Idea that is either good or evil; but the willing subject" (Wittgenstein, 1961, p. 79e); "You say that it is just as it is for the eye and the visual fields. But you do *not* actually see the eye" (p. 80e); "I objectively confront every object. But not the I" (p. 80e); "How can man be happy at all, since he cannot ward off the misery of this world?" (p. 81e); and "The work of art is the object seen sub specie aeternitatis; and the good life is the world seen sub specie aeternitatas. This is the connection between art and ethics" (p. 83e).

Our concern, however, is with the self or the reference of "I." As we have seen earlier in Schopenhauer, "I" does not refer to any substantive or individuated substance in the world. It is not illusory. Although

Wittgenstein says such things as, "it is true that the knowing subject is not in the world, that there is no knowing subject" (1961, p. 86e), and "The I is not an object" (p. 80e) what he means (à la Schopenhauer) is that the I is not an object that I objectively confront in the world: "I objectively confront every object. But not the I" (p. 80e). Because of this, he continues, "there really is a way in which there can and must be mention of the I in a *non-psychological sense* in philosophy" (p. 80e). It must not be psychological because the psychological I could be confronted objectively in the world, and the I that is the concern of both Schopenhauer and Wittgenstein is not an object in the world. It is not that there is no I but rather that the I cannot be discussed in the same way as objects in the world: objectivism, if we may call it that, is inapplicable to the I. The I is given in a non-objective way. This is not, therefore, a merely negative conclusion at this stage.

Here Wittgenstein seems to be parting company with Schopenhauer, because, whereas Schopenhauer says that all that philosophy can do on the notion of the I is take one to the brink and that mysticism must take over, in the *Notebooks*, as we have quoted, Wittgenstein says that philosophy can and must elucidate this notion of the I. On these issues Janaway suggests (1989, p. 321) that it is almost as if Wittgenstein has Schopenhauer's vocabulary but that he is unclear as to how to use it: "I am conscious of the complete unclarity of these sentences" (Wittgenstein, 1961, p. 79e). This concern is expressed before a series of remarks that can be seen as attempts to make those sentences clear (p. 79–89e).

Where he does part company with Schopenhauer is on metaphysics and on the interpretation of the notion that the world is my world. First, Schopenhauer makes much of metaphysics, for example, in relation to space and time and to ideas, but Wittgenstein will have little of that. Perhaps his position is best summarized in the *Blue Book*: metaphysics "leads the philosopher into complete darkness" (1958, p. 48).

Second, Schopenhauer seems caught with the notion of an I as an eye that mirrors the world, but Wittgenstein says the world is my world because of language. In the *Tractatus* at 5.62 he says: "The world is *my* world: this is manifest in the fact that the limits of *language* (of that language which alone I understand) mean the limits of *my* world." If there is any mirroring of "how I found the world" (Wittgenstein, 1961, p. 82e), it is not through the eye but through the logic of the language, which reflects the structure of the world. This is the position in *Tractatus*, and it is presaged in *Notebooks*.

Wittgenstein continues (1961, p. 82e, compare 1971, 5.641):

The philosophical I is not the human being, not the human body or the human soul with the psychological properties, but the metaphysical subject, the

boundary (not a part) of the world. The human body, however, my body in particular, is a part of the world among others, among animals, plants, stones, etc., etc.

Whoever realises this will not want to procure a pre-eminent place for his own
body or the human body.

Thus, it is a mistake to see the I as in the world but, insofar as the I sets the
limits to the world, to how I find the world, it is a proper aspect of philosophical inquiry for Wittgenstein, and not merely a Schopenhauerean
focal point for the mirroring of the world, clouded in mysticism. The
point that arises here is whether Wittgenstein has transgressed his position on philosophy, moving down a path toward a philosophical theory
of the self. Fogelin (1996, p. 45) believes that he has transgressed this self-
imposed stricture on philosophical theorizing, but he does not believe
that the transgression is sufficiently serious to be compromising for
Wittgenstein. To see if this is the case we need to look at how he treats
statements that both contain the first person "I" and contain references to
mental states such as pain. The central move, as we shall see in the next
chapter, is to treat first person statements of, for example, pain, as essentially similar to natural expressions of pain.

In summary at this point it can be said that if "I" does not refer to a
substantive individuated object in the world then "I am LW" is not a
contingent identity statement. "I" does not refer and therefore cannot be a
place holder in a contingent identity statement of logical form a = b.
Wittgenstein, like Schopenhauer, is left with the I as a mysterious entity,
but, in part, that may be because Wittgenstein has been asking the wrong
type of question, namely a what question: "*What* is the I?"

4

The Self:
Wittgenstein,
Nietzsche, Foucault

How one becomes what one is
                    — Nietzsche, 1992, p. 1

Neither Wittgenstein nor Foucault saluted each other in person or explicitly in print. When Wittgenstein died in April 1951 Foucault, still a student at École Normal Supérieure, was preparing for his second attempt at the *aggrégation*, after which he was to continue studies at the Fondation Thiers, and then take a lowly teaching position at the University of Lille in 1952. Wittgenstein would not have been aware of Foucault's existence.

However, Foucault was aware of Wittgenstein, although he has claimed that he did not study him in detail (Miller, 1993, p. 131, quoting from an interview in 1989 with Hans Sluga, a Wittgenstein scholar). Arnold Davidson (1997, p. 2) draws our attention, however, to a lecture given by Foucault in Japan in 1978 (Foucault, 1978, p. 540f.): "For a long time one has known that the role of philosophy is not to discover what is hidden, but to make visible precisely what is visible, that is to say, to make evident what is so close, so immediate, so intimately linked to us, that because of that we do not perceive it. Whereas the role of science is to reveal what we do not see, the role of philosophy is to let us see what we see."

There are a number of passages in Wittgenstein's *Philosophical Investigations* that bear close similarities to what Foucault has said in this brief extract, for example, "Philosophy may in no way interfere with the actual use of language: it can only describe it" (1953, #124); philosophy "simply puts everything before us, and neither explains nor deduces anything" (#126); "the aspects of things that are most important to us are hidden because of their simplicity and familiarity" (#129); and "our considerations could not be scientific ones. . . . The problems are solved not by giving new information, but by arranging what we have always known" (#109), because, "what is hidden, for example, is of no interest to us" (#126).

In the same source Foucault talks of analytic philosophy and uses the term to refer explicitly to Anglo-American philosophy, drawing a parallel between how analytic philosophy provides a critical analysis of thought "on the basis of the way in which one says things," and "in the same way, a philosophy that would have as its task to analyse what happens every day in relations of power" (Foucault, 1978, p. 541). The latter is to be a philosophy that bears not on Wittgensteinian language games but on relations of power. It is not to give a theory of power but a description of power, laying out what is visible and what we can see, in games of power.

Foucault refers to Wittgenstein explicitly in at least two sources (Foucault, 1966, 1977). Foucault also explicitly acknowledged parallels to the work of John Searle (private letter to Searle, May 15, 1979 cited in Dreyfus & Rabinow, 1983, p. 46). We do not wish to rest here, however, but to advance the comparison between Wittgenstein and Foucault by considering the notion of the self or the subject. Such a comparison is touched upon, but only very briefly by Sluga (1996b, p. 349). The structure of the chapter will be to attempt to advance from the mystical and pessimistic notion of the self or "I" with which we were left at the end of the preceeding chapter. We attempt to rectify this pessimistic conclusion on Wittgenstein by advancing an expressivist approach to identity statements, based upon Wittgenstein's notion that first person statements like "I am in pain" express pain and do not describe a mental state. The account will then shift to Foucault who, although believing in Wittgensteinian fashion that the "I" refers to nothing substantial, yet shows us how we can care for or nurture the self. His account of the self, although having parallels to Wittgenstein, is more optimistic and goes beyond the expressivist account of "I" statements.

"I" DOES NOT REFER

In the preceding chapter we saw how the "I" was treated as a non-referring term. In that case what kind of term is it? Grammatically it occupies the subject position in the sentence "I am LW," but logically it does not operate in that manner. Hacker (1990, pp. 479–81) identifies in *Tractatus* a more logico-linguistic analysis of the "I." As we have seen in Wittgenstein's analysis of "A believes that p" this is to be analyzed as "'p' says p." "I believe that p" is to be analyzed in a similar way. For Wittgenstein the

"I" in "I believe that p" does not operate as a logically proper name signifying a simple substance or a self. According to Hacker the Wittgenstein of the *Tractatus* thought that the "I" would disappear on analysis. Presumably this would be some form of logical analysis like that provided by Russell when he analyzed the proposition "The King of France is bald," when there is no such entity as the "the King of France." Russell's analysis transferred the term "King of France" into a predicate position so that its ascription to an entity "x" was merely false and not meaningless — that is, the problem of non-reference of the term had been bypassed and its meaningfulness retained. If Wittgenstein still held to some form of Schopenhauerean mysticism as late as 1916 (Wittgenstein, 1961, p. 82e) this, Hacker says, is to be abandoned later.

There are stronger arguments available to the effect that "I" is not a referring expression, for example in Anscombe's (1981) "The First Person." In that source she argues against a "common sense" view of "I," in which there are two components that can be called the referential and the indexical views. She notes problems with the reflexive pronoun "I" as "the explanation of the word 'I' as 'the word which each of us uses to speak of himself' is hardly an explanation" (1981, p. 23). Where did a self get into the picture and how do we explain "himself" (would that require an "I" for instance)?

In typically Wittgensteinian fashion she says that it is treating "I" as a sort of proper name that "gets us into this jam" (Anscombe, 1981, p. 23). In other words we have taken the grammatical occurrence of "I" and treated it as a proper name — this is the fault, she says, of logicians (for example, Russell, 1967, pp. 27–28). Thus any such question as "What does 'I' stand for?" is the wrong kind of question because it leads us down the murky track to Descartes' quagmire of substances and later, selves. Here the influence of Wittgenstein on (traditional and academic) philosophical questions is clear.

Instead Anscombe compares "I" with other demonstratives such as "this" and "that" (1981, p. 27). Because one can fail in trying to make reference with demonstratives such as "this" and "that," their use must always in principle require the removal of ambiguity. They are to be contrasted, however, because this cannot happen with the use of "I" — getting hold of the wrong object is excluded (p. 32). If we continue with "I" as a referring expression, however, as a logically proper name, then she concludes that Descartes was right — "I" refers to an immaterial Cartesian ego. Here her argument stops because she treats this conclusion as a *reductio* of the belief that "I" refers. For Anscombe, at best, "I" is like "it," as in "it is raining."

The other commonsense view that she attacks is the indexical view, according to which in each use of "I" the reference of the utterance is fixed by a rule to the effect that "I" in each particular use is to be taken as the producer of the utterance. Her argument against this view maintains that such a position is untenable because it does not allow for the inevitable fact that our "I" judgments manifest self-consciousness. Garrett (1997) claims that her examples in the argument only establish that the manifest fact of self-consciousness is not explained, and not that the indexical view is incompatible with that incontrovertible fact. Thus, she has at best a weak position. (Garrett also objects to other aspects of Anscombe's position.)

Although her position has Wittgensteinian influences, Wittgenstein did not go down the "it" as in "it is raining" track. Instead his treatment of first person statements is meant to bypass these problems and bridge the dichotomies between inner and outer, mind and body, and subjective-objective. This bridge depends upon an expressivist account of first person statements.

EXPRESSING PAIN

In the *Notebooks* Wittgenstein says: "the thinking subject is surely mere illusion," adding "the I is not an object" (1961, p. 80e). If we take his comment that it is false that I am not LW, alongside his comments that "I" does not refer to any substantive or individuated self and his general comments about the grammar of propositions, then we must return and look at the grammar of statements containing "I," especially those concerned with mental states, that is, those that ascribe thoughts, intentions, sensations to an "I." We are looking here for an account of the grammar of first person statements ascribing mental states that make them unique — expressions of natural feelings rather than descriptions of inner mental states.

The possibility of this is opened by Wittgenstein in the *Philosophical Investigations*, at least as early as #142. In the immediately preceding sections he had been discussing normal and abnormal cases of applying the picture of a cube, concluding (1953, #141): "I want to say: we have here a *normal* case, and abnormal cases." He continues (#142) that it is only in normal cases that the use of a word is clearly prescribed and that in abnormal cases we may not know what to say. If the rule becomes the exception and vice versa this would make our language games "lose their point." In particular we need characteristic expressions of pain, fear, and joy. Wittgenstein is ambiguous here as to whether first person statements of pain are expressions of pain. He is not yet saying explicitly that first person statements concerning pain, fear, and joy are expressions of pain, fear, and joy, but only that they must be understood against our characteristic expressions of pain behavior.

In the private language argument Wittgenstein asks (1953, #244): "How do words refer to sensations?" Wittgenstein explicitly makes the point here that first person statements ascribing pain sensations do not refer to sensations but express pain.

How does a human being learn the meaning of the names of sensations? — of the word "pain" for example. Here is one possibility: words are connected with the primitive, the natural, expressions of the sensation and used in their place. A child has hurt himself and he cries; and then adults talk to him and teach him explanations and, later, sentences. They teach the child new pain behaviour. "So you are saying that the word `pain' really means crying?" — On the contrary: the verbal expression of pain replaces crying and does not describe it.

The interpretation of this passage has been controversial. However, according to Fogelin (1996, p. 44): "there are a great many passages in the *Philosophical Investigations* and in his other writings that suggest that Wittgenstein was committed — in outline at the least — to something like an expressivist account of first person mental utterances." Fogelin states that Wittgenstein's expressivist approach to first person mental utterances is the outcome of intractable problems caused by the uncritical assumption that mental terms like "pain" get their meanings because they refer to inner states or processes. Treating first person mental utterances as similar to natural expressions of feeling — pain with a cry, for example — is an attempt to break away from these problems of reference and objectivity. Wittgenstein (1953, #302) talks of the subject of pain being the "person who gives it expression." However, Wittgenstein has also to break the notion that the expression of thought is a proposition and the expression of pain a cry (#317): "As if the purpose of the proposition were to convey to one person how it is with another: only, so to speak, in his thinking part and not in his stomach." The problem of the reference of "pain" is raised often, for example, at #288. Wittgenstein's central point is that we cannot be mistaken in our own case that we are in pain, because if I claimed to know how to use "pain" but didn't know whether this, what I have now, was pain, then we would seriously question my ability to use "pain." To search for a criterion of pain is to reopen the possibility that I can be mistaken that I am in pain.

Later in the *Investigations* (Wittgenstein, 1953, #293ff.) there is a detailed discussion of propositions ascribing pain to the first and third persons. What Wittgenstein is to reject here is the notion of a private language through the well-known beetle in the box argument. He continues in relation to the paradox of a nothing serving as well as a something in the box, to assert (#304): "The paradox disappears only if we make a radical break with the idea that language always functions in one way, always serves the same purpose to convey thoughts — which may be about houses, pains, good and evil, or anything else you please."

Wittgenstein's position is that first person statements ascribing pain to an "I" do not function descriptively but expressively, as expressions of pain behavior, much the same as a cry of pain. Also, these expressions of pain are learned.

AN EXPRESSIVE ACCOUNT OF IDENTITY

The hypothesis to be advanced is that first person statements of identity should be construed as expressions of identity and that they are not like normal contingent identity statements. On the normal interpretation, a = b is assumed to have the logical form a R b, whereby two objects stand in a relation R to one another. Thus we can substitute for "R" relations such as "to the left of" and "is identical with." In the case where "I" is substituted for "a," "LW" for "b," and "identical with" for "R," and the normal interpretation applied we have, according to Wittgenstein, an example of taking the apparent grammar as the real grammar.

We have already seen that for Frege, the early Wittgenstein, and Tarski identity is not necessary in logic. Why introduce it then? We will start from the Wittgensteinean notion of "I" being used to explain a name — introduced earlier in the quote from *Philosophical Investigations* (#410). How does "I" explain a name like "LW"? A child learns the use of "I" and names such as "Ludwig" almost simultaneously. However, the child who learns how to use these terms must already be a language user, limited as this notion may be for the child. Learning the use of a language in general for the child is not something that can be taught through the use of language (1975, #6). It can only be shown in use. Wittgenstein makes much of intentions in relation to the use of language, for example, at *Philosophical Remarks*, #20: "If you exclude the element of intention from language, its whole function then collapses." How does "I am LW" function in language?

First, said by LW, "I am LW" cannot normally be false, because I cannot be mistaken about who I am. Of course I can be ill, deluded, or dreaming as I can in cases of "I have a pain," but in general I cannot be mistaken in saying "I am LW." Adding that I might be mistaken would either be seen as saying something nonsensical or odd and in need of further amplification. This much "I am LW" shares with "I am in pain." If "I am in pain" is then an expression of pain, then "I am LW" might also be considered as an expression rather than as a description of identity. What is an expression of identity? Identity is certainly not like a sensation, or feeling, or attitude, although the latter has some possibilities. For example, we express attitudes through various bodily gestures, such as a smile, a nod of support, or by clapping our hands. We also say such things as "that's right" or "we're with you" where we are not describing states of affairs so much as expressing where we stand, as what our attitudes are to some proposal or belief. In "we're with you" we do not need to stand beside to express our attitude of support. Nor should "we stand with you" be taken as describing some literal state of affairs (although it can) but usually it involves an expression of an attitude.

However, "I am LW" does not quite express an attitude in those senses. As we have seen, Wittgenstein said (1953, #410) that "I," "here," and "this" are not names, but earlier he had said (#253): "I have seen a person in a discussion on this subject [pain] strike himself on the breast and say: 'But surely another person can't have THIS pain!' — The answer to this is that one does not define a criterion of identity by emphatic stressing of the word 'this.' Rather, what the emphasis does is to suggest the case in which we are conversant with such a criterion of identity, *but have to be reminded of it*" (emphasis added).

"I" then functions to remind people of certain things in statements such as "I am LW." First that the name "LW" is to be associated with criteria of identity such as "the Austrian philosopher," "the relentless truth-seeker," "the person who gave away a fortune," and so forth (compare Waismann, 1965). Second, that a center of consciousness that cannot be mistaken about "I am LW" is associated with those criteria and that in expressing that identity the center of consciousness in question has a certain world view, because the "I" is an eye at the boundary of the world of representation (Schopenhauer) and of language (Wittgenstein). If the listener has or learns the criteria of identity of LW, or some of the criteria, then that listener can identify LW but not the I, because the "I" does not refer to an object in the world; it is not something that can be represented to the listener or identifier.

My intention in asserting "I am LW," a truth about which I cannot be mistaken or uncertain, is that a particular center, or eye, or boundary point of language can be identified via the criteria for identity for LW (the Austrian philosopher and so forth). The fact that a thought is true depends upon the thought and the fact (1975, #21): my thought that I am LW cannot be false, and the fact that a mouth is speaking, saying "I am LW" identifies a center or focus of representation, will, and intention for Schopenhauer, and a center of language and intentional use for Wittgenstein. Because the criteria of identity used by those who know LW to identify LW are in the world and objects for my representation also, my expression of identity functions correctly and cannot be mistaken.

As for Schopenhauer the eye or I is not in the world, as "I" does not refer to an object in the world, but the "I" is not a nothing either. "I am LW" is not a descriptive statement or an example of a contingent identity statement but functions to explain identity through first person expressions of identity about which, in our own case, we cannot be mistaken. In *The Blue Book* Wittgenstein returns to the reference of "I." He says that it has two uses, as object and as subject (1958, p. 66). He uses "I" or "my" to refer to an object when he is talking of the body — "my arm is broken" — and "I" as subject when we speak of mental states, and so forth — "I hear so and so," or "I see so and so," or "I have a toothache." Wittgenstein continues his anti-object theme in relation to the second use. "'I' in 'I have a pain' does not denote a particular body" (1958, p. 74). This only drives us into Cartesianism if we retain a referential account for the substantive "I." Wittgenstein of course abandons referentialism.

So "this is LW," or "here is LW," or "I am LW" do not state criteria of identity but reassert or remind us of criteria of identity. They are not reminding us of the truth of some such proposition as "I am LW," but of who we are, as we express who we are: "this is me!" What is the logical grammar of that utterance? For Wittgenstein "this" is not a name, as we have seen (1953, #410), so either "me" cannot be a name, or the proposition "this is me" is not of the same logical form as the traditional contingent identity statement a = b.

NIETZSCHE

Nietzsche was strongly influenced and heavily indebted to Schopenhauer's *The World as Will and Representation*. According to Janaway (1989, p. 342) Nietzsche's most radical views can be traced to Schopenhauer's conception of the subject as both willing and knowing. However, what Nietzsche adopted was not adopted uncritically, and in his later writings he moved on and away, proclaiming Schopenhauer's metaphysics to be false. Russell (1946, p. 788) says that although Nietzsche is the successor of Schopenhauer he was superior to Schopenhauer especially in the consistency and coherence of his thought. Although his writing effectively ceased in the last decade of the nineteenth century, it is in the later half of the twentieth century that his influence has been felt.

Early in his professional life Nietzsche published the essay *Schopenhauer as Educator*, in which he extols Schopenhauer at the expense of various university professors of philosophy. In this early period of his writing culture is extolled for producing the genius or creative artist, poet, or musician (especially Wagner), and he attacks Socrates the rationalist. In the second period of his writing he is to reverse his view on Socrates, to prefer science over poetry, to adopt an almost positivistic attack on metaphysics, and to challenge almost all accepted beliefs and customs (Coppleston 1965, p. 166). (Russell refers to him as representing aristocratic anarchism [1946, p. 789].)

A central criticism by Nietzsche of Schopenhauer is that the self remains a riddle, an it, to which Schopenhauer can only offer a guess: the will. The "I" as a thing in itself is indefensible according to Nietzsche and cannot be predicated with the attributes that Schopenhauer wishes to attach to the will. "A totally obscure, inconceivable x is draped with predicates, as with bright coloured clothes which are taken from a world alien to it, the world of appearance. Then the demand is that we should regard the surrounding clothes, that is the predicates, as the thing itself" (Janaway 1989, p. 343).

In *The Birth of Tragedy* Nietzsche introduces Schopenhauer's distinction between the self as the eye, or pure representing subject and the self as will. Schopenhauer is used there to introduce the two great gods of Greek tragedy, Apollo and Dionysus. The Greeks, according to Nietzsche, were well aware that life could be inexplicable, dangerous, and at times terrible, but this did not result in a pessimism and a turning of their back upon life, as in the case of Schopenhauer. Rather they attempted to transcend this terrible world by transmuting it (and the life of human beings) through art (Coppleston, 1965, p. 171). There were two broad approaches to this transformation: the Apollonian and the Dionysian. Nietzsche begins by comparing Apollo and Dionysus respectively with the contrasts between (plastic) sculpture and (non-plastic) music, dreams, and drunkenness. Apollo, in *The Birth of Tragedy*, is the god of all plastic energies and the soothsayer, the "shining one," a god of restraint, of freedom from the wilder emotions, and of philosophical calm. Here Nietzsche quotes from Schopenhauer on the man wrapped in the veil of Mâyâ (1923, p. 455): this is the notion of a man swept by tempests in a small boat at sea yet supported by his principles, in that case: "the way in which the individual knows things as phenomena . . . his ephemeral person, his extensionless present, his momentary satisfaction, this alone has reality for him; and he does all to maintain this, so long as his eyes are not opened to better knowledge."

Yet, Nietzsche suggests, Schopenhauer has depicted for us a terrible awe that seizes us when man is suddenly bereft of reason to account for some phenomenon or phenomena. If , on the contrary, we grasp the blissful awe that arises at the inability, if the not the collapse of reason, we gain insight into the Dionysian (1956, p. 23): "He feels as if the veil of Mâyâ has been torn aside. . . . In song and dance man expresses himself as a member of a higher community, he has forgotten how to walk and speak; he is about to take a dancing flight in the air . . . he is no longer an artist, he has become a work of art; in these paroxysms of intoxication the artistic power of all nature reveals itself."

In effect Nietzsche is introducing under the guises of Apollo and Dionysus the notions from Schopenhauer of the self as a pure representing subject and of the self as will. This is the central dichotomy of *The Birth of Tragedy*, and a dichotomy some vestige of which Nietzsche never gave up (Janaway, 1989, p. 345).

The artistic for the Dionysian bursts forth from nature itself and does not require the mediation of the human artist (in contrast to the Apollonian [1956, p. 24]). Even so every artist is an imitator according to

Nietzsche: the Apollonian of dreams and the Dionysian of ecstasies. The Apollonian artist is hiding the reality behind imposed perfect aesthetic forms, whereas the Dionysian artist is embracing and affirming existence no matter what terrors are to be found. On the one hand these are represented by epics and the plastic arts and on the other by tragedy and music. He goes on to talk of the Dionysian festivals as involving a return to or a communing with nature, the overthrowing of Apollo and reason, and a return to nature and to the frenzy and daring of the world. Thus (1956, p. 23): "Under the charm of the Dionysian not only is the union between man and man reaffirmed, but Nature which has become estranged, hostile, or subjugated, celebrates once more her reconciliation with her prodigal son, man. Freely earth offers her gifts, and peacefully the beasts of prey approach from desert and mountain. The chariot of Dionysus is bedecked with flowers and garlands."

These two "approaches" are to be considered as artistic energies: "the mediation of the human artist" and its antithesis, seen "as energies which bursts forth from nature herself . . . energies in which nature's art-impulses are satisfied in the most immediate and direct way . . . in the pictorial world of dreams . . . and . . . as drunken reality" (1956, p. 24).

Thus Spake Zarathustra, which has been said to be "the work least popular among philosophers, at least in the Anglo-American tradition," although "probably his most famous work" (Magnus & Higgins, 1996, p. 39), depends upon a fictional form and upon rhetoric; for example, "*thus spake Zarathustra*" ends many of the sections. However, Zarathustra does not merely pronounce or tell stories because, according to Heidegger (1961), Zarathustra teaches "by showing." According to Deleuze (1983, p. xiii), "*Zarathustra* can only be read as a modern opera and seen and heard as such." Thus, in Book IV, sometimes seen as out of place to the commentators, he shows the way out to the highermen or philosophers, by uniting again (or ascending) with the earth and the animals in a drunken and joyous celebration marked by laughter. Laughter as a way out of philosophy is to be recommended by Foucault.

The Superman is introduced early, in the prologue to *Thus Spake Zarathustra*, Book I (1961, p. 28): "Let your will say: The Superman *shall be the meaning of the earth!* . . . I conjure you my brethren, *remain true to the earth*, and believe not those who speak unto you of superearthly hopes! Poisoners are they, whether they know it or not." The relationship of the Superman to the earth is emphasized immediately, in an attack upon souls and God, and any notions of a future world: "To blaspheme the earth is now the dreadfulest sin, and to rate the heart of the unknowable higher than the meaning of the earth!" (p. 28). Then he moves to reinstate the body over the unknowable soul (p. 28), because the body is to be the ground of all meaning and knowledge: "Once the soul looked contemptuously on the body, and then that contempt was the supreme thing: — the soul wished the body meagre, ghastly and finished. Thus it thought to escape from the body and the earth . . . what doth your body say about the soul? Is your soul not poverty and pollution and wretched complacency. . . . Verily a polluted stream is man. One must be a sea, to receive a polluted stream without becoming impure . . . the Superman: he is the sea."

However, he reverts in the emphasis on the earth and the body to the frenzy of Dionysus (1961, p. 43): "Where is the lightning to lick you with its tongue? Where is the frenzy with which you should be innoculated? Lo I teach you the Superman: he is that lightning, he is that frenzy!"

For Nietzsche it was important to live a life of challenge and danger, indeed the Superman must be willing to risk all in the service of humanity. He must be Dionysian (1961, p. 46): "I tell you: one must still have the chaos in one, to give birth to a dancing star. I tell you: ye still have chaos in you." In the prologue when talking to the dying tightrope walker Zarathustra says (1961, p. 48): "thou hast made danger thy calling; therein there is nothing contemptible. Now thou perishest by thy calling: therefore will I bury you with my own hands."

Not much is said about the Superman in *Thus Spake Zarathustra* but he is contrasted with the last man and the higher man. The last man is Appolonian, tied down by a lack of desire, seeking security, comfort, and happiness. Then there are the higher men, Appolonian in that they adopt aspects of Zarathustra's teachings but in fundamental and differing ways between one another, thus distorting Zarathustra's perspective. To a certain extent they epitomize the fundamental differences that arise between academic philosophers in relation to perennial philosophical problems. For Zarathustra the way out is to return, if not ascend, to a communion with the earth and the animals, to a drunken frenzy and to laughter. As he sets off down the hill a chastened but wiser Zarathustra, an interlocutor says to him (1961, p. 313): "One thing however do I know, — from thyself did I learn it once, O Zarathustra: he who wanteth to kill most thoroughly, *laugheth*. 'Not by wrath but by laughter doth one kill' — thus spakest thou once, O Zarathustra*, thou hidden one, though destroyer without wrath, thou dangerous saint, — thou art a rogue!"

Thus, in summary at this stage it can be seen that although Nietzsche introduces Schopenhauer's distinction between the world as representation and the world as will in his early work *The Birth of Tragedy* and develops this more forcefully in the allegorical and rhetorical *Thus Spake Zarathustra*, he is to move beyond Schopenhauer in *Beyond Good and Evil* and later writings where he develops this dichotomy and treats this major idea more formally. For Nietzsche it can be said that the world of will is not just a negative attitude to preserve life, and withdraw from it as much as possible as in Schopenhauer, but a much more positive attitude to affirm life through the will to power. Clearly for Nietzsche the objective world is a fabrication, because the eye (I) of representation cannot found any subject transcendent reality. If we fabricate the world according to our needs then it is not merely to sustain life but to attain mastery over the world according to Nietzsche. It is not a will to life but a will to power that motivates us. It is unclear, however, whether the will to power is an ontological fact, "what there is," or whether it too is a fabrication, at best some kind of principle to be fashioned and fostered by the genius or Superman.

For Nietzsche the subject always interprets something. For it to be a subject it must experience something. However, how we interpret is always dependent upon the will. Consequently, the mirror is always distorted or dimmed and the pure object cannot be experienced. The object cannot be experienced, therefore, as a pure uninterpreted thing in itself, as in Schopenhauer's aesthetic mode of contemplation. Objectivity can at best only be aspired to by removing differences between perspectives or appearances, by agreeing on the motives, or particular wills to power, in relation to objects. In Nietzschean fashion Foucault refers to the natural sciences as no longer being wracked by such disagreement and multiple perspectives, by maximizing as far as possible shared or agreed perspectives.

According to Deleuze (1983, p. xiif.) Nietzsche's approach to concepts has been misunderstood. This has led, he believes, to interpretations of the will to power as "wanting, coveting or seeking power" instead of Nietzsche's intentions, associated with giving, making, or creating. Nietzsche maintained, according to Deleuze, that there is "the deepest relationship between concept and affect," but that these analyses must always be understood in the atmosphere, situations, and contexts provided by Nietzsche, and not be substituted in, or understood against, different situations. Thus Deleuze maintains: the master-slave relationship should not be characterized by deserved domination; the will to power is not to be seen as a will that wants and seeks to own power; and nihilism is a not a totalizing attitude held by Nietzsche but is itself defined in terms of the triumph of reactive forces and negative interpretations of the will to power; the eternal recurrence or return is to be conceived not as a tedious return of the same, but as a transmutation (see e.g., 1961, IV); and the Superman should not be seen as exemplifying a master race. Otherwise, Deleuze suggests, "Nietzsche will appear a nihilist, or worse, a fascist and at best as an obscure and terrifying prophet" (1983, p. xii).

FOUCAULT

Michel Foucault began to pursue questions of the self vigorously from 1979, culminating in the final two volumes of *The History of Sexuality*. The questions about the self were posed explicitly in his important article "What is Enlightenment?" (Foucault, 1979). His question was: "who are we in the present, what is this fragile moment from which we can't detach our identity and which will carry that identity away with itself?" In Nietzschean fashion he is to answer this question slowly by turning to experience, as opposed to a committed position, to Dionysian practice rather than an Apollonian higher ground or vantage point (for example, as in the case of the engaged intellectual of Sartre). Here traditional philosophy was of little account, because in order to grasp our experience one must stay close to the modern — to everyday events — and to experience them, be willing to be affected by them, and to effect them. This is, no doubt, an outcome of his experiences post-1968, as professor of philosophy at Vincennes and engaged intellectual in the 1970s (for details see, for example, Eribon, 1991; Macey, 1993), because what mattered was "experience *with* . . . rather than engagement *in*" (quoted in Rabinow, 1997, p. xix, emphasis added). "Who one was, Foucault wrote, emerges acutely out of the problems with which one struggles" (p. xix).

Foucault says little about Nietzsche and how, or to what extent, he was influenced by him (in spite of two articles on Nietzsche [Foucault, 1977; 1986]). Like Wittgenstein he was silent on such matters. If "God is dead" was an aphorism of Nietzsche then so was "man is dead" for Foucault. Precisely what is meant by this is an interesting question. The normal answer is that it is the man of the human sciences, the humanistic construction of subjects by philosophers from Descartes to Sartre and Beauvoir. To a certain extent that is true, but it ignores the "I" of Schopenhauer and its interpretation and realignment to the physical world by Nietzsche. In order to explore these issues we will start with an important point by Maurice Merleau-Ponty, because Foucault respected Merleau-Ponty (Eribon, 1991, p. 32). In an almost Schopenhauerean comment Merleau-Ponty says in the preface to *The Phenomenology of Perception*:

I cannot conceive myself as nothing but a bit of the world, a mere object of biological, psychological or sociological investigation. I cannot shut myself up within the realm of science. All my knowledge of the world, even my scientific knowledge, is gained from my own particular point of view, or from some experience of the world without which the symbols of science would be meaningless. The whole universe of science is built upon the world as directly experienced, and if we want to subject science itself to rigorous scrutiny and arrive at a precise assessment of its meaning and scope, we must begin by reawakening the basic experience of the world which we perceive, for the simple reason that it is a rationale of that world. I am, not a "living creature" nor even a "man" or again even "a consciousness" . . . *I am the absolute source*, my existence does not stem from my antecedents, from my physical and social environment; instead it moves outward towards them and sustains them, for I alone bring into being for myself (and therefore into being in the only sense that the word can have for me) the tradition which I elect to carry on . . . or the horizon I wish to abolish. (emphasis added)

In this passage Merleau-Ponty makes a sharp and clear distinction between the "I" (eye) as subject and as object for others, including the human sciences. In asserting the primacy of the "I" as source and the primacy of the world as experience — the absolute source of notions such as living creature or man — Merleau-Ponty is making similar points to Schopenhauer, to Nietzsche, and to the Wittgenstein of the *Notebooks* and *Tractatus*. He is also drawing a distinction between the attributes that the "I" might accord to the body and those that the human sciences might accord. In asserting that the "I" sustains and "moves out towards" the sciences, including the human sciences, Merleau-Ponty is driving a wedge between the truths of the human sciences and the truths known by the "I," a wedge between psychological descriptions of the self that both Schopenhauer and Wittgenstein could agree with. For Schopenhauer these are concerned with the will as manifested by the body; for Nietzsche as the communion of the "I" with the world; and for Wittgenstein as the immersion and sustenance of the "I" in the form of life and in language.

However, Foucault does not hold the mystical view of the "I" that is to be found in Schopenhauer and in Wittgenstein. He seems to follow Nietzsche in the self being part of the organic (and inorganic) world, but it is not something that is open to biological, sociological, and so forth description. Insofar as man is dead for Foucault, it is, therefore, not just the man of the human sciences, with all of the humanistic baggage that man there carries, who is dead and cannot serve as a posit of human theory. It is the subject post Kant to which these attributes are accorded, and not the self of Schopenhauer, Nietzsche, Wittgenstein, and Foucault. For Schopenhauer because the "I" is not logically amenable to any such attributions, it cannot be part of the objective world or the world of experience. As we saw earlier this was Nietzsche's critique of Schopenhauer — adorning the "I" with clothes that (logically) it could not wear. The attribution of scientific qualities to the self would of course be doubly mistaken for Schopenhauer.

Foucault's message was always that the self is not something that is given. Rather he adopted a position enunciated early by Nietzsche (1983, p. 127): "Be yourself! All you are now doing, thinking, desiring, is not you yourself." Miller (1993, p. 69) says that this was Schopenhauer's influence upon Nietzsche and Nietzsche's upon Foucault. (Interestingly neither Macey [1993] nor Eribon [1991] refer to Schopenhauer.) For both Nietzsche and Foucault: "Our body is but a social structure" (Nietzsche, 1989, 21:19), and our self is contingent and hanging because of shifting social and cultural forces (1968, p. 552). Hence, they both reject the metaphysics of Schopenhauer's "I." Nevertheless, both see the self as being constructed by customs, practices, and institutions in which we live and grow (compare Wittgenstein on forms of life). The point is that these are not ultimate givens, and therefore we can change. Nietzsche thought that we had come to hate the body and its Dionysian untamed frenzies because of Christianity, and thus deeply immersed in social and cultural traditions it was difficult "to become what one is." For Nietzsche of *Thus Spake Zarathustra* it begins with the discovery of the Dionysian frenzy of life by communing again with the world, and to transcend the self that appears as a given. For the later Foucault it is to care for the self. For both: "No one can construct for you the bridge upon which precisely you must cross the stream of life, no one but you yourself alone" (Nietzsche, 1983, p. 129).

Foucault in his earlier writings on the constitution of the self sees coercive forces and practices as dominating selves. He treats power as repressive and there is talk of the hostile engagement of warlike forces in the domination of individuals, groups, and in the constitution of the self. Although repression is a form of domination, it is not an extension or abuse of legal powers, but rather is a continuation of a perpetual relation of forceful domination, not by manifold forms, but exercised within society as technologies of domination at a capillary level and by each and every member of that society; on the underside of the law, as he describes it. His concern is with the power or knowledge that underlies, or that is a set of conditions that permit and legitimate certain particular claims to truth.

In his later writings Foucault is to drop the concept of repression, because "repression is quite inadequate for capturing what is precisely the productive aspect of power . . . [and] this [repression] is a wholly negative, narrow skeletar conception of power" (1980b, p. 119), although the warlike metaphors are retained as late as 1983. Here he becomes more Nietzschean: power is productive, it creates or makes people, it can be positive and not merely negative. He uses this positive conception of power in his later writings, particularly volumes II and III of *The History of Sexuality* (Foucault, 1985; 1990).

In Volume I of the *History of Sexuality* (Foucault, 1980a) the key to technologies of the self is the belief, now common in Western culture, that it is possible to tell the truth about one's self. It has almost become a basic tenet of Western culture that with the help of professionals truth about one's self can be discovered through the self-examination of consciousness and the confession of one's feelings, attitudes, desires, thoughts, and acts. The belief that the body and its desires reveal the deepest truths about one's self has become almost commonplace and is embedded in what Foucault calls sexuality. By telling the truth about one's sexuality, where the deepest truth is embedded in the discourse and discursive practices of sexuality, the individual becomes an object of knowledge both to himself and to others. In telling the truth one knows oneself and is known to others in a process that is both therapeutic and controlling. However, if sexuality structures the deepest truths, there are other areas

in which we tell the truth. These discourses and the set of discursive practices associated with them are part of what Foucault calls the human
sciences: they penetrate, permeate, and inform, for example, medicine,
psychiatry, psychology, the law, and education.

These technologies are developed from medical models in parallel clinical methods in the nineteenth century. However, according to Foucault, a
fundamental shift in clinical methods took place. There was a shift in
tasks from the strict medical clinical model. In that model the patient
confessed to the doctor as part of the examination and the attempt to clas-
sify objectively the medical problem that needs correction. In the new
model the confession and the examination are part of a process of
constructing the sexuality of subjects, so that their discourse is controlled
and they become individuals of a certain form. The truth, or knowing
one's self, is essentially therapeutic.

This structure and discourse meant that eventually the subject could no
longer understand what was being said and could no longer, therefore, be
the arbiter on the deepest truths. This role fell to the authority, the scientist, not only to incite the truth and to interpret these deep truths but also
to reconstruct the subject's experience of sexuality and discourse and,
thereby, control the subject. In knowing one's true self one has not only to
tell the truth in the confession but also to speak the truth in the concepts of
the discourse on sexuality. In speaking this truth, in knowing one's true
self, one constructs the experience of sex, and one reconstructs one's self
by adopting new descriptions and hopefully new practices. The therapy
comes about; from telling the truth, which can itself involve vicarious
pleasurable and liberating effects; from thereby knowing one's self
through speaking the truth; and thereby liberating one's self from the
repressive aspects by the acts of speaking and reconstructing the self.

According to Foucault the Delphic maxim, "to know yourself" has
taken over from the other notion of Greek antiquity, "to take care of yourself." He argues that the "need to take care for oneself brought the
Delphic maxim into operation," and that the latter was subordinated to
the former. This is not the case in modern Western culture, he claims, as
the notion of caring for oneself has come to be seen as an immorality, a
means of escape from rules and respect for law. Given further the Chris-
tian inheritance that the road to salvation lies through self-renunciation,
to know oneself seems paradoxically the road to self-renunciation and
salvation. Secondly, he argues, theoretical philosophy since Descartes has
placed ever-increasing importance upon knowledge of the self as the first
step in epistemology. His conclusion is that the order of priority of these
two maxims has become reversed — "know thyself" has priority over
"care for the self."

Care for the self is to be a form of exercise upon the self and not
a Schopenhauerean renunciation of the self. It is not that the self is a

mystical entity, but it is certainly not corporeal, because if the "I" is a self to be cared for it is not a self to be known through the human sciences, but it does involve the exercise of reason. In *The Order of Things* Foucault described how in the human sciences "the thinking subject defines itself as a speaking, living, working individual" (Foucault, 1984, p. 281), but in his lectures at Le Collège de France he is to shift from coercive practices (as for example, in *Discipline and Punish*) to "an exercise of the self on the self, by which one attempts to develop and transform oneself, and to attain to a certain mode of being" (1984a, p. 282). In returning to the ancient Greeks he was emphasizing practices of freedom over practices of liberation. Care of the self was necessary in order to know oneself. Only then could ethos as a way of being through a practice of freedom take a shape that was "good, beautiful, honourable, estimable, memorable and exemplary" (p. 286). This is not a form of narcissisim, because care for the self is always "in a certain sense" "a way of caring for others," although not necessarily of first caring for others, because care for the self is ethically prior (p. 287).

Foucault is not advancing a theory of the subject. Here as in many other genealogies his question is "How?" (1984a, p. 290): "What I rejected was the idea of starting out with a theory of the subject. . . . What I wanted to try to show was how the subject constituted itself, in one specific form or another . . . it is not a substance. It is a form, and this form is not always identical to itself . . . in each case one plays, one establishes a different relation to oneself."

By classifying the subject or self as a form he seems to see it as conceptual, as the form that our conceptualizing of ourselves at any particular time may take in a complex interplay of intellect, character, and action. Thus, you may not have the same relationship to yourself when you constitute yourself as a political subject to speak at a meeting and as a father speaking to a daughter or son prior to the meeting. These two forms, he says, may not be identical. Thus, we cannot assert an identity relationship such as a = b between these two forms. Put another way his concern is with how the intellect, character, and action can be reconciled in living in the context of practical affairs in the present, and that the singularity of the present in its games of truth and practices of power may either require a certain form of the self or present the opportunity to constitute one's self actively in a form of transfiguration of other forms of the self. These practices are not something entirely invented, because we are influenced by models: in Foucault's case by Kant on the historical singularity of reason and Baudelaire on the stylization of the self, although not in an artistic or narcissistic sense (Rabinow, 1997, p. xxxii). Other models are available and are proposed and suggested (sometimes imposed) by the culture, society, and social group (Foucault, 1984a, p.

293). All of these models must be subjected to historical and philosophical examination.

This knowledge that one has of the forms that the self takes (self-knowing) is active and highly political as it was for the Greeks. For the philosopher this becomes doubly so, "in terms of intensity, in the degree of zeal for the self, and consequently, also for others, the place of the philosopher is not that of just any free man" (Foucault, 1984a, p. 293). Here Foucault was assigning a special role for the philosopher that Wittgenstein was reluctant to assign. In Foucault's case it was a role that was academic because it was also scholarly, although it was philosophy not in the normal and more traditional academic sense but in a very overt sense of the political. This was foreshadowed by the curriculum that he had established as professor of philosophy at Vincennes, and that was to be criticized by Minister of Education Oliver Guichard, and ultimately excluded from the national accreditation of degrees in philosophy in 1970 (Eribon, 1991, p. 207).

Foucault was to respond with these questions in *Le Nouvel Observateur* (quoted in Eribon, 1991): "What is the reason for this quarantine? What is so dangerous about philosophy that so much care must go into protecting it? And what is so dangerous about people from Vincennes?" These were questions that might well have been posed to the critics of Wittgenstein and his works. More recently they are applicable to the violent rejection by many philosophers of the recent proposal to offer Jacques Derrida an honorary degree at Cambridge.

CONCLUSION

For both Wittgenstein and Foucault there is no such thing as a self, if we mean by that a substance referred to by "I." Foucault sees it as a kind of logical form, not fixed or immutable, capable of change through care by the self of the self, and a concomitant reconceptualizing of the self. (We will discuss this notion of care in Chapter 11.) This is not, however, a metaphysical notion of the self like that of Schopenhauer, vestiges of which remained with Wittgenstein.

5

Wittgenstein, Psychology, and Freud

In this chapter we will consider a number of the issues raised by Wittgenstein in relation to psychology and provide an introduction to Freud. We discuss Freud more fully in the next chapter. Freud used the term "psychoanalysis" to refer to his own work. In his polemical *History of the Psychoanalytical Movement* in 1914 he said: "Psychoanalysis is my creation. . . . For ten years I was the only one occupied with it. . . . Nobody knows better than I what psychoanalysis is." Why then should Wittgenstein often refer to him and his work with the notion of psychology (although there are exceptions, for example, Wittgenstein, 1982, p. 787)? That is one issue to be pursued, although a minor issue. The other more major issues to be considered in this chapter and the next are: the scientific status of Freud's work (was it more like philosophy than science?), the analysis of dreams, rationality and dreams and madness, the therapeutic effects of analysis, and the indignity of Freud's notion of free association or the talking cure. First, we will explore Wittgenstein's approach to psychology and then provide a general introduction to Freud, Freud's Vienna, and psychoanalysis.

PHILOSOPHY AND PSYCHOLOGY

Wittgenstein did not change his views on philosophy. According to Baker and Hacker (1980, p. 463): "This is one of the main threads of continuity in Wittgenstein's opera." For him philosophy "clarifies which questions are intelligible and which investigations are in principle relevant or irrelevant for answering them. This view Wittgenstein held and argued throughout his career" (Baker & Hacker, 1980, p. 457).

It is certainly not a kind of science. In *Philosophical Investigations* (Wittgenstein, 1953, #109, compare 1981, #455) he says:

It was true to say that our considerations could not be scientific ones. It was not of any possible interest to us to find out empirically "that, contrary to our precon-ceived ideas, it is possible to think such-and-such" — whatever that may mean (the conception of thought as a gaseous medium). And we may not advance any kind of theory. There must not be anything hypothetical in our considerations. We must do away with all *explanation*, and description alone must take its place. And this description gets its light, that is to say its purpose, from the philosophical problems. These are, of course, not empirical problems; they are solved, rather, by looking into the windows of our language, and that in such a way as to make us recognize those workings.

We can say then that philosophy cannot provide the foundations of science, because there are no deductions that can be made from philoso-phy and in this sense, as opposed to science, philosophy is "flat" (Baker & Hacker, 1980, p. 463). (Insofar as psychology is a science, or purports to be, then philosophy may have little to say to psychology, apart from suggestions for conceptual clarification.) Instead, it provides in a purely descriptive manner, the form of scientific, that is, empirical, propositions. Philosophy as a purely descriptive enterprise explains nothing and constructs no theories. Philosophical problems are resolved not by advancing theories but by "looking into the workings of our language" and providing descriptions of how we use our language in a rearrange-ment of familiar linguistic facts, that is, facts that are available to us but the details of which have become hidden or obscured. Because they have become obscured philosophical puzzles have arisen, and psychology provides one kind of theoretical answer to such puzzles. For Wittgen-stein, philosophy has asked the wrong sort of question and psychology has provided the wrong kind of answer. A different view of philosophy is held by Wittgenstein: Instead, "philosophy is a battle against the bewitch-ment of our intelligence by means of language" (1953, #109).

It was these views that underlay his approach to psychology, because psychology not only lays claim to being a science but also bewitches us by its improper use of language and of theory. Essentially Wittgenstein saw psychology as both conceptually confused and philosophically confusing. Hence, if it were a science, and therefore philosophy could not either provide foundations or contribute to it as a science, yet philosophy was concerned with the limits of language, with the general forms of language use that were possible. Here, because of what he saw as severe conceptual confusion in psychology, Wittgenstein felt able to comment and clarify misleading conceptual claims, for example, concerning the use of concepts, such as thinking, believing, and expecting.

Wittgenstein also saw philosophy as being very difficult. First, there is a considerable battle to be waged against being seduced by the archetype of science — something that in Wittgenstein's view Russell, for example, was unable to resist — and that psychology had embraced. Second, and in relation to his discussions of psychology, there are problems with the surface grammar of statements. Thus when we say "I am in pain," it appears from the traditional grammatical subject-predicate distinction that a subject referred to by "I" has a predicate "pain" ascribed to it, so that the sentence is used to describe a mental state of the person uttering the statement. Wittgenstein argues at great length that the surface grammar of "I am in pain" (it is a major example that he uses) masks the logical grammar of this statement, because it is more like a cry of pain and operates in our language as a sophisticated expression of pain — see Chapter 4. The general point here is that we do not use language merely to describe or to give information. We also tend to project grammar onto reality. Thus, bewitched by the surface grammar of first person statements, "I" has been projected upon reality to yield various versions of the self, when, as Wittgenstein says (1961, p. 80e): "The I, the I is what is deeply mysterious. The I is not an object. I objectively confront every object. But not the I." We discussed Wittgenstein on the self in Chapter 4.

Although he saw ordinary language as being in order as it was, nevertheless it carries with it many metaphors and pictures (including mental state) — for example, the river of time, the inner and the outer, mind and body — and these pictures and metaphors need to be unpacked while, at the same time, resisting their obscuring effects.

Second, the concept of pain, for example, is used by us in our normal everyday utterances, as we have learned how to use it, but it has been appropriated and used by psychologists to refer to an inner mental state. However, if there are inner mental states, not open in principle to observation, there must be outer criteria capable of observation if psychology is not to abandon its scientific claims and retreat to metaphysics and mythology. This involves a conflation of the concept of pain with the criteria for pain. If there are mental states, then the criteria may be observable, Wittgenstein concedes, but this is not our concept of pain.

Finally there were a number of intellectual prejudices to be overcome in philosophy. The archetype of science has already been discussed. Secondly there were philosophical schools (or mythologies) that had been erected and refined mainly by academic philosophy. These schools provided the wrong type of answer to philosophical puzzles, according to Wittgenstein. They sought among other things to provide a holistic picture, caught by such terms as "idealism," "pragmatism," and "realism," as opposed to clarifying a limited and particular domain — how we use the personal pronoun "I," for example. Also, there were priorities, such as the sharp over the vague, the simple and elegant over the complex and prolix, of explanation over description, and of formal logic over informal logic.

WITTGENSTEIN AND PSYCHOLOGY

These philosophical concerns can be seen in Wittgenstein's antithetical discussions of psychology. Wittgenstein had always been concerned by psychology, and although this can be identified in his thought at least as early as the *Tractatus*, it becomes more explicit in his later writing. When he was at Cambridge before 1914 he had thought psychology to be a waste of time (conversation with Rush Rhees [Wittgenstein, 1967, p. 41]). His aversion to psychology was noted by Paul Engelmann (1967, p. 99) in his remarks on the *Tractatus*. Engelmann states that Wittgenstein carefully avoided in *Tractatus* any use of psychologistic terms or implications, and describes this careful avoidance in terms of a "surgeon's painstaking care in keeping his instruments clean" (p. 100). According to Engelmann, *Tractatus* is "not only free from psychology but anti-psychologistic" (p. 100). This is a stronger theme than just an avoidance of psychologistic terms but a claim that the avoidance was explicitly antipsychology. What is also important here is that Engelmann had seen very early drafts of *Tractatus* from 1916 onward, and in fact retained one typescript until very late in his life when, living in Tel Aviv, he donated it to the Bodleian library. In order to understand Wittgenstein's aversion to psychology, we need to understand what he saw as the improper intrusion of pyschology into the use of psychological terms like "pain," "thinking," and "reading."

Wittgenstein argues that psychology does not formulate laws and in this respect does not fare well, compared with the science of physics, for example. Nor can we use quantitative measures in psychology to investigate mental states and processes, although we can of course use quantitative methods in relation to observed behaviors, but these are mistakenly taken, as we shall see below, for criteria of these alleged inner mental states and processes, referred to by psychological terms like "thinking." These problems permeate psychology, according to Wittgenstein.

It is not a contingent failure that there are no laws in psychology, because it is a problem deep within psychology itself and will not be solved by time as psychologists work harder and longer. Thus, in *Remarks on the Philosophy of Psychology*, Vol. 1 (1980b, #1039) he says:

The confusion in psychology is not to be explained by its being a "young science." Its state isn't at all to be compared with, e.g., that of physics in its early period. Rather with that of certain branches of mathematics. (Set Theory). For there exists on the one hand a certain experimental method, and on the other conceptual confusion and methods of proof . . . in psychology there are experiments which are regarded as methods of solving the problems, even though they quite by-pass the thing that is worrying us.

Because psychology cannot formulate general laws and because its experimental method, which depends upon observing what people do and say, is not to investigate mental states and processes but to observe what people do and say, it is not a science according to Wittgenstein. That what people say and do are taken as criteria for such mental states is to accept the psychologists' questions and answers, and their account of concepts referred to by psychological verbs, such as think and believe. This is why the psychologists, searching for a description of an inner mental state, for example, pain, must turn back instead to the phenomena or events in which pain behavior is exhibited. This provides an entrée for Wittgenstein to confront again the events or phenomena to redescribe them, and to not accept the psychologist's answers concerning mental states. In any case to use such concepts as thinking and feeling to describe these inner mental states is to revert to a nonscientific use of concepts. These are terms taken from everyday language, but within psychology they are not defined fastidiously enough, so that they both carry the earlier baggage of wide use and, in turn, have infected that concept claiming priority for the mental state version of the concept.

Such general criticisms of psychology are neither unique nor original. However, as Wittgenstein notes, although there is a relationship between some psychic phenomena and action this is not a law like causal relation. Indeed: "the fact that there *aren't* actually any such laws seems important" (Wittgenstein, 1973, p. 77). If changes in mental phenomena do not happen by chance either, and if there are no causal laws, then there must be some form of necessity, even if it does not take the form of a causal law. What this might be for Wittgenstein depends upon our understandings of such things as feelings and motivation and their relations to action. Feelings and motivations can be reasons for action but not, in Wittgenstein's book, causes of actions. Our understanding of mental concepts is, therefore, important if we are to understand why changes in mental phenomena do not happen by chance, without being caused.

In such passages as *Remarks on the Philosophy of Psychology* (1980b, Vol. 1, #1039), Wittgenstein raises the issues of conceptual confusion in psychology. This is a twofold criticism. First, there is confusion over particular concepts like thinking and reading that have a use in ordinary language but are converted to refer to inner mental states or processes. Second, there is the major confusion between the notions of reason and cause. We will look now in detail at Wittgenstein's first criticism, that of conceptual confusion.

As to be expected Wittgenstein starts with words used in our everyday language games. He makes the non-exceptional point that the words used in psychology are similar to words we use in everyday language. Topics we would expect in psychology books he cites as (1980b, vol. 2, #19); "Man thinks, is afraid, etc." The words think and fear (afraid) occur there as we would expect. Wittgenstein notes this at #21, but adds a qualification: "Psychological words are similar to those which pass over from everyday into medical language ('Shock.')." The point provided by the notion of shock here is that in medical terminology "shock" refers essentially to a physiological somatic state accompanied by a psychic state: it has been given a sharp medical definition. However, in ordinary language the term is used much more widely and can be used in contexts where there may be no accompanying physiological states, for example, "I was shocked to learn of her accident," or "I was shocked to read of the burglary in the next street," and so forth. In reference to the specific psychological term "thinking" he says (1980b, vol. 2, #20, compare 1981, #113): "Where do we get the concept 'thinking' from, which we now want to consider here? From everyday language. What first fixes the direction of our attention is the word 'thinking.' But the use of this word is tangled. Nor can we expect anything else. And that can of course be said of all psychological verbs. Their employment is not so clear or so easy to get a synoptic view of, as that of terms in mechanics, for example."

Wittgenstein continues much later in the same source to say on the tangled use of psychological words like "think" (1980b, vol. 2, #3730): "As if the word `violin' referred not only to the instrument, but sometimes to the violinist, the violin part, the sound, or even the playing the violin." Thus, "think" is tangled in two senses. First in ordinary language where, like "shock," it has a number of uses connected by a family resemblance, but second in psychology it is not used in a definite sense like "force" in physics, or "shock" even in medicine. In one sense psychology carries the tangled web of use from everyday language into its theories, slipping and sliding between the former and older meanings, when it should be seeking to define concepts rigorously and quantitatively. In psychology this problem is well exemplified in the theories of intelligence where, for example, it is said that intelligence quotient (IQ) measures intelligence. Critics point out that IQ tests measure whatever they measure, and that such scores cannot be extended to other areas of cognitive or affective performance. In particular they cannot be used to predict ability or potential. Intelligence is a much more tangled web than such tests might suggest or claim (Gould, 1981). In fact IQ exhibits the fallacy of conflating an alleged mental state (an ability) — intelligence — with a, or the, observable and measurable criterion(-ia) of the mental state. This is not the concept of intelligence, which has wide and multifarious uses, sharing family resemblances.

In education there have been critiques of the notion of ability. Tuck (1983) for example raises general questions about ability talk in psychology, as to what ability is and how it is to be measured and used, and reaches several conclusions. First, if it is anything at all it is not substantive and cannot be identified. Then, in Wittgensteinian fashion, he turns to the observed behavior of people on IQ tests and asks different questions about answers to the items. What they measure (or more properly indicate), he argues, are the social and cultural heritage of the person — who their parents were, which school they went to, and who taught them. Becaue these measure phenomena in the past that are mainly contingent they cannot be used to predict what might happen in the future, especially under changed conditions.

Wittgenstein continues in more forceful terms, in striking at the notion that concepts used in psychology are scientific (1980b, vol. 2, #62): "Psychological concepts are just everyday concepts. They are not concepts newly fashioned by science for its own purpose, as are the concepts of physics and chemistry. Psychological concepts are related to those of the exact sciences as the concepts of the science of medicine are to those of old women who spend their time nursing the sick."

Wittgenstein is not dismissing the potential for psychology to become an empirical science because it does have a valid realm of phenomena (1980b, vol. 2, #35): "I would like to say: Psychology deals with certain *aspects* of human life. Or with certain phenomena. — But the words 'thinking', 'fearing' etc., etc. do *not* refer to these phenomena."

This is a half-hearted concession from Wittgenstein because although conceding this scientific possibility, it would be something in which he would have little interest because it was scientific. Psychologists believe that they are dealing with phenomena referred to by terms such as "think" and "fear," but in reality they are talking of other things and investigating other things, and these may be important aspects of human life to investigate. However, they are not referred to by terms such as "thinking" and "fearing." Wittgenstein illustrates this problem by reference to what psychologists do in laboratories (1980b, vol. 1, #287): "If someone does a psychological experiment — what does he report? — What the subject says, what he does, what has happened to him in the past and how he has reacted to it. — And not: what the subject *thinks*, what he *sees, feels, believes, experiences*?" (emphasis added).

There are differences between the phenomena of psychology, which are concerned with what the subject says, does, and so forth and with what he thinks or feels; that is, between what the psychologist says as he observes and what the subject of the observation experiences. If psychology is about our utterances or expressions of thinking, feeling, pain, then these are not the same as psychological reports such as the subject said "I feel tired." Wittgenstein expresses this firmly: "I want to say that our 'utterances,' with which psychology has to do, absolutely are not all descriptions of experience-contents" (1980b, vol. 1, #693). It is these utterances or expressions of pain and so forth that should be of concern, but how is scientific method to investigate these? Experimental method then can only "by-pass the thing that is worrying us," and one cannot even be certain of the fruitfulness of the experiments (1980b, vol. 1, #1039). Wittgenstein believes that this is a vast conceptual muddle and confusion, using the wrong concepts to go down a theoretical and (allegedly?) scientific path.

Wittgenstein's wider conceptual point here is that it is a mistake to believe that "think" refers at all. His point is that attempts to define thinking, by ostensive definition (1988, p. 4) or as an activity, say (p. 7), are inconclusive and may lead to philosophical problems and theories. We have learned the use of the word and we are not puzzled by its use, but we are puzzled if we try to define (describe) it (p. 5): "Why should we be puzzled by the use of a word? We can certainly use the word 'think,' but we cannot *describe* the use. But why should this bother us?" Also, at page 7, "Philosophical problems arise when a man has the King's English use of 'thinking' but describes it wrongly . . . a child 'picks up' psychological expressions. No explanation is ever given . . . the child picks it up. If we are asked to describe the use, we are bewildered. Any explanation that comes into our head is always wrong."

If these words do not refer to psychological phenomena at all, then Wittgenstein is also arguing that there is a realm of psychic phenomena to which psychology is not applicable. This is asserted (Wittgenstein, 1980b, vol. 2, #107): "The sentence `Imagination is subject to the will' is not a sentence of psychology." This sentence is not merely meaningful but may be used in important human contexts, such as the teaching of the practicing arts, or in the creative pursuit of the sciences, and the words "imagination" and "will" have been learned by the child in use. We cannot define these words but must look at the situations in which they have been learned and are then used.

Changes in psychic phenomena do not occur by chance but because of our conceptual understanding of concepts like "think" and "fear." We know that we can become fearful because of thinking, because fear can be influenced by thinking, but the thinking does not cause the fear. Thinking about an incident not seen initially as personally threatening can result in the incident being seen as threatening because of thinking about it. The thinking did not cause the fear, as it could have been otherwise, if I were stronger, or if I were more perceptive. Thus, "thinking about X made me fear X" does not describe a causal state of affairs, even though I was made to fear X as a result of thinking about X. Thinking about X made me realize that there were conceptual connections between an X and thinking about an X — people confronted with X's sometimes exhibit fear and we understand this from our immersion in a form of life. Fearing X was not then a chance outcome of thinking about X because, on account of these conceptual connections, I was made to fear X; made, but not caused.

DIFFERENCES AMONG PSYCHOLOGICAL CONCEPTS

Wittgenstein (1953, #571) begins an examination of psychological concepts and differences among them. In particular he wishes to argue that not all such notions described by these psychological terms are states. The preceding discussion of linguistic meaning in *Philosophical Investigations* is suspended and the investigations shift to the examination of a number of psychological expressions. The suspension or shift, however, is only temporary, because he needs to clarify psychological concepts before returning to confront the idea that acts of meaning giving also give words and utterances their life (Baker & Hacker, 1996, p. 394). His first point, familiar enough, is that it is misleading to think that "psychology treats of processes in the psychical sphere, as does physics in the physical" (p. 394). Again he asserts of physicists and psychologists that the: "physicist sees, hears, and thinks about and informs us of these phenomena [for example, electricity], and the psychologist observes the external reactions (the behaviour) of the subject" (p. 394).

However, the psychologist claims to be examining similar things to electricity, for example, mental states. According to Wittgenstein, the notion of a mental state is not something referred to by psychological words such as "thinking," "believing," and "reading." We have already looked at his general criticisms of this notion. The notion of a mental state is used improperly in another way to subsume under it "expecting, hoping, believing," as if they are just like the other mental states of "thinking" and "feeling" (Baker & Hacker, 1996, p. 394). Wittgenstein, however, wishes to distinguish, for example, "expecting," "hoping," and "believing" from "thinking" and "feeling." Although they may grammatically be said to be a state (Wittgenstein, 1953, #572), this surface grammar is misleading, and classifying and treating them as homogeneous, as psychological mental states, hides important differences between them.

Wittgenstein immediately invites us to look again at the phenomena that are characteristic of these states (1953, #572): "in order to understand the grammar of these states it is necessary to ask: `What counts as a criterion for anyone's being in such a state?'" He commences with the state of having an opinion. What is it a state of? he asks (#573). He dismisses notions such as the soul or the mind, to state that it is correct to say that a person has an opinion, although, as this does not help very much, we must instead turn to the criteria for a person having an opinion. What counts as a criterion for someone being of such-and-such an opinion? When do we say that a person has reached an opinion, or when do we say that a person has altered an opinion? It is these criteria that are important in knowing how to ascribe an opinion to a person. Instead, in psychology, these criteria for holding an opinion become identified with the concept of opinion, and are then in turn treated first, grammatically as a state and then, second, psychologically and theoretically as behavioral criteria of the mental state, so that the concept is to be taken as referring to a mental state. There may be mental states that are appropriate for study by psychologists, but if there are (and they are of little interest to Wittgenstein), they have little to do with how we use the concept, with how we are able and prepared to say that someone holds an opinion. Thus, in order to understand the concept "opinion" we must confront these criteria or phenomena again and refuse to accept that because "opinion" appears grammatically as a state that this grammatical fact permits us to impose a mental state upon the person said to hold an opinion. Surely something mental — a process or an activity — must be going on. Perhaps there is, but that is not an answer to questions of the meaning of what it is to hold an opinion, according to Wittgenstein. We also do not need to accept the psychologists' answer to the puzzle generated by the grammatical fact that opinion is a state. We must resist philosophical and theoretical answers to this puzzle and instead describe our use of language in relation to "opinion" and "holding an opinion."

Next (commencing at Wittgenstein, 1953, #574) Wittgenstein distinguishes believing from hoping and expecting, and all three from thinking and feeling. There are connections but there also are varying differences. For example, believing may not involve conscious thinking of something to be the case (#574): "When I sat on this chair, of course I believed it would bear me. I had no thought of its possibly collapsing." He adds, however, sometimes thinking may accompany believing — when a belief is renewed or revised, for example. Thinking need not accompany an expectation as in high excitement I watch the progress of the burning of a match or a wick toward an explosive. I need not think here at all (#576). If I am expecting someone to come this need not occupy my thoughts, because expecting may only mean here that I would be surprised if he did not come, although again thinking may accompany expectation when I eagerly await someone (#577) or anxiously await someone, who is perhaps already late — a friend or fellow climber on a difficult climb.

Beliefs are also not to be equated with feelings (Wittgenstein, 1953, #578–79). Wittgenstein commences by asking, "What does it mean to believe Goldbach's theorem?" Is it a feeling of certainty as we think about the theorem, or state it, or hear it? If it is said that the feeling is a particular coloring of our thoughts, where does this come from? He wishes to return to questions about phenomena, in this case connections between the belief and the proposition. We need to look at the consequences of this belief — that I search for a proof for the proposition (the expression of

Goldbach's theorem) may be one — and if so, he asks, what does this searching consist in? We must look and see how this feeling of confidence is manifested in our behavior (#579). It is these manifestations — the outward criteria that must stand for inner processes — that constitute a feeling of confidence in a belief, but in this case the criteria for believing and having a feeling of confidence in the theorem seem to be the same. However, the consequences of a belief and of a (real) feeling are not the same. The consequences of a belief are such things as searching for a proof, whereas the consequences of a feeling may be multifarious. In all cases our understanding of such things depends upon the circumstances in which they are embedded. A feeling of significance cannot arise from one aspect alone of a complex event like a coronation. It is the whole event that gives particular aspects within such a scene of pomp and dignity its significance. We must, therefore, return to descriptions of the events or phenomena as to when it is appropriate to talk of a belief or of a feeling, because these concepts acquire their use (meaning) in these circumstances and do not describe inner mental states.

Sensations and states of anxiety are more like feelings. Thus, "I am in pain" is an expression of pain (see later) and not a description of pain, as is "I am afraid" an expression of fear. They are manifestations or expressions of fear and pain, and not descriptions of inner states. "I feel confident in this theorem" and "I believe this theorem" depend upon the same sort of criteria for use whereas my manifestation of fear, the expressive, "It'll go off now" (said of the match and explosives case earlier) is different from "I believe that it will go off now," or "I expect that it will go off now."

In these sorts of ways Wittgenstein distinguishes expecting, hoping, and believing from one another, distinguishes them from both thinking and feeling, and distinguishes between thinking and feeling. This is ultimately to describe a considerable complexity in the descriptions of the use of these words, and this complexity is obscured or hidden by the generality of the psychologists' notion of an inner mental state.

In general Wittgenstein is both critical and antagonistic to psychology. There may be a science of psychology possible, but if so it needs to define its concepts more rigorously and not believe that it is providing understanding of the meaning of our traditional psychological words such as thinking, believing, hoping, feeling, and expecting. At present it is conceptually confused by employing terms from ordinary language, where the meaning has been established by use in a form of life, and it mistakes criteria for the use of such words as among the criteria of inner mental states or processes referred to by those terms. We learn and understand these words by being inducted into a form of life. We know how to use those words, although we may not be able rigorously to define or describe their uses, because there is no one definition or use but multifarious uses in family resemblances.

INTRODUCTION TO FREUD

Wittgenstein says of Freud's explanations (Wittgenstein, 1980a, p. 55e): "Freud's fanciful pseudo-explanations (precisely because they are brilliant) perform a disservice. (Now any ass has these pictures available to use in 'explaining' symptoms of illness.)" On science in the same source he was to say (p. 79e): "I may find scientific questions interesting, but they never really grip me. Only *conceptual* and *aesthetic* questions do that. At bottom I am indifferent to the solution of scientific problems: but not the other sort."

This presents us with something of a dilemma. Wittgenstein is not gripped by scientific questions, presumably because they are theoretical and not philosophical in his sense but, as a matter of fact, he was not indifferent to Freud but was interested in him. Although Freud claimed to be scientific, Wittgenstein passes contradictory judgments on Freud as scientist, because sometimes he is said to be scientific and at other times he is criticized for not being scientific. Perhaps Wittgenstein saw Freud as being more philosophical than scientific, as raising conceptual issues rather than empirical physiological questions, but even then in pursuing a theory of dreams it had to be ultimately in the theoretical sense of philosophy that raised Wittgenstein's ire. Either way as scientist (or pseudo or bad scientist) or as philosopher, he was therefore also theoretical, and in that sense mistaken in Wittgenstein's view.

In general we will hold that Wittgenstein's position was that Freud was not scientific, and that Freud was not scientific on his own positivistic grounds of what counted as science. Our general point will be based upon the claim that Wittgenstein awards the status of science to Freud in passing and perhaps isolated comments, but that where he provides sustained comment and analysis he judges Freud as not being scientific and as being mistaken philosophically. So what interested Wittgenstein in Freud?

We believe that it was Freud's interest in advancing reasons (although he mistook these for causes), and therefore Wittgenstein's interest was in Freud's language. To disregard the Freudian metaphysics, the alleged causes of mental illness, and to concentrate on the language is, in psychoanalytic history, to take a path opened by Lacan, although Lacan was most probably not available to Wittgenstein.

Wittgenstein often referred to Freud. Sometimes, as in a letter to Norman Malcolm, he is quite positive: for example, he refers to "Freud's extraordinary scientific achievement," yet he often attacked psychoanalysis as being unscientific, as being merely *"une façon de parler."* Often it seems unclear as to what Wittgenstein perceived the problem with psychoanalysis to be: was there something inherently inconsistent or incomprehensible with psychoanalysis — was it science and so forth or was the problem with the use of it, and with the asses who would seize it and use it in an age like ours (Bouveresse, 1995, p. xix)? Here Foucault's attacks upon the use of psychoanalytical techniques, as, for example, in *The History of Sexuality*, Vol. 1, are quite apposite. Wittgenstein would have shared much of Foucault's concerns about the indignities of the confessional and pseudo-medical examination that had come to permeate psychoanalysis — in the free association of ideas that permit the analyst to explore areas of silence and resistance. For example he was quite indignant about the examination that he was required to undergo in 1926 when he left teaching. If a good use of psychoanalytic theory were possible or existed, Wittgenstein seemed to doubt that such uses were fulfilled in practice. However, he did believe that philosophical clarity might save us from such misuses.

At first sight this remark on Freud and science to Malcolm seems out of place. Whereas philosophers of a scientific bent (for example, Carnap and other members of the Vienna Circle) might have welcomed psychoanalysis as a rationalistic and progressive approach to the scientific study of mental phenomena, Wittgenstein was under no such expectations or illusions concerning the onward march of science in general. In any case he often remarked that Freud was not scientific. Thus (1967, p. 44): "Freud is constantly claiming to be scientific. But what he gives is *speculation* — something prior even to the formation of a hypothesis." Yet, trained in the Helmholtz school of medicine, Freud tried to say what man is, seeing himself as a loyal member of the positivistic tradition (Miller, 1966, p. 267).

Freud published his major work, *The Interpretation of Dreams*, in 1900, but it was almost another decade before he received recognition and began to attract adherents. Wittgenstein was later to send a copy of this book to his friend M. O'C. Drury, telling him that when he had first read it he said to himself: "here at last is a psychologist who has something to say" (Monk, 1991, p. 356). Bouveresse implies (1995, p. 3), following Rhees (Wittgenstein, 1973, p. 76), that Wittgenstein first read Freud after 1919, but Rhees does not say "first," only that it was something in reading Freud after 1919 that surprised him, and he saw that Freud had something to say. Wittgenstein must have read Freud earlier. He must have read Freud's earlier work with Breuer, *Studies in Hysteria* (1895), which was in the Wittgenstein family library, and Wittgenstein is later to be complementary to Breuer (Wittgenstein, 1980a, p. 36e), suggesting that it was Breuer who had sown "the real germ of psychoanalysis." Was Wittgenstein's early understanding of Freud obtained by osmosis, as suggested by McGuinness (1988)? There must be something stronger than osmosis, because Wittgenstein was clearly interested in psychic phenomena before

World War II, and it is known that he underwent hypnosis in 1913 (Bouveresse, 1995).

At the turn of the century it would have been very difficult to avoid Freud in Vienna, and in Wittgenstein's case this was doubly so. Sexuality was a major talking point in Vienna at that time — Cioffi (1973, p. 5) refers to "the currency of his [Freud's] intellectual themes, particularly with reference to the neuroses." For example there was the work by Otto Weininger, *Sex and Character*, published in 1903, and Wittgenstein was influenced by Wieninger. Then there were the ongoing attacks by Karl Kraus on the dehumanizing forces operating in Vienna, including his support of both prostitution and homosexuality, in his anti-newspaper *Die Fackel* (see Janik & Toulmin, 1973, chap. 3). Kraus also influenced Wittgenstein. Also, there was Freud and a growing coterie of friends. Psychoanalysis was not only a major talking point in Viennese circles but Wittgenstein's elder sister, Margarete (Gretl), who had been an early supporter of Freud (Monk, 1991, p. 16), had been analyzed by Freud and maintained personal relations with him until his departure for England in 1938. She was an intellectual and had introduced her younger brother to Kraus's newspaper, *Die Fackel*, founded in 1899 (Monk, 1991). It would have been impossible to have lived as Wittgenstein did without being aware of psychoanalysis and, in Wittgenstein's case, not be curious about it. We do know that he was interested in psychic phenomena, had probably read Freud, and would have been aware of Kraus's attacks upon Freud. There must have been more than osmosis of Freud's general ideas by Wittgenstein.

No doubt Wittgenstein was influenced by Kraus on Freud (and on other social issues). A much quoted remark from Kraus was (quoted by Janik & Toulmin, 1973, p. 75): "Psychoanalysis is that spiritual disease of which it considers itself the cure." Wittgenstein comes close to the position expressed by Kraus' aphorism in his own position on psychoanalysis. Kraus' attacks were leveled against Freud's distorted picture of human nature, because he held that Freud and his followers were merely replacing bourgeois Judeo-Christian myths about sexuality with new myths. In addition he saw Freud's id and its control by the ego and super ego as severing all ties with creativity, which was for him the source of all that is healthy in human affairs. He also believed that a change in social mores would do more for the hysterical Viennese wife than a dose of free association with Freud — what he referred to as "the running milk of motherhood" (Janik & Toulmin, 1973, p. 77). Furthermore, with its emphases on adjustment to society, Kraus saw it as but a further attack on the originality and creativity of the artist — in Foucault's terms the production of people to lead useful, docile, and practical lives. Thus, psychoanalysis was for Kraus a mere manifestation of the ills it sought to cure (Janik & Toulmin, 1973, p. 75). These worries as expressed by Kraus seem to have been summarized later by Wittgenstein (1967, p. 26): "Freud has very intelligent reasons for saying what he says, a great imagination and colossal prejudice, and prejudice which is likely to mislead people." Yet this may have been unfair to Freud, because Freud was attacking the remnants of the Middle Ages, which had lingered into the end of the nineteenth century. This was seen clearly by C. G. Jung (1973). Freud was also not responsible for much of the political elements of the psychoanalytic movement that was to sweep the world, especially North America, early in the twentieth century.

Freud was certainly advocating a radical theory in his insistence on the central importance of the unconsciousness to our mental life and in his view that repression was a central controlling force upon human beings. It was radical also, in the times of the march of scientific rationalism, in that it proposed that conscious rational thinking may not be the bedrock to be relied upon — for example, in the notion of the rational, autonomous person. As Fromm says (1982, p. 133): "Freud deprived man of his pride in his rationality." Freud's thought had radical and revolutionary potential, but his theory of the unconscious had little or no revolutionary social consequences or impact. The theoretical point is that if the root of our social malaise rests with our individual sexual problems, then there would be no need to examine economic and social institutions and structures. This point was seen by Kraus. Thus, even if it were true that Freud saw himself as a liberal and as liberating human beings, the theoretical and practical effects of his theory can be seen as reactionary if not controlling of human beings. Individual liberation at the best does not entail or effect social liberation. If Fromm is right (1982, p. 134f.), in talking of the early psychoanalysts, that "hardly more than a handful of psychoanalysts had radical beliefs," and that as a member of the intellectual middle class "Freud thought as a child of his time," this may not be so surprising.

Jung, however, sees Freud not as being merely reactionary and conservative but as being a great critic of the nineteenth century (Jung, 1973) and as a person of the status of Nietzsche and James Joyce, who strove frantically to destroy the moralizing, bourgeois respectability, religious ideas, and political truths of the Middle Ages, which still lingered on despite the Enlightenment. Jung argues that it is the decay of these controlling ideas along with developing ideas of materialism and rationalism that provide "the matrix out of which Freud grew" (Jung, 1973, p. 51). Freud rejects the more typical middle class manner of seeing the world in a rosy light and of glossing over social, economic, and political issues, because these were seen by Freud as illusions, hypocrisy, half ignorance, morally shallow, and artificial. For Freud they hid a deeper unhealthiness that rested on the dark background of infantile sexuality (Jung, 1973, p. 51). Far from marking him out as "the herald of new ways and new truths . . . (he should be seen) . . . as a great destroyer who breaks the chain of the past . . . who liberates us from the unhealthy pressure of an ancient world of rotten habits" (p. 51). This is not the Freud of Kraus, who saw him as continuing these middle-class hypocrisies, or of Fromm.

In general psychoanalytic theory was not welcomed intellectually outside of Austria and Germany, although it had many adherents in practice in the psychoanalytical and political movement, particularly in North America. Cioffi (1973, intro.) refers to a number of sources that paint a picture of Freud as being surrounded theoretically by a skeptical and hostile world. A number of reasons are advanced by Cioffi (1973). These are: a failure to explicitly and quickly repudiate abandoned hypotheses or concepts; delays in translation from German; the rejection of his views on sexuality; anti-Semitism; a rejection of things perceived as German after World War I; and a failure to distinguish between psychoanalytical thought and the psychoanalytical movement. This latter point is important, because although Freud dissociated his thought from many of the therapeutic interventions advanced in its name, he would also appear to have been guilty of not only cutting off those with whom he disagreed intellectually, but of actively opposing their membership in societies (Cioffi, 1973, pp. 8–9). Finally, if Freud's thought was that psychoanalysis could be liberating, parts of the movement were to prescribe intercourse as a therapeutic measure. Not only did this raise social hackles but also such prescription can be seen as controlling rather than liberating. When such prescription is combined with Freud's notion of transference to the analyst, this raised further ethical issues. These prescriptions of course brought considerable opprobrium upon the movement, even though they are not to be found in Freud's thought or manifested in his own life by the puritanical Freud. Although we have noted the controlling effects of psychoanalytic theory, this exploitive version of control would not have been of the type supported by middle-class reactionaries and reactionary medical associations.

With this brief introduction to Freud, his development of psychoanalysis and psychoanalytic theory, and Wittgenstein's caustic approach to psychology, we can now turn to the particular criticisms that Wittgenstein made of Freud's approach to the analysis of dreams. We should note an early ambiguous interpretation of Freud by Wittgenstein that perhaps hardens later, post–World War I, to be harder on Freud, and with his increasing use of the importance, not of a technical language (1963), but of the way in which everyday language is embedded in human practices or in forms of life. Thus, for Wittgenstein meaning and understanding are to be grasped through use and not through representation, through knowing how an expression has been learned and works in our everyday forms of communication, even if we have forgotten some of these things and have gone astray, so that language has gone on holiday. If Wittgenstein's

initial interest in Freud was concerned with the language of interpretation, the symbolization of Freudian theory — the posited relationships
between dream symbol and real world — which he saw as more or less
random if not arbitrary, was incompatible with what he understood by
language (that is, a public language).

6

Wittgenstein, Freud, and Dreams: *Une Façon de Parler*

Freud is to coin the term "psychoanalysis," but his earlier medical training was in neurology, and he was to move to psychology and to work with the psychologist Joseph Breuer on the use of hypnosis in treating hysteria. In 1895 they published together, but already by then Freud was developing the idea of free association. It was this notion that was crucial for the development of psychoanalysis (Miller, 1966, p. 254). It was also to raise the ire of Wittgenstein, and as practiced, of Foucault (1980a).

According to Wittgenstein, Freud "wanted to find some one explanation which would show what dreaming is. He wanted to find the essence of dreaming" (Wittgenstein, 1973, p. 82). To this extent Freud had scientific ambitions, but these were to be exercised in a positivistic manner, and on his own positivistic grounds he was found wanting. On this latter point Wittgenstein is not the only critic of Freud. The critical work for understanding Wittgenstein's criticisms of Freud is *The Interpretation of Dreams* (Freud, 1932).

FREUD AND *THE INTERPRETATION OF DREAMS*

Freud begins *The Interpretation of Dreams* by claiming that "there is a psychological technique which makes it possible to interpret dreams" (p. 19), lamenting almost immediately, that "in spite of thousands of years of endeavour, little progress has been made in the scientific understanding of dreams" (p. 19). The science to which Freud was committed, theoretically or in principle, was positivistic and he was to postulate a positivistic notion of the causality of dreams. "We start with the assumption that dreams are a phenomenon of our own psychic activity" (p. 61), but the phenomena of dreams are different from the phenomena of the waking state: "the distinguishing characteristic of the waking state is the fact that its psychic activity occurs in the form of ideas . . . but the dream occurs mainly in visual images" (p. 61). This is an assumption and is not tackled empirically. Freud is determined "to explain as many as possible of its (the dream) observed characteristics from a single point of view . . . [to provide] . . . a theory of the dream" (p. 85). What he had found almost universally lacking in scientific theories of the dream was room for "a problem of dream interpretation" (p. 105). This was because these theories treated the dream as a somatic (that is, physical) process and not as psychic (that is, non-physical) activity. A theory of dream interpretation may be different from a causal theory about dreaming, but Freud does not distinguish between these two possibilities in part, we believe, because of his conceptual confusions. This will be developed later in relation to Wittgenstein.

On the contrary Freud suggests that the unscientific world "has always endeavoured to interpret dreams" (1932, p. 105). Thus, for Freud his starting point is positivistic common sense or givens of experience: "an ancient and stubbornly retained popular belief seems to have come nearer to the truth of the matter than the opinion of modern science" (p. 108). Passages such as these must have been attractive to Wittgenstein because, in spite of Freud's thrust toward theory, he is starting from what we know well, from a collective and expressed experience and views about the role of dreams in ways of life. How we understand dreams would have to start from what we know, because what we must bring forward for Wittgenstein is that which is there to be seen and understood, that which is partially hidden because it is too familiar.

For Freud, rather, there must be some cause, conscious or unconscious, of the events in the dream. He does not start with the dream as a whole but takes the parts and the events of the dream instead (1932, p. 113). He did not conceive these more particular events as senseless, "for dreams really do possess a meaning," and one that "can be recognized as a wish fulfillment" (p. 128). The events in dreams, moreover, are seen by him as symbols that refer to personal matters and that can arouse deep emotions. If the dream is also conceived as preserving sleep (a further assumption) then it can be argued that these deep personal emotions cannot appear directly, as then, in their eruption, they would disturb sleep. Therefore, if they are to appear then they must appear indirectly. Thus, for Freud they appear indirectly, in a harmless symbolic form. This form of expression through symbols hides deeper issues concerned with infant sexuality. These symbolic forms are substitutions for deep personal emotions, and the task for the analyst is to uncover these symbols and recover these deep emotions and wish fulfilments, even in anxiety dreams. This involves the interpretation of the dream, which, in turn, requires a theory to interpret the dream. This turn to theory is mistaken in Wittgenstein's view.

That is the bare bones but bones upon which Wittgenstein is to gnaw. Wittgenstein appreciated that Freud had something to say, even when he thought Freud wrong, but this was not the Freud of the psychoanalytical movement. Here he seemed to share the views of Karl Kraus on psychoanalysis — that it was part of its own problem. This was not the critique of Kraus that psychoanalysis presented a distorted picture of human nature (Janik & Toulmin, 1973, p. 75), but a more general problem with psychoanalysis itself. It was a personal attack upon himself that made Kraus pay attention to the dangers inherent in the psychoanalytic movement (Janik & Toulmin, 1973), that is, that almost any wild speculation could be justified in terms of analysis. This concern was shared with Wittgenstein. A related problem has surfaced more recently in attempts to recover memories of children's sexual abuse through consciousness-altering techniques similar to notions of free association. Considerable concern has been raised about such procedures and the British Royal College of Psychiatrists has effectively banned the use of recovered memory techniques according to the *New Zealand Herald* (1997, p. A3).

What Wittgenstein attempted was to separate what was valuable in Freud from what was not. That which he saw as valuable was that the dream was a way of saying something. He also seemed to see himself and Freud as involved in a therapeutic mission to liberate people, although in different ways and for different reasons. Whereas Freud was concerned to liberate people from repression, because he believed that truth would set one free, Wittgenstein was concerned with freeing people from searching for truth through certain forms of philosophical theory, because he was obsessed with these types of questions that intruded, forced themselves upon people, and held them captive. For Wittgenstein it is certain pursuits of truth that were controlling and made people unfree, and the search for truth, as for example, in science, was not important to Wittgenstein.

WITTGENSTEIN AND THE STATUS OF FREUD'S *THE INTERPRETATION OF DREAMS*

Wittgenstein notes that psychology does not formulate laws and in this respect does not fare well, as in the science of physics for example. We also cannot use quantitative measures in psychology. These problems permeate psychology, according to Wittgenstein, and the fact that there are no laws is not a contingent failure, and that we only need to work longer at formulating laws but, rather, it is a problem deep within psychology itself. He says (1980b, vol. 1, #1039, compare 1953, #232): "The confusion in psychology is not to be explained by its being a 'young science.' Its state isn't at all to be compared with, e.g., that of physics in its early period." Wittgenstein would agree with Freud, however, that changes in mental phenomena are not guided by chance, but not that they are guided by laws like those of physics. (For a fuller discussion of these problems see Chapter 5.)

So far these general criticisms of psychology are neither unique nor original. However, as he notes, although there is a relationship between some psychic phenomena and action, this is not a law like causal relation. Indeed: "the fact that there *aren't* actually any such laws seems important" (1973, p. 77). If changes in mental phenomena do not happen by chance, and if there are no causal laws, then there must be some form of necessity, even if it does not take the form of a causal law. What this might be for Wittgenstein depends upon our understandings of such things as feelings and motivation and their relations to action. Our understanding of mental concepts is, therefore, important if we are to understand why changes in mental phenomena do not happen by chance, without being caused (see further Chapter 5).

Psychoanalysis is unscientific in further ways, according to Wittgenstein. As we saw earlier whatever happens in a dream for Freud, the events in the dream, are to be understood as symbols that in turn represent some wish. This wish can be brought forward by the analyst through the practice of analysis and the notion of free association. It should also be noted that there may be several wishes and that these can be stratified, hence adding to the analyst's difficulties (Freud, 1932, p. 215). According to Wittgenstein "this procedure of free association and so on is queer, because Freud never shows how we know how to stop — where is the right solution" (Wittgenstein, 1973, p. 77). First, it is unclear in Freud as to which is the right solution and who is to be the judge of this — is the decision made by the analyst or the patient? Second, the right interpretation of the dream depends upon the correct identification of wishes symbolized in the events of the dream. Certainly many dreams cannot on the surface be interpreted as fulfillments of those wishes, because there are nightmares and anxiety dreams that do not seem to be representative of wishes and do not involve wish fulfilments. Freud's response is that these are sadomasochistic wishes that are being fulfilled in the anxiety dream. In a similar vein Fromm (1982, p. 72) objects that "many dreams do not contain a wish but offer an insight into one's own situation or into the personality of others." To convert all dreams into wishes and wishes of a certain kind is, according to Wittgenstein, a speculation, and a speculation is "not put forward as a result of detailed examination" (1973, p. 78). Wittgenstein's point is that Freud has no adequate empirical evidence of a variety of cases upon which to base a hypothesis about wishes and dreams (note, he is not making some claim about the use of induction).

Elsewhere he says that a causal relationship depends upon experience (1953, #169): "Causation is surely something established by experiments."

Also, one cannot predict from some Freudian hypotheses. This can be seen from the use of an example offered by Fromm (1982, p. 20) on homosexuality, although we use it for a slightly different purpose. If Freud is correct that homosexuality may be repressed, one cannot predict on Freudian grounds that a particular person is or is not a repressed homosexual. Thus, from the hypothesis of a repressed wish for homosexual relationships it is possible on Freudian grounds that a person is not interested in the opposite sex, although not sexually active, and that another person is a profligate in heterosexual relations. These appear to be incompatible outcomes of hypothesis. According to Freudian theory, either of the observed and incompatible behaviors is consistent with repressed homosexual wishes. Because the hypothesis of repressed homosexuality leads to incompatible and observed behaviors, how could one ever falsify the hypothesis that patient x was a repressed homosexual? Because of this problem Fromm notes (1982, p. 20): "the absence of homosexuality can never be proven and not rarely analysis has continued for years in search of unconscious homosexuality." For Wittgenstein "what he gives is speculation — something prior even to the formation of an hypothesis" (1973, p. 79), and he (p. 86) "has not given a scientific explanation of the ancient myth. What he has done is to propound a new myth."

WITTGENSTEIN AND *THE INTERPRETATION OF DREAMS*

According to Wittgenstein (1980a, p. 68e) "in Freudian analysis a dream is dismantled. . . . It loses its original sense *completely* . . . but all the same the dream story has a charm of its own, like a painting that attracts and inspires us . . . the dream-image inspires us." On (Shakespeare and) dreams (p. 83e) he says: "A dream is all wrong, absurd, composite, and yet at the same time it is completely right: put together in *this* strange way it makes an impression. Why? I don't know."

Wittgenstein sees the dream holistically and does not dismantle the dream as Freud does in positivistic manner, so as to isolate particular events in the dream and identify them as the symbols of repressed sexual wishes. Freud sees the dream as at best a protection of sleep or a controlling aspect of the personality that prevents the eruption of intense desires and emotions. Except that the dream can be used positively and analyzed in the process of therapy, Freud seems to conceive the dream in negative terms. This is clearly not the case with Wittgenstein. He sees the dream as making an impression that is attractive and inspiring, yet unrealistic (1980a, p. 83e). In relating the dream to Shakespeare he is making points about the uniqueness of the dream, that it has a law of its own, that is not true to life, that he is in wonder at Shakespeare who seemed to present as uniquely and unrealistically as the dream, but that he would not try to place or categorize him for that would place him wrongly (p. 84e). The view that Freud has on dreams, that they are not rational, but in some sense hallucinations, has a long history in Western philosophy and is traceable to at least Descartes, who excluded dreams from the realm of the rational in his *Meditations*.

The central starting point for Wittgenstein's critique of Freud is Freud's theoretical claim that everything that happens in the dream can be divided into discrete events, each of which can be seen as symbolic for some other wish, person, earlier childhood incident, sexual object, entity, and so forth. Analysis of the dream through free association connects the events of the dream with some sexually repressed wish or wishes. Wittgenstein protests (1973, p. 77), "Freud never shows how we know where to stop — where is the right solution." As we have seen already the absence of homosexuality cannot be proven, but what counts as success-fully proving its presence? Is the patient or the analyst to be the judge? If the patient does not accept the doctor's analysis, is the patient wrong? In what ways could the patient refuse the doctor's judgment?

What Wittgenstein (1973) does not discuss here but, for example, Foucault (1980a) does, is the power relationships that are brought into play between the analyst and the patient, or to put it another way, the power that is exercised by the analyst over the patient. Freud had himself practiced as both neurologist and psychologist before developing his theory, which he called a psychoanalytical theory. It involves a humanistic theory of a subject formed causally and a technical language with concepts such as id, ego, superego, free association, transference, libido, and pleasure principle, to name but a few. How are patients to understand this language unless they are also theoreticians familiar with psychoanalytical theory?

In general the analyst must convince the patient to accept a redescription of the presented condition essentially in the language of psychoanalytical theory. Of course many of the terms in the description of the patient's condition are not strictly speaking technical terms, although they may be used technically in the theory. Rather, as Wittgenstein has pointed out, the terms are taken from everyday language and carry meanings there that overlap with the use of the terms in the technical theory. Thus, the redescription is probably intelligible to the patient. Even so, the patient must accept a redescription of the self in the new technical language — arguably that of a different self, one that is not rosy and normal (in bourgeois terms), but sexually repressed. How could such a redescription be refused when offered by an expert, who is a doctor and skilled in such examinations, practices, and theories?

Wittgenstein is aware that "many people are inclined to accept" the explanations provided by Freudian analysis (1973, p. 78), but the reasons he gives for this are not those advanced above. According to Wittgenstein, Freud claims "that people are disinclined to accept them," but if that is so "it is highly probable that it is also one which they are *inclined* to accept. And this is what Freud actually brought out" (Wittgenstein, 1973, p. 78). His argument is that Freud does not actually employ scientifically grounded notions, such as the child's anxiety at birth, but mythological notions that say that what is happening now is a repetition of that earlier anxiety. How can it be shown empirically that present anxiety is a repetition of an earlier anxiety at birth or even that there is any such thing as anxiety at birth?

Wittgenstein does not consider either the status of the analyst as a knowledgeable professional, or the matrix of other discourses, for example, on sexuality, child development, and pedagogy, that intermeshed with psychoanalytic discourse, that provided wider support at *fin de siècle* Vienna, and that would have tended to incline people to accept the psychoanalytic descriptions of themselves and explanations of how they came to be in need of therapy. We are talking about people who were middle class, sophisticated, and reasonably well educated after all.

Freud's notion of symbols and symbolization also attracted critique from Wittgenstein (1973): "top hats are regularly phallic symbols, wooden things like tables are women, etc. His historical explanation of these symbols is absurd." Wittgenstein is thinking, no doubt, of this sort of historical claim made and supported by Freud on sexual symbolization (Freud, 1932, p. 334). "What is today symbolically connected was probably united, in primitive times, by conceptual and linguistic identity. The symbolic relationship seems to be a residue and reminder of a former identity . . . [adding in a footnote referring to the work of Hans Serber] . . . primitive words denoted sexual things exclusively, and subsequently lost their sexual significance and were applied to other things and activities, which were compared with the sexual."

Yet Wittgenstein himself nearly falls into the same kind of trap because he states (1973, p. 78) that "it is the most natural thing in the world that a table (women) should be that sort of symbol." The point, however, is that all such claims on the history of symbolization must be speculation.

In any case Wittgenstein's proper target in Freud's writing is that there is no clear way of knowing that x is a symbol of A — for example, that the branch is a symbol for the phallus ("the branch has long been used to represent the male organ" [Freud, 1932, p. 331]). What has to be determined, Wittgenstein argues, is whether the branch is always a symbol of the phallus. Might it not be a symbol for a gibbet, or of peace (the olive branch)? In other words although "it may be used to refer to a . . . phallus [it] may also be used not to refer to that at all" (Wittgenstein, 1973, p. 78).

Freud acknowledges this problem (for example, 1932, p. 269) where he talks of playing with a picture puzzle (the analysis of the dream) and replacing each image "by a syllable or word which it may represent by virtue of some allusion or relation." What the image is a symbol of is to be decided by its relation to the whole, so that "put together they are no longer meaningless, but might constitute the most beautiful and pregnant aphorism." However, acknowledging the problem is one thing and providing criteria for the meaningfulness of the whole and the reference of symbols is another. Although the branch may be symbolic for a phallus under some circumstances, this does not mean in art, for example, that the artist meant it that way in a particular painting. Similarly with the dream, Wittgenstein is saying. The fact that there is a branch lying on the ground in my dream does not mean that it is to be interpreted as a symbol for the phallus — (as Freud does [1932, p. 331]) — sometimes it may, but sometimes it may not.

There is the further problem raised by Wittgenstein that an event in a dream may not be recognized as a symbol, or that no symbolic interpretation can be given to it. If a holistic picture puzzle is then imposed upon the dream then the symbol may be given an interpretation, post fact, so to say, although it was not understood earlier as an event to contribute to the interpretation of the dream. It is these sorts of difficulties that befuddle symbolization that bring Wittgenstein to claim (1973, p. 79) that what Freud "gives is speculation." "Couldn't the whole thing have been differently treated?"

When a dream is interpreted, Wittgenstein continues, "it is fitted into a context in which it ceases to be puzzling." Contrary to Freud's "one-stop shop" method, "what is done in interpreting dreams is not all of one sort"(Wittgenstein, 1973, p. 81). For example when the dream is brought into relation with other recent events, or other things remembered, then the dream changes and all of this "still belongs to the dream, in a way." It is not at all clear that the dream interpretation must be as determined by the Freudian analyst. Even in the examples that Freud gives, he claims, "there is not a single example of a straightforward sexual dream," and "it seems muddled to say that *all* dreams are hallucinated wish fulfillments" (p. 82). He concludes at this point: "It is probable that there are many different sorts of dreams, and that there is no single line of explanation for all of them. Just as there are many different sorts of jokes. Or just as there are many different sorts of language."

Although there are certain similarities with language, dreams cannot be considered as a language, because that would require a regular symbolism (rule-following) and it would need to be translatable into German or into another language, say English or French. There does not seem to be a regular symbolism on Freud's own admission, and if one can translate from dream to the other language one cannot translate from English or German to a dream language.

Finally, Wittgenstein argues that there is no reason why we dream. We just do. Similarly (1973, p. 84): "There is no reason why people talk. A small child babbles often just for the pleasure of making noises. This is also one reason why adults talk. And there are countless others . . . why should not dream hallucinations be the perfectly normal thing in sleep, not requiring any extraordinary force at all. . . . The truth is that there is no one reason [for dreams]."

REASONS AND CAUSES

Underlying much of the discussion above is a confusion between a cause and a reason. According to Wittgenstein one is led to this confusion by the ambiguity of the word "why," and this confusion bedevils Freud's thinking. He says (1953, p. 15): "The double use of the word 'why,' asking for a cause and asking for the motive, together with the idea that we can know, and not only conjecture, our motives, gives rise to the confusion that a motive is a cause of which we are immediately aware, a cause seen from the inside, or a cause experienced — Giving a reason is like giving a calculation by which you have arrived at a certain result."

More forcefully (Wittgenstein, 1988, p. 82): "Motive doesn't mean cause. Cause is a matter of observed regularity; whereas I *know* my motive. . . . Giving the motive is a specific language game." Essentially causal thinking is hypothetical. It depends upon a relationship between observed events, so that for event A to be a cause of event B, there must have been no counter-instances to the regular sequence of events, A then B. The relation is seen as contingent, that is, that a B type event might not follow an A type event. However (p. 82): "In order to know the reason which you had for making a certain statement, acting in a particular way, etc., no number of agreeing experiences is necessary, and the statement of your reason is not a hypothesis."

For Wittgenstein we can (logically) only make conjectures about causes but we can (logically) know the reason. It is not clear what Freud is doing: is he formulating hypotheses and making causal conjectures, or is he advancing reasons? Clearly the method of arriving at an hypothesis and the verification of a causal connection differ from the offering and verification of a reason for doing something. The former normally requires a number of repeated experiences of the consecutive nature of events A and B, but for the latter to be known as the reason for acting in a particular instance one need only be immediately aware of an action being done for a particular reason, whether or not one has acted for that reason in the same way in the past. The confusion arises, Wittgenstein says, because we treat a motive as "a cause of which we are immediately aware, a cause 'seen from the inside', or a cause experienced" (1988, p. 82). Here he clearly parts company with Schopenhauer (Bouveresse, 1995, p. 71). Wittgenstein's interest is not so much in how causes and reasons are discovered or recognized but in the (logical) grammar of causal statements and reason-giving statements. His philosophical point is that their grammars are fundamentally different.

The fundamental points here have already been introduced in part by consideration of concepts such as think and feel (see Chapter 4), which have a wider application than to particular psychological phenomena (Wittgenstein, 1980b, vol. 2, #35), and Wittgenstein's claim that psychological utterances are not reducible to scientific statements. His point is not whether there are psychological truths but that the grammar of scientific psychological statements is different from the grammar of reason-giving statements. If the explanations offered are different not only in their concepts, their grammar, their interpretation of "why?" and in their manner of verification, then it would seem that they are incompatible.

Bouveresse (1995, p. 76f.) argues that Wittgenstein should not be interpreted in this manner. From the facts of difference of grammar nothing can be established concerning the priority of one form of statement over the other. Even if Wittgenstein seems to favor reason-giving over scientific psychological statements, this might be because, as we saw earlier, he is not interested in science. His concern is with reason giving, the role that plays in a language game, and the type of understanding provided. If reason-giving statements cannot be reduced to scientific psychological statements it does not follow that they are also incompatible. Bouveresse claims that (p. 76f.): "It would be rather excessive then to impute to Wittgenstein the claim that the explanation by reasons and the explanation by causes are incompatible."

Indeed, in some sources Wittgenstein seems almost to be saying that a reason can be a cause. Certainly he says nothing that excludes this possibility (Bouveresse, 1995), and even suggests the possibility (Wittgenstein, 1988, pp. 82–83): "The expression of fear or delight contains an object. (It is irrelevant that there is also fear of nothing.) Giving the motive of an action is like stating the object of fear or delight; the motive, or the object, *may* also be a cause." The reason is accepted as a motive because it is "a *likely cause* of the action" (pp. 82–83). So there is a regularity of a kind that provides understanding of the action in terms of the reason. Nevertheless, motive does not mean cause.

It is not our intention to pursue these issues as such further because they have received ample coverage in the philosophical literature. What can we say here of Freud and Wittgenstein on the reason-cause issue in way of some summary? Freud believed that he was advancing the science of psychology through a form of analysis that would uncover underlying sexual wish fulfillments. If we understand Wittgenstein correctly, he saw

Freud as identifying reasons only and not the underlying scientific causes. To the extent that he confused reasons (motives) and causes he was mistaken, according to Wittgenstein, and far from entering the scientific psychological language game, he remained at the level of everyday language and teleological forms of explanation. The scientific claims granted a legitimacy to psychoanalysis that was not warranted conceptually (on the reason-cause issue, as well as on those other issues discussed earlier).

Nonetheless, Freud was offering a new set of reasons for acting in certain ways, and this may have been what Wittgenstein recognized and applauded in his more complementary comments on Freud and psychoanalysis. Thus, as Bouveresse says (1995, p. 76f.): "We can say of Freud that he succeeded quite remarkably in extending the realm of teleological explanation by showing that a considerable quantity of mental phenomena and behaviour which at first sight seem to make no sense can indeed be made intelligible in these terms and given an explanation that can be qualified as generally intentional."

So, on the one hand, Freud has extended the range of phenomena open to reason-giving explanation, but, on the other hand, he wanted to treat these same phenomena in the ways in which they were treated in the natural sciences. Although some reasons could also be seen as causes, for Wittgenstein this was not normally the case, because motives could not be causes.

THE NORMAL AND THE ABNORMAL: DREAMS AND MADNESS

Freud was criticized early in his work for bringing the abnormal to the forefront of human affairs and for explaining human behavior in terms of sexual forces. What might have been seen as normal, dreaming, is now seen in Freudian theory as preventing such forces erupting violently and disturbing sleep if not worse (in the hands of certain non-Freudian analysts). There was, therefore, considerable rejection of early Freudian psychoanalytic theory by the middle class and the intelligentsia. What else had he done that must have rocked philosophical (c)oracles? We will consider three issues that are associated with normal and abnormal behavior, and with dreaming and madness.

First, he had attacked the priority of reason in action. Second, he had relegated dreaming beyond the citadel of rationality, from which it had been excluded at least since the time of Descartes. Third, he had attacked the distinctions between being rational and between dreaming, hallucinating, and being mad. The first distinction, that the irrational unconscious might be the cause of action, has been dealt with above and we will not pursue that issue further.

As to the second point, Descartes had relegated or excluded dreaming from the realm of reason in the Second Meditation. Descartes discussed three possible ways in which we might be deceived. According to Descartes we can be deceived by the senses, because we are dreaming, or because we are mad. He argues that we can only be deceived by the senses if there is a way of knowing when we are deceived. If we are deceived all the time then we would not know it. So for deception and falsity there must also be certainty and truth. Certainly we can be deceived, but that is because sometimes we can be certain. Sometimes we must be certain — as Wittgenstein says, although for rather different reasons (Wittgenstein, 1969, p. 163): "For whenever we test anything, we are already presupposing something that is not tested. . . . Doesn't testing come to an end."

Descartes treats dreaming in a similar fashion to how he treats deception of the senses, arguing that the dream only makes sense against the background of waking life, that is, that there is a veridical background against which we know that we are dreaming. To know that we are dreaming we must be able to compare the dream against veridical waking states, because if there were no veridical states, then not merely could we not know that we were dreaming, because everything would be dreaming, but also we could have no concept of dreaming. There must be, therefore, according to this argument, an irrevocable and foundational or basic notion of a veridical state, contrary to dreaming. As Foucault said about both of these arguments (Foucault, 1961, p. 57): "Neither the images created in sleep, nor the certain awareness that the sense can be deceived, can take doubt to the extreme point of its universality; suppose we are asleep; truth will not entirely escape into the night."

For Foucault this does not mean that the dream is to be relegated to the realm of unreason or excluded from the citadel of reason. Foucault in his later writings explores the importance accorded to the dream in earlier civilizations (Foucault, 1988, p. 39):

There were experts who were able to interpret dreams, including Pythagoras and some of the stoics, and some experts who wrote to teach people to interpret their own dreams. There were huge amounts of literature on how to do it, but the only surviving dream manual is *the Interpretation of Dreams* by Artemidorus (2nd century A.D.). Dream interpretation was important because in antiquity the meaning of a dream was an announcement of a future event . . . one had to interpret one's own dreams; one had to be a self interpreter. To do it, one had to remember not only one's own dreams but the events before and after. One had to record what happened every day.

If this were the case then clearly the dream is not seen as being irrational. It has a rational connection with what has happened in the past and what will happen in the future. By recording the connections between past, dream, and post-dream events, one can learn how to make rational connections between dream and past and thereby predict future occurrences. Thus, the dream is seen as being rational. No doubt this is but one of Freud's mythical and metaphysical understandings of dreams, especially in relation to the symbolic interpretation of the dream and the notion of a scientific prediction. However, Freud did not have the right sense of scientific prediction either.

In early writing Foucault saw the dream positively. In the foreword to Ludwig Binswanger's *Dream and Existence* he takes a radical if not revolutionary stance to the role of the dream in our conceptions of human being and reason. Far from being excluded from or peripheral to rationality Foucault argues that dreams are a central aspect of rationality. They do not represent pale shadows of the real and integral aspects of human experience and they do not have little value in and of themselves. Both Binswanger and Foucault accepted the challenge laid down by Freud to consider the dream as important in human experience. The early Foucault's thesis is that the imagination is epistemologically grounded in the dream and serves as a condition of the imagination.

There are similar echoes in Wittgenstein (1980a, p. 83e): "A dream is all wrong, absurd, composite, and yet at the same time it is completely right . . . it makes an impression." He says that Shakespeare's genius is that the corpus of his works "create their own language and world," like a dream. Wittgenstein, like the early Foucault, is relating the dream directly to the imagination and, in Shakespeare's case, to creativity and genius.

On this matter there may be lingering influences on Wittgenstein from Schopenhauer, because he had claimed that experience is, or is at least like, a dream or an illusion (Janaway, 1989, p. 167). Indeed Schopenhauer quoted approvingly from Shakespeare's *The Tempest*: "We are such stuff as dreams are made of." Schopenhauer was unable to specify any sure criteria for distinguishing dreams from wakening experiences, rejecting both vividness (how can they be compared?) and the comparative causal coherence between the two (Janaway, 1989, p. 167). Wittgenstein does not make this close comparison with the waking state as does Schopenhauer. He sees the dream as being a story, sometimes vivid, which is not causally connected to events in his life, but is more "like a painting that attracts and inspires us" (Wittgenstein, 1980a, pp. 68–69e). It is associated with the rational and not excluded, because the story of the dream can be compared and contrasted with veridical accounts of events and be seen as a true or a distorted story. Indeed Descartes must contrast dreams with waking states to show that dreams are not veridical and, thus, cannot be a source for the thinking subject, but Wittgenstein wishes to incorporate the dream for the thinking subject into the areas of the creative and the imaginative, because he sees the dream as inspiring: "The dream affects us as does an idea pregnant with possible developments" (pp. 68–69e). It is, therefore, as a source for the imagination and creativity that can lead to other developments that Wittgenstein, along with the Schopenhauerian Kraus, sees as being so important. For Wittgenstein the thinking subject needs the dream.

Descartes also excluded any possibility that madness has anything to offer to rationality and the thinking subject. However, in the *Meditations* he treats madness differently from the deception of the senses and the hallucinations given in dreams. It is the objects of perception or dreams that are in question in cases of deception and hallucination, and not the thinking subject. In the discussion of madness consideration shifts to the thinking subject, and it is the impossibility of being mad to the subject who thinks to which Descartes appeals. Essentially he declares that he, the thinker, cannot be mad. Madness is then excluded from his method of inquiry through clear and distinct ideas. For Foucault (1961, p. 58): "unreason is plunged deeper under the ground, there no doubt to disappear, but there also to take root."

In many passages Wittgenstein seems to take madness as clear-cut or as a given (for example, 1980b, vol. 1, pp. 148, 965). He does not equate madness with the nonsensical, because the latter may only indicate failure to understand concepts. However, in *Culture and Value* and in letters to Drury (1984) Wittgenstein begins to comment that we may need to rethink our notion of madness. Our commonsense view of it must be in question. As he said to Drury (p. 166): "The thing I would dread most, if I became mentally ill, would be your adopting a commonsense attitude; that you could take it for granted that I was deluded."

Wittgenstein notes that people can become mistrustful of others, withdrawn and devoid of love, "in the ordinary course of events" (1980a, p. 54e). There may be reasons for this, but there need not be. There need be no compelling reasons for our understanding of such people, but it does not follow that they are mad, because such things happen in the ordinary course of events. Yet at some point common sense might say that such people were mad. The grounds seem unclear and hence the need may have come for us to think differently about mental illness (p. 55e). His positive remark here is (p. 54e): "Madness need not be regarded as an illness. Why shouldn't it be seen as a sudden — more or less sudden — change of character?" Here he notes Freud's "fanciful pseudo-explanations" as performing a disservice, so any new approach to mental illness should avoid Freudian theory. However, we do not find further suggestions from Wittgenstein as to how we are to proceed

If we are to rethink mental illness as a change in character then by not labelling people as mad we do not exclude them, or by classifying them open up the possibilities of treatment which, as we know in *One Flew Over the Cuckoo's Nest*, can be very threatening and permanent. Foucault saw these points too and the dangers inherent in caring for the mentally ill, but again, although for different reasons, he advances no program.

UNE FAÇON DE PARLER

Wittgenstein looks upon psychoanalysis as telling a story, a new myth, as a way of speaking. As we have seen, he does not consider it as a language because it is not translatable with other languages. There also are other reasons.

Thomas Mann raised the possibility of the use of psychoanalytic theory in literature, drawing parallels between literature and psychoanalytic theory, and identifying general parallels between the thought of Schopenhauer, Nietzsche, and Freud, connections that Freud did not seem to have recognized. In an address on the occasion of Freud's eightieth birthday in 1936 Mann says (1973, p. 60):

Through abnormality we have succeeded in penetrating most deeply into the darkness of human nature; that the study of disease has revealed itself as a first class technique of anthropological research . . .the literary artist should be the last person to be surprised at the fact. Sooner might he be surprised that he . . . should have so late become aware of the close sympathetic relations which connected his own existence with psychoanalytical research and the life work of Sigmund Freud . . . when I began to occupy myself with the literature of psychoanalysis I recognized . . . much that had long been familiar to me through my youthful mental experiences.

Although acknowledging the spread of Freud's medical theory to "every field of science, and every domain of the intellect," including literature, Mann is quite clear in this source that psychoanalysis and psychoanalytic theory are not a new form of experience or in Wittgenstein's sense a new form of life, but are dependent upon actual experience or the experience that is presented as lived by the characters in a novel. Psychoanalysis tries to explain experience and to this extent it is parasitic upon human experience. Mann says that psychoanalytic research is "connected to [one's] own existence" (Mann, 1973, p. 60) and, although he was to realize this connection, it was not to present a new way of expressing that experience, as the surrealists tended to see it (Descombes, 1995, p. viii). Thus, although connected they must be separately identifiable, with psychoanalytic theory a means of explaining that experience.

Thus, it would be mistaken to replace the languages of literature by a language derived from or based upon the core concepts of psychoanalytic theory, if there were such a language. Even though psychoanalytic theory is *une façon de parler* it is not a language or story that can portray experience, although it can help to explain it. This point is recognized in its full force by Simone de Beauvoir in her novel *The Mandarins* (which won her the prestigious Prix Goncourt).

In this novel Anne, the major character, is both a practicing and theoretical psychoanalyst. In the novel there is no talk of analysis per se until Chapter 8, 524 or so pages into the novel, when she is brought to face up to the breakdown of a friend Paula. Paula's interpretations of her rapidly decaying relationship with her husband Henri are full of psychoanalytic symbolism. These are interpretations by Paula of conversations, letters, incidents, and events in which either Henri or both are involved. The incident that causes the recognition of an explicit need for psychoanalysis, however, is a bizarre dinner party organized by Paula. This incident in the novel is based upon a true incident, described in *The Prime of Life* (1965, pp. 167–79), along with other incidents that occur in *The Mandarins* in relation to Paula. Beauvoir's two main points are that psychoanalysis is deployed as a possible explanation and therapy for Paula's bizarre behavior and her dinner party, real experiences in the novel, but secondly these are descriptions of real incidents in Beauvoir's life, because she insisted that personal experience must be used in literature. Until this severe abnormality surfaces the novel does not need psychoanalytic theory and practice explicitly as part of the story of the novel, although it is there implicitly in terms of Paula's interpretations of her relationship with Henri. Only in Chapter 8 does the reader who is not aware of psychoanalytic symbolization grasp the significance of Paula's account of events.

In addition, as in all of Beauvoir's work, there is much detailed psychological and philosophical reflection upon the human situations portrayed in the novel. Some French philosophers, especially Sartre and Merleau-Ponty, were receptive to the novelty of Freudian ideas even if they were highly critical, and Freudian contributions were welcomed to *Les Temps Modernes* (Descombes, 1995, p. viii). Although Beauvoir is not mentioned by Descombes, she must have been well aware of Freudian ideas through her association with *Les Temps Modernes*, which commenced publishing in 1945, 11 years before the publication of *The Mandarins*. She notes that she was reading about Freud in July 1956 (Beauvoir, 1968, pp. 441–43). However, her interpretation of Freud is that his work is "so different from that of both the philosopher and the scientist" (p. 442, compare Wittgenstein). To make this judgment on Freud Beauvoir must have formed this position prior to completing *The Mandarins*. Indeed she was asked after its publication when she had practiced psychoanalysis (p. 329). Given Beauvoir's insistence of the importance of the inclusion of primary experience to the writing of literature, such a question might not have been improper. However, such questions miss the philosophical point, so often expressed forcefully by Wittgenstein, that we are familiar with such things as a person like Paula who is "radically alienated from herself by an exclusive attachment to one man" (Beauvoir, 1968, p. 278), and we do understand such things because they are part of a form of life. What psychoanalytic theory offers is a different way of accounting for such things. Paula's exclusive attachment is not just an obsession, like keeping fit or reading, it is not just alienation because of the failure of the relationship: it is all those, but there is an underlying psychic cause of such obsession and alienation, which brings to the surface an abnormality.

Beauvoir used personal experiences in her novels as exemplifications of philosophical ideas (see for example, *She Came to Stay* and *The Blood of Others*). If Paula's behavior in her exclusive attachment to Henri, in imposing upon herself the model of the supportive wife and upon Henri the model of the confused husband, is seen first as exemplifying bad faith, later it is to be explained by Freudian theory. This is not to do philosophy but rather to show that what appears as bad faith has another non-philosophical explanation. The psychoanalytic explanation in fact supports the philosophical concept of bad faith while at the same time emphasizing other aspects of the human condition, experiences of which are used to exemply her philosophical position. In conclusion Beauvoir says in this novel the point that Thomas Mann was so delicately expressing in his respectful address on the occasion of Freud's eightieth birthday.

There is another way in which Wittgenstein might have interpreted Freud. Wittgenstein saw psychoanalysis as being therapeutic even though it was not causes that Freud was uncovering but, instead, reasons for action. Freud does not elaborate upon the functions that these new reasons might play for human beings. In his earliest published work, *Mental Illness and Psychology* (1987), Foucault addressed this Freudian issue.

Foucault was quite critical of Freud arguing (as he was to more fully later) that although the natural sciences can be correct about physical and organic nature, there is no human nature for the human sciences to be correct about. Thus, he is able to reject Freud's libidinal view of human nature, based as it is upon a "certain psychological substance [Freud's libido, Janet's psychic force]" (Foucault, 1987, p. 24). The notion of regression to the child is rejected because we must "accept the specificity of the morbid personality; the pathological structure of the psyche is not a return to origins; it is strictly original" (p. 26). For Foucault in this source a structural description of mental illness (p. 26): "would not involve explaining pathological structures, but simply placing them in a perspective that would make the facts of individual or social regression observed by Freud and Janet coherent and comprehensible."

What Foucault goes on to claim is that we have to follow Freud, not on his pseudo-biology, but to reach for the historical dimension of the human psyche, in particular why the patient has derealized the present through a notion of psychological defense (1987, p. 36): "Psychoanalysis . . . is tending more and more to turn its attention to the defence mechanisms and finally to admit that the subject reproduces his history only because he responds to a present situation."

Thus, Foucault, in talking of laying out the individual psychic history to see why someone has become mentally ill — alienated madness as he calls it (1987, p. 76) — has similarities to Wittgenstein's notion of "placing things side by side." In commenting on Fraser's *Golden Bough* Wittgenstein says (1979, p. 3e): "We only have to put together in the right way what we know, without adding anything, and the satisfaction we are trying to get from the explanation comes of itself . . . and the explanation isn't what satisfies us here anyway . . . we can only *describe* and say, human life is like that."

Here we can see parallels between Foucault (certainly in Foucault [1987]) and Wittgenstein (Marshall, 1995b). They are both highly skeptical of the claims of the human sciences and in this area suspicious of theoretical approaches, because they can be manipulative. They both have positive but critical approaches to Freud. Thus, they both: reject the scientistic form of explanation offered by Freud; accept that Freud did have something important to say; believe that description is the way to understanding human behavior through a laying out of the facts; believe that what is distinctively human is to be found in this manner and not through scientistic psychology; see that mental illness is in some way alienating of humans (Foucault), but that it may be only a change of character that is usually interpreted badly (Wittgenstein); and that psychoanalysis, therefore, is *une façon de parler*, and not a new and independent language or language game.

They differ, however, on a number of points. First they differ, at least in what was said or written, on the amount of harm that can be caused by psychoanalysis. For Wittgenstein analysis "is likely to do harm": for Foucault analysis is more than likely to do harm, because it is always potentially dangerous, and at the time of writing *Mental Illness and Psychology* he was very familiar with Heidegger's views on such matters. These Heideggerian views, toughened intellectually by immersion in Nietzsche, were to underline Foucault's writings until at least *The History of Sexuality*, Vol. 1. Foucault obtained two advanced qualifications, in psychology (1949) and psychopathology (1952). Thus, he had studied and worked in hospitals, which implies considerably more detailed knowledge of the psychological field than that of Wittgenstein. Certainly Wittgenstein did not have the detailed knowledge and understanding in psychology that he had in mathematics. Although Foucault was sensitive to language and associated practices, this was different from Wittgenstein's views of language and forms of life. For him when description came to an end some things could only be shown, but for Foucault there were hidden power relationships, associated with depth knowledge, which needed to be brought to the surface and made visible.

7

Metanarratives, Nihilism, and the End of Metaphysics: Wittgenstein and Lyotard

Context: The "linguistic turn" of Western philosophy (Heidegger's later works, the penetration of Anglo-American philosophies into European thought, the development of language technologies); and correlatively, the decline of universalist discourses (the metaphysical doctrines of modern times: narratives of progress, of socialism, of abundance, of knowledge). The weariness with regard to "theory," and the miserable slackening that goes along with it (new this, new that, post-this, post-that, etc.). The time has come to philosophize.
— Lyotard, 1988, p. xiii

In short, it [nihilism] stands like an extreme that cannot be gotten beyond, and yet it is the only true path of going beyond; it is the principle of a new beginning. . . . God is dead. God: this means God, but also everything else that, in rapid succession, has tried to take its place — e.g., the ideal, consciousness, reason, the certainty of progress, the happiness of the masses, culture, etc. Everything not without value nevertheless has no absolute value of its own — there is nothing man can rely on, nothing of any value other than the meaning given to it in an endless process.
— Blanchot, 1987, p. 36

In *The Postmodern Condition* Jean-François Lyotard (1984) locates the problem of the legitimation of knowledge within the general context of the crisis of narratives and distinguishes between the modern and the postmodern in terms of the appeal to a metalanguage. The postmodern, he defines simply as "incredulity towards metanarratives" (Lyotard, 1984, p. xxiv). The rule of consensus that governed Enlightenment narratives and cast truth as a product of agreement between rational minds has been rent asunder; the narrative function has been dispersed into many language elements, each with its own pragmatic valencies. In arguing this position Lyotard views himself as philosophizing "after" Wittgenstein. This chapter interprets the work of both later Wittgenstein and Lyotard as philosophical responses to European nihilism and the end of metaphysics and discusses the question of European nihilism in terms of Lyotard's notion of the end of grand narratives, before considering at greater length Lyotard's *The Differend* as a positive response to nihilism.

There is a section in *The Postmodern Condition* that in a few pages suggestively wields together, if only momentarily, Lyotard's thoughts regarding delegitimation following the crisis of scientific knowledge, with Nietzsche's sense of European nihilism and Wittgenstein's notion of language games in a way that sheds light on both how and what it might mean to philosophize at the close of the twentieth century. Lyotard's notion of delegitimation refers to the state of contemporary culture and society following the decline of the grand narratives. In short he argues that the culture of advanced liberal capitalism, renewing itself after its retreat in the 1930s and the protection subsequently afforded by the Keynesian economic settlement, has eliminated the communist alternative and now functions as a scientific secular culture undergoing an advanced process of disintegration. It is as if after the death of God, whereas Nietzsche maintains the highest values have devaluated themselves, the new scientific values have proved themselves incapable of legitimation and nihilism still stands at the door. Lyotard sees in Wittgenstein's *Philosophical Investigations* a way of philosophizing in face of this cultural disintegration and pessimism, which leads in new ethicopolitical directions. He self-consciously positions Wittgenstein's *Philosophical Investigations* and his own philosophy of the *differend* as philosophical responses to European nihilism and cultural pessimism — both attempts to outline a kind of legitimation not based upon the performativity of the system as a whole. Lyotard's "Wittgenstein" and his own philosophy provide responses to the forces of cultural disintegration and pessimism that some scholars take as both one of the major characteristics of the postmodern condition and the greatest challenge confronting contemporary education.

Lyotard holds that capitalist renewal and the upsurge of technology have led to a crisis of scientific knowledge and to an internal erosion of the very prospect of legitimation. He locates the seeds of such delegitimation, which he also refers to as nihilism, in the decline of the legitimating power of the grand narratives of the nineteenth century. The speculative narrative of the unity of all knowledge held that knowledge is worthy of its name only if it can generate a second-order discourse that functions to legitimate it, otherwise such knowledge would amount to mere ideology. The process of delegitimation — an intellectual enterprise carried out by both Nietzsche and Wittgenstein[1] — has revealed that science not only plays its own language game (and consequently is both on a par with and incapable of legitimating other language games) but also is incapable of legitimating itself as speculation assumed it could.[2]

In the brief passage under investigation Lyotard (1984, p. 39) suggests that in order to play the speculative game we must first assume that the positive sciences represent the general mode of knowledge and, second, "that we understand this language to imply certain formal and axiomatic presuppositions that it must always make explicit."[3] It is in this context that Lyotard mentions Nietzsche for the first time: "This is exactly what Nietzsche is doing, though with a different terminology, when he shows that 'European nihilism' results from the truth requirement of science being turned against itself." His accompanying footnote (p. 125) refers to Nietzsche's notion of "European Nihilism." In the same context Lyotard (1984, p. 41) refers to Wittgenstein's conception of language games and, in particular, to the modern development of new language games. Wittgenstein himself mentions the symbolism of chemistry and the notation of infinitesimal calculus; Lyotard lists the growth of machine languages, the matrices of game theory, new systems of musical notation, systems of notation for denotative forms of logic, the language of the genetic code, graphs of phonological structures, and so on. In relation to this proliferation, he writes: "We may form a pessimistic impression of this splintering: nobody speaks all of those languages, they have no universal metalanguage, the project of the system-subject is a failure, the goal of emancipation has nothing to do with science, we are all stuck in the positivism of this or that discipline of learning, the learned scholars have turned into scientists, the diminished tasks of research have become compartmentalized and no one can master them all" (Lyotard, 1984, p. 41). Under these conditions, he suggests, philosophy is forced to relinquish its legitimation duties and is reduced to the study of logic or the history of ideas. European nihilism for Lyotard is represented most clearly in the process of cultural disintegration symbolized most clearly by the end of metaphysics or, more correctly, the end of philosophy as the universal metalanguage — as that master-discipline able to underwrite all claims to knowledge and, thereby, to unify the rest of culture.

The pessimism associated with this cultural disintegration and the accompanying sense of delegitimation crystallized in turn-of-the-century Vienna. Lyotard writes in this regard:

Turn-of-the-century Vienna was weaned on this pessimism: not just artists such as Musil, Kraus, Hofmannsthal, Loos, Schönberg, and Broch, but also philosophers

Mach and Wittgenstein. They carried awareness of and theoretical and artistic responsibility for delegitimation as far as it could be taken. We can say today that the mourning process has been completed. There is no need to start all over again. Wittgenstein's strength is that he did not opt for the positivism that was being developed by the Vienna Circle, but outlined in his investigation of language games a kind of legitimation not based on performativity. That is what the postmodern world is all about. Most people have lost the nostalgia for the lost narrative. It in no way follows that they are reduced to barbarity. What saves them from it is their knowledge that legitimation can only spring from their own linguistic practice and communicational interaction. (Lyotard, 1984, p. 41)

Central to Lyotard's analysis is the revival or recovery of the notion of narrative that he develops at the local and popular level as a form of customary, cultural, or ethnic knowledge — a "knowing how," "knowing how to live" and "knowing how to listen" — against the totalizing and globalizing tendencies of older master narratives of legitimation that operate, albeit in crisis mode, in the service of the great historical actors of the nation-state, the proletariat, the party, and, increasingly (one might add), the world policy agencies (for example, World Bank, Organization for Economic Cooperation and Development), the G-7, "the new world order."[4] Lyotard develops what he calls a "pragmatics of narrative knowledge" in which narratives determine criteria of competence and performance, defining rights of what can be said and done in a particular culture. Local or little narratives, in sharp contrast to the game of legitimacy played in the West, provide immediate legitimation: as he says, "they are legitimated by the simple fact that they do what they do" (Lyotard, 1984, p. 23).

Lyotard has subsequently revised his analysis of the role of narratives. In "Apostil on Narratives" he acknowledges that in *The Postmodern Condition* he exaggerated the importance of the narrative genre, and he says, "specifically, . . . [I] went too far in identifying knowledge with narrative" (Lyotard, 1992, p. 31). He argues that on the whole, scientific theory does not take the form of narrative and that within general narratology there remains an ineliminable metaphysics that accords hegemony to the genre of narrative over all others. In accordance with his passage to the *differend*, Lyotard now wishes to forgo this metaphysical element by emphasizing the different regimes of phrases and different genres of discourse without attributing any one regime or genre privilege or precedence. In "Missive on Universal History," Lyotard writes: "It is inadvisable to grant the narrative genre an absolute privilege over other genres of discourse in the analysis of human, and specifically linguistic (ideological), phenomenon, particularly when the approach is philosophical. Some of my earlier reflections may have succumbed to this 'transcendental appearance,' 'Presentations,' *Instructions Païennes*, even *The Postmodern Condition*" (Lyotard, 1992, p. 35).

His concern not to privilege narrative — to eliminate any residue of metaphysics — brings his thinking into line with Wittgenstein of the *Philosophical Investigations*. Both the later Wittgenstein and Kant of the third *Critique* provide "epilogues to modernity and prologues to an honourable postmodernity. They draw up the affidavit ascertaining the decline of universalist doctrines (Leibnizian or Russellian metaphysics). They question the terms in which these doctrines thought they could settle differends (reality, subject, community, finality)" (Lyotard, 1988, p. xiii).[5]

By maintaining that the signification of a term is its use and by disentangling language games, Wittgenstein lays the ground for a new kind of diasporic thought or a thought of dispersal that shapes our contemporary context. Wittgenstein's legacy, Lyotard argues, must be yet relieved of its debt to anthropomorphism — an anthropomorphism that is empirical in Wittgenstein and involves the notion of use. This is a task that Lyotard sets himself in *The Differend*.

LANGUAGE GAMES AND
THE POSTMODERN CONDITION

Lyotard in *The Postmodern Condition* champions Wittgenstein's language games as the basis of his analysis of the crisis of narratives. He emphasizes the pluralistic nature of language games to advance an attack on the conception of universal reason and of the unity of both language and the subject. There is no one reason, only reasons, he argues, where no one form of reason takes precedence over others. The traumatic aspect of *The Postmodern Condition* points to the tearing apart of old organic bodies that regulate thinking. Although Habermas and critical theory emphasize the bifurcation of reason into its instrumental (positivistic) and moral-practical forms, Lyotard (following Wittgenstein) and Foucault emphasize the (postmodern) multiplicity and proliferation of forms of reason, defined by the rules of particular discourses or language games. Each of the various types of utterance — denotative, prescriptive, performative, and so forth — comprises a language game with its own body of rules. The rules are irreducible and there exists an incommensurability among different games. Lyotard makes three observations concerning language games. First, he argues in true Wittgensteinian fashion that the rules do not have a bedrock justification, nor do they carry with them their own legitimation. Where Wittgenstein might say they are constituted in practice, Lyotard claims they are the object of a contract, explicit or not, between players that gives rise to an agonistics of language. Second, "if there are no rules, there is no game." Third, "every utterance should be thought of as a 'move' in the game" (Lyotard, 1984, p. 10). Indeed, the social bond is comprised of such moves.

This is the basis of Lyotard's innovation, because he emphasizes a notion of language games that is based upon the idea of struggle and conflict. In one deft stroke Lyotard politicizes Wittgenstein's conception of language. Two principles underlie Lyotard's (1984, p. 10) adopted method as a whole: "To speak is to fight, in the sense of playing, and speech acts fall within the domain of a general agonistics." As Fredric Jameson (1984, p. xi) explains, utterances are not conceived of either as a process of transmission of information or messages, or a network of signs, or even in terms of a semiotics as a signifying system: rather they are seen as an agonistics of language — "an unstable exchange between communicational adversaries." This elevates the conflictual view of language as a model for understanding the nature of the social bond: "Each of us lives at the intersection of many of these [language games]. However, we do not necessarily establish stable language combinations, and the properties of the ones we do establish are not necessarily communicable" (Lyotard, 1984, p. xxiv). Against both the functionalist view (Talcott Parsons), which represents society as a functional whole and the Marxist view, which represents society as a duality based on the principle of class struggle, Lyotard advances a postmodern conception of the social bond based squarely upon the notion of language games. Each one of us is located at nodal points in circuits of communication or at posts through which messages pass. The social is thus atomized into flexible networks of language games. Yet, as Lyotard argues: "No one, not even the least privileged among us, is ever entirely powerless over the messages that traverse and position him at the post of sender, addressee, or referent" (Lyotard, 1984, p. 15). As Lyotard suggests:

After Wittgenstein, the first task is that of overcoming this humanist obstacle to the analysis of phrase regimes, to make philosophy inhuman. Humanity is not the user of language, nor even its guardian; there is no more one subject than there is one language. Phrases situate names and pronouns (or their equivalent) in the universes they present. Philosophy is the discourse that has as its rule the search for its rule (and that of other discourses), a discourse in which phrases thus try themselves out without rules and link themselves guided only by amazement at the fact that everything has not been said, that a new phrase occurs, that it is not the case that nothing happens. (Lyotard, 1984, p. 15)

In his interpretation, Lyotard thinks that Wittgenstein is still too humanistic, too wedded to the anthropocentrism that accompanies forms of life, as the given. This is why Lyotard jettisons the language-game analysis in his later writings to embrace "phrase regimes" and also why he argues that the first task "after Wittgenstein" is "to make philosophy inhuman." Lyotard argues that this inhumanity and its implications for the social bond yet remain to be analyzed.

LYOTARD'S PASSAGE TO *THE DIFFEREND*

Lyotard in *The Differend* proclaims "Now is the time to philosophize." For Lyotard consensus disguises the conflict among players within and between language games and, more importantly, it disguises the fact that consensus can only be established on the basis of acts of exclusion. For Lyotard, both Marxism and liberalism are examples of totalizing discourses, based on foundational Enlightenment metanarratives, which claim to be able to express the truth without residue. These metanarratives, Lyotard argues, do not speak the truth so much as express the desire for truth; they embody moral ideals about which we should remain skeptical or incredulous. Accordingly, it is easy to understand how Lyotard self-consciously locates himself after Wittgenstein.

In "Wittgenstein 'After'," Lyotard (1993) acknowledges the way in which his thinking takes place "after" and links up with Wittgenstein's. He clarifies the ethicopolitical background of Wittgenstein's response to the general sense of nihilism and delegitimation characterizing European culture following two world wars. Wittgenstein's rejection of philosophy as a metalanguage, his emphasis upon the diversity of language usage, and the incommensurability of language games are seen as part of Wittgenstein's philosophical response to his sense of contingency and uprootedness following the decline or disintegration of European cultural unity in midcentury. For Lyotard, this same sense of cultural disintegration is represented in the figure of Auschwitz. In *The Differend*, Auschwitz functions as a model that designates an experience of language that brings speculative discourse to an end because, as Lyotard maintains, it invalidates the presupposition of that philosophical discourse (namely, that all that is real is rational and that all that is rational is real). For Lyotard (1988, pp. 152–60) Auschwitz serves as the symbolic end or liquidation of the project of modernity. It symbolizes the "tragic incompletion of modernity" by pointing to the moral that universal history does not move inevitably toward the better, that history does not have a universal finality. The transition from language games in *The Postmodern Condition* to phrase regimes in *The Differend* is Lyotard's major theoretical innovation and philosophical response to the ethicopolitical demands following the loss of innocence in a time "diseased by language" and dominated by "industrial technoscience." As Lyotard writes: "Mourning for the unity of language [and of the subject] — a certain 'joy' in the description of its strengths and its weaknesses, the refusal to have recourse to metaphysical entities like finality, the will to power, or even thought — ought to make Wittgenstein familiar to us" (Lyotard, 1993, p. 21).

We are encouraged in this interpretation by Plinio Prado's (1991) Wittgensteinian interpretation of Lyotard's *The Differend*. He shows how and why Wittgenstein comes to form an unavoidable passage for

Lyotard's thinking on the *differend* and charts the first references to the later Wittgenstein in Lyotard's work after his withdrawal from the grand narrative and practical critique of radical Marxism. Lyotard, he says, does not approach Wittgenstein's work from the viewpoint of a professional philosopher interested in questions of logical truth, rather he welcomes Wittgenstein "as a result of ethical and political questions concerning 'delegitimation': that is, on the basis of the crisis 'which resides in any attempt to moralise politics.' . . . The passage is signalled to us by the general context of nihilism and by the ethico-political stakes of justice. . . . Henceforth, the Idea (in the Kantian sense) of justice, regulating the political realm, is placed . . . under the Wittgensteinian rule of divergence" (Prado, 1991, p. 96).

The problem of justice and the refusal of a metalanguage, Prado (1991, p. 98) suggests, constitutes the guiding thought of Wittgenstein's work: "For Wittgenstein, 'injustice' lies precisely in the claim to occupy the meta-viewpoint, to 'universalise'; that is, to impose one's rules and criteria upon other games, leaving one's own language in order to 'attack' others." He views Wittgenstein's remarks upon Frazer's ethnology as pointing to a classical and eminently political example of such aggression. He refers to von Wright's (1982) description of Wittgenstein in relation to his times as evidence of the way in which Wittgenstein was profoundly affected by the nihilism that struck European culture, "by the collapse of 'grand' aims," the dispersion and dissolution of resemblances conferring a unity upon culture. This experience of rootlessness and contingency — "the disappearance of culture" — Prado maintains, can be seen in the Wittgensteinian leitmotif of the indetermination or of the paradox of the rule. There is no solution to the paradox of the rule; there is always a "gaping abyss" (Wittgenstein) separating the rule from the case, a structural discontinuity between the general (the rule) and the particular (the case) that can always give rise to disagreement and conflict. To determine without rules whether a particular case falls under a rule or not is what we call reflective judgement. The stakes of the ethical and the political are located precisely in the gap that opens up between the rule and the case. Prado puts his case in the following terms, linking Lyotard to Wittgenstein: "The open multiplicity of language games, autonomous and always irreducible to each other, the refusal of any meta-game, the indetermination and contingency of 'moves' (words, actions, gestures) constitute . . . the horizon of a reflection on justice in the 'age' of nihilism and of the collapse of any metaphysical authority (Spirit, Meaning, Progress, Ideals, Ends)" (Prado, 1991, pp. 100–101).

The Differend, Prado argues, approaches the question of nothing, of being, and non-being — the gaping abyss — from the perspective of an ontology of sentences (phrases). If there is no correct way to follow a rule, we are left only with the pure contingency of linkage — between sentences, between the rule and the case — that can only be bridged through the use of reflective judgment. Wittgenstein's thought opens up the path to a justice of multiplicity where "the pretension of one game to prevail over others . . . would be injustice itself" (Prado, 1990, p. 96). In this Wittgensteinian conception, the ethicopolitical stakes are placed at the heart of the indetermination of the rule allowing Lyotard to resume the task of critical practice in the form of a politics of judgment that has its primary goal "to detect the undetermined, to listen and bring to hearing the differend hidden under the alleged universal" (Prado, 1991, p. 96).[6] As Lyotard clearly states: "that a universal rule of judgement between heterogenous genres is lacking in general" (1988, p. xi), or that "there is no genre whose hegemony over others would be just" (p. 158). A *differend*, as Lyotard defines it, is "a case of conflict, between (at least) two parties, that cannot be equitably resolved for lack of a rule of judgement applicable to both arguments" (p. xi). The aim of philosophy in this situation, Lyotard argues, is to detect differends (a cognitive task) and to bear witness to them (an ethical obligation).[7]

One of the clearest pictures of the implications of Lyotard's Wittgenstein-inspired philosophy for the ethicopolitical question of other cultures comes from Bill Readings (1992, p. 168) who, in reference to Australian aborigines, argues that "Lyotard's rethinking of philosophy as a process of experimental or pagan judgement allows the question of justice to be kept alive in late capitalism."[8] Readings exercises experimental judgment in Lyotard's sense in the case of the relation between the republican nation-state of Australia and its indigenous peoples, a case that exemplifies for him the clash between "the metanarrative of a unitary state claiming to embody universal values and more fragmentary or explicitly local or minoritarian groups" (p. 169).[9] He argues that the claim to a universal history (dedicated to the idea of humanity) in this case is not the ground for global community but rather of victimization and terror. The *differend* between the Commonwealth government and the aborigines illustrates such an injustice: the representational structure of a republican "we" reduces aboriginal identity — an identity radically untranslatable and inaccessible to Western modernist rationality — to an abstract human nature assimilable to a community of a homogenous "we." It is, Readings argues, an inherently integrationist "we," a self-authorizing, republican "we" that builds its definition of community in terms of a universal claim to humanity. However, such consensual republican community building represses difference in the name of "we" the people and prevents the possibility of asking the question "who are we to speak?" As Readings (p. 175) explains: "Any culture that doesn't understand itself as a 'self', or as potentially human, is silenced, suppressed." Cultural differences are referred to in the universal language of liberty and freedom, which forces thinking of difference into the mold of abstract identity based on atomistic individualism. Readings concludes:

> The assumption of universal human nature . . . lights the way to terror even as it upholds the torch of human rights. The problem of averting genocide demands a respect for difference, a deconstructive ethics, that is prepared to relinquish the concept of the human, to separate liberty from fraternity. Deconstruction rephrases the political, not by adding race along with gender and class to the categories by which we calculate oppression but by invoking an incalculable difference, an unrepresentable other, in the face of which any claim to community must be staked. (pp. 186–87)

The analysis of other cultures provided by Readings in terms of difference is not an isolated one. We mention it here because of its relevance to an Australian audience. Paul Patton (1995) has provided a similar analysis of Australian society in terms of the philosophy of difference, focusing on the Mabo debate and utilizing a poststructuralist approach to political questions. Patton (1995, p. 167) makes clear, contra Rorty on cultural difference, that Rawl's theory "reflects a deep commitment within liberal theory: to a principle of sameness or identity among members of the political community." In the idea of difference, he suggests, difference understood as specificity or variation rather than opposition or exclusion, "we can find some intimations of a different idea of both society and justice, one that does not entail the assimilation of one culture by another."[10]

Lyotard's later work provides a basis for rethinking philosophy of education and of making central to it the ethicopolitical question of other cultures. His notion of pagan judgment allows the question of judgment to be kept alive in the era of globalization, where the claim to a universal history is not the ground for a global community but rather one of terror and victimization. Lyotard's philosophy enables us to stop trying to force cultural differences into the universal language of liberty and freedom, a discourse that reinterprets difference in the mold of abstract identity based upon atomistic individualism.

NOTES

Parts of Chapter 7 are based on "Metanarratives, Nihilism and the End of Metaphysics: Wittgenstein and Lyotard," a paper presented by Michael Peters at the conference "Narrative and Metaphor: Across the Disciplines," The University of Auckland, New Zealand, July 8–10, 1996, and Peters (1995b, pp. 189–204).

1. Lyotard (1984, p. 40) also mentions Martin Buber and Emmanel Levinas as developing philosophies in response to delegitimation or nihilism.
2. By reference to modern developments in logic and arithmetic Lyotard shows that the principle of a universal metalanguage required for demonstrating

the truth of denotative statements has given way to the principle of a plurality of formal and axiomatic systems. In terms of the properties required of the syntax of any formal system (consistency, completeness, decidability, and independence of axioms), it is possible to generalize from Kurt Gödel's incompleteness theorem that all formal systems have internal limitations. The metalanguage used by logicians to describe a formal axiomatic system is natural. It is also universal (in the sense that all other languages can be translated into it) but not consistent with respect to negation, because it allows the formation of paradoxes.

3.   See also Lyotard (1989a).

4.   Note Jameson's (1984, p. xii) remark that the great master narratives have not disappeared but gone underground, so to speak, to operate with an unconscious effectivity.

5.   See also Rosen (1962). Rosen defines nihilism as a theoretical form (or, ultimately, a formlessness) to be found in the writings of Nietzsche, Heidegger, and Wittgenstein (especially, ordinary language philosophy considered as a form of epistemology).

6.   Prado also countenances and qualifies Lyotard's critique of Wittgenstein's anthropological empiricism.

7.   Lyotard's term "paganism," as Prado (1991, p. 96) points out, refers to the universe of "games incommunicable with each other" resistant to being synthetized in a "unifying meta-discourse" and his associated notion of "political minorities" understood as "territories of language." As he writes: "each one of us belongs to several minorities and, what is very important, not one of them prevails. It is only in this sense that one could say that society is just," Lyotard & Thébaud (1985, p. 181).

8.   See also Readings (1993a), especially the sections entitled "Intellectuals: Speaking for Others" and "An Endless Politics," where he writes "Politics becomes a matter of justice, of handling differences, rather than of establishing truth or even countertruth" (p. xxiv). See also Peters (1994b) for a review of Lyotard's *Political Writings*.

9.   Readings explores the *differend* between aborigines and the West as it is witnessed in Werner Herzog's *Where the Green Ants Dream*.

10.   The literature on the philosophy and politics of difference is now quite extensive: see, for example, Lyotard (1989b), Young (1990), Yeatman (1992, 1994), and Wilson and Yeatman (1995). For a discussion of the politics of difference in the educational literature see Peters (1994a, pp. 72–75; 1995c).

8

Rorty, Wittgenstein, and Postmodernism: Neopragmatism and the Politics of the *Ethnos*

David Hollinger (1995) in his recent *Postethnic America: Beyond Multiculturalism* argues for a rooted cosmopolitanism — a position associated with the Enlightenment of the eighteenth century that rejects the discourse of multiculturalism based on the psychological concept of identity in favor of the more social and performative notion of affiliation.[1] Affiliation is seen to be based upon a modest choice-maximizing principle in contrast to the prescription that accompanies the discourse of multiculturalism and so-called communities of descent. A postethnic perspective emphasizes the question of U.S. nationality by focusing upon the civic character of the U.S. nation-state. Hollinger (1995) in developing his position traces the shift from species to ethnos — from a universalism (and ethnocentrism) characterizing the species-centered discourse typified by the work of Alfred Kinsey and others, to a new sense of historical particularity typified in the work of Thomas Kuhn. The former argued for universalism by erasing human (sexual) differences and biologizing essences, the latter demonstrated the impossibility of escaping ethnocentrism by emphasizing the "contingent, temporally, and socially situated character of our beliefs and values, of our institutions and practices" (p. 60). If Kuhn's work drew our attention to the way that scientific truths were dependent upon a set of historically specific practices that comprised a community, then it became "more plausible to view the Bill of Rights as just another tribal code" (p. 61). Kuhn's historicism gelled with the work of other influential scholars: Clifford Geertz emphasized local knowledge, Michael Walzer had accented membership of community in his particularist *Spheres of Justice*, and even John Rawls by the 1980s had recognized the force of historicist arguments relocating questions of justice within a more particular social setting. In the context of this narrative, Hollinger showcases Richard Rorty as the paradigm epitomizing the shift from an ethnocentrism (in the mid-1980s) to developing a more inclusive notion of the *ethnos* in the 1990s. It is Rorty's position, above all, that Hollinger takes to be definitive of a kind of postethnic liberal politics he advocates for the United States. Hollinger derives great philosophical comfort from Rorty's changed views, insisting that they help inspire a postethnic disposition toward issues of affiliation.

Hollinger (1995, pp. 71–77) elaborates Rorty's earlier view focusing upon his pragmatic witness against the old universalism. In Hollinger's eyes Rorty attempts to avoid the species-centered discourse by construing principles of human dignity, not by invoking a (Judeo-Christian derived) universalism but simply by recognizing that such an appeal to dignity is a contingent feature of the moral community comprising our particular Western *ethnos*. Rorty disposes of the Kantian rationalists, who search for human essences, by substituting a notion of human solidarity. Yet by the end of the 1980s Rorty begins to extend the "circle of the we" (Hollinger, 1995, p. 74) attempting to build "an ever larger and more variegated *ethnos*" (Rorty, 1989, p. 192). The crucial aspect of our *ethnos*, Rorty maintains, is its traditional distrust of ethnocentrism. As Hollinger (1995, p. 74) observes: "By 1993 Rorty was calling for the creation of a 'planetary community' defined by 'human rights'." Having once jettisoned the old metaphysical baggage concerning an essential human nature, all that is left to do is to spread "human rights culture" through "sentimental education," rather than through "moral knowledge." As Hollinger (1995: 75) explains:

The most salient features of Rorty's position in 1993 were his fierce attack on tribalism, his uninhibited embrace of all humankind as the potential beneficiary of human rights culture derived from Christianity and the Enlightenment, and his uncompromising willingness to defend human rights culture against the claims of cultures that failed to support these rights. Even Rorty, then, has come around to insisting that full recognition of the historically particular character of our discourses should not be taken as a license for abandoning a traditional human rights commitment.

Hollinger, thus, takes Rorty's current position as one that supports his own — a cosmopolitan postethnic liberal politics based upon the extension of a human rights culture. This is his answer for the destiny of the U.S. civic community (and by extension, the rest of the world) against the ethnos-centered discourse of multiculturalists and their implicit attacks upon the West, Western essentialism, and Western neo-imperialism. It is clear that Rorty believes that the primary task facing philosophers, social theorists, and others in the next few centuries is the building of a multi-cultural global utopia, a task to be undertaken by first unravelling each culture (understood as shared habits of action) into "a multiplicity of fine component threads" and weaving these threads together with equally fine threads from other cultures to form a global cultural tapestry exhibit-ing a variety-in-unity characteristic that promotes a kind of rationality based on tolerance and freedom (Rorty, 1993, p. 593). It is an answer that rests upon a form of liberal democracy that views the polity as an aggre-gation of freely affiliated individuals. It is an answer also that, in our view, is both a dangerous description of liberal politics in the postmodern condition and one peculiarly inappropriate for Aotearoa/New Zealand.[2]

In this chapter we first briefly trace the development of Rorty's (1983) thought and examine his "postmodernist bourgeois liberalism" in terms of the politics of the *ethnos*. We argue that Rorty's position, originally inspired by Wittgenstein, falls down in its approach to the question of other cultures precisely to the extent that it shifted or deviated over time from a Wittgensteinian view. In the second part of the chapter we exam-ine some of these points of tension or deviation, concluding that Rorty's current position provides a dangerous description for liberal politics in the postmodern condition.

RORTY'S PHILOSOPHICAL TRAJECTORY

Claiming Wittgenstein, Heidegger, and Dewey as his heroes, Rorty (1980) in *Philosophy and the Mirror of Nature* emerged as one of the leading philosophers in the English-speaking world to inquire of the status and role of his discipline after the collapse of the Kantian enterprise. His antirepresentationalism, based upon readings of Sellars, Quine, and Davidson, led him to a radical historization of philosophy: if there is no distinction between the necessary and the contingent, no distinction between scheme and content, then, he argues, it is no longer clear what counts as analysis or what role philosophy can serve. Rorty (1980, p. 169) stressed the indispensability of the Kantian framework for modern analytic philosophy: "If we do not have the distinction between what is 'given' and what is 'added by the mind,' or that between the 'contingent' (because influenced by what is given) and the 'necessary' (because entirely 'within' the mind and under its control), then we will not know what would count as a 'rational reconstruction' of our knowledge." A little further on, he remarks: "Analytic philosophy, *cannot*, I suspect, be written without one or other of these distinctions. If there are no intu-itions into which to resolve concepts (in a manner of the *Aufbau*) nor any internal relations among concepts to make possible 'grammatical discov-eries' (in the manner of Oxford philosophy), then indeed it is hard to imagine what an 'analysis' might be. Wisely few analytic philosophers any longer try to explain what it is to offer an analysis" (Rorty, 1980, p. 172). It is on the basis of this relatively early analysis that Rorty rejects liberals who are Kantian rationalists — those who search for a universal essence of human nature as a basis for justifying human rights.

In developing an alternative role for philosophy in post-Kantian culture, Rorty rejects philosophy-as-epistemology to embrace philosophy-as-hermeneutics, that is, philosophy as an edifying conversation. In doing so, he begins to bridge the gap between Anglo-American analytic philosophy and its Continental counterpart, forging something of a neopragmatist alliance with poststructuralism.

Rorty, more recently, suggests that in his imagination Dewey has come to eclipse both Wittgenstein and Heidegger, and in his later writings he has self-consciously styled himself as a defender of what he calls Deweyan liberalism. The full political consequences of his brand of liberalism, however, have only recently become evident in a series of papers on democracy, cosmopolitanism, and liberalism — a position, at one point, he flippantly calls "Postmodernist Bourgeois Liberalism" (Rorty, 1991a). It is a position that openly espouses a kind of ethnocentrism as an inescapable condition of liberal culture, although recently, in answer to his neo-Marxist critics, he has come to differentiate between ethnocentrism and the *ethnos*. Rorty's position represents, perhaps, the most fully fledged and deliberate attempt to work through the consequences of pragmatism and to link the politics of liberalism with postmodernism.[3] Yet the term "postmodernist" is a problematic label to apply to Rorty for a number of reasons. Not only has he now distanced himself from his previous uses of the term,[4] but his professed sympathies with postmodern philosophers like Jacques Derrida and Michel Foucault have taken a decidedly chilly turn, especially after the left critique of his political liberalism based upon what is perceived to be his use of a colonizing, imperialistic, and encompassing liberal "we."[5] Rorty is simply dismissive of Marx and the neo-Marxist critics who attacked him — they are essentialists, after all! Rorty's real quarry is postmodern political theory. He is scathing about what he calls the Foucauldian left, which he maintains has given up on the idea of democratic politics, is mired in critique, and is unable to deliver an alternative utopian vision. The best parts of what Rorty now calls "the post-Nietzschean tradition of Franco-German thought" (1991b, p. 1), by which he appears to mean the thought of Heidegger and Derrida, are those parts that "help us see how things look under nonrepresentationalist, nonlogocentrist descriptions" (p. 5). The worst parts are those parts that engage politics. Rorty's criticism is that post-Nietzschean politics is obsessed with radical critique and infected with a despair and general sense of cultural pessimism: "So the only sort of politics with which this tradition is continuous is not the actual discourse of the surviving democratic nations, but a kind of pseudo-politics reminiscent of Marxist study-groups of the thirties — a sort of continual self-correction of theory, with no conceivable relation to practice" (Rorty, 1991b, p. 24). By contrast, a Deweyan vision of the modern world is dominated by social hope and is directed to actual problems of contemporary democratic societies, which it addresses in a reformist and pragmatic spirit. With the exception of Dewey and possibly Weber, "Our political imagination has not been enlarged by the philosophy of our century," (p. 26) and in any case our social democratic vocabulary is all right as it is and does not require any further sophistication by philosophers.

We think that there is a deeper reason for the shift, a reason in part to do with Rorty's philosophical development and trajectory, which has become clearer over time — a shift symbolized in Rorty's writings by the gradual eclipsing of Wittgenstein by Dewey. In more sophisticated terms, we might say that the Rorty of *Philosophy and the Mirror of Nature* was a radical philosopher, providing a critique of analytic philosophy and deconstructing the Western tradition of philosophy-as-epistemology in a Wittgensteinian manner. Yet Rorty does not follow through on his Wittgensteinian insights because he is still anchored in or tied to the analytic movement in crucial ways, albeit its second U.S. phase, a phase dominated by Quine and Davidson. We first came across this suggestive reading in a book of interviews with contemporary U.S. philosophers carried out by Giovanna Borradori (1994, pp. 103–4), who makes the following remark in the preface to his interview with Rorty: "The point of departure of Rorty's neo-pragmatist discourse is precisely a critique of analytic philosophy. However, he directs his criticism mainly at its first phase, the most orthodox one, born following the immigration of Viennese logical positivism to the United States. In fact, a second phase of analyticism, embracing authors such as Quine and Davidson, whose proximity to pragmatism is emphasized by Rorty, remains untouched by his attack." The second phase not only remains untouched but also becomes an important part of Rorty's reworking of philosophy of language and pragmatism based upon developments in the work of Quine and Davidson, somewhat against their own evaluations.[6] Rorty's second phase analytics promulgated in the name of pragmatism and liberalism sits awkwardly with Rorty's reading of the later Wittgenstein. This awkwardness becomes clearest in relation to the question of other cultures.

The differences between Rorty and Wittgenstein can be seen as a deeper reflection of their own cultural affiliations: Wittgenstein, as a figure of the Austrian and counter-Enlightenment tradition, is strongly influenced by Schopenhauer, Kraus, and Spengler, among others. He has, so to speak, lived "the decline of the West" and has been weaned on European cultural pessimism.[7] Rorty, by contrast, as a philosopher of the New

World who became disenchanted with the U.S. transplant of Old World positivism, attempts to revive a U.S. public intellectual tradition going back to Dewey. He is, by contrast, full of optimism and social hope and imbued with a New World utopianism.

RORTY'S POSTMODERNIST BOURGEOIS LIBERALISM

Rorty's antirepresentationalism puts natural science on a par with the rest of culture: knowledge is not a matter of getting reality right, rather it is a matter of acquiring the appropriate habits of action for coping with reality. Rorty sees himself as the Wittgensteinian physician of culture freeing us of the picture that has held us captive for almost a century. His therapeutic desire is to rescue us from a set of pseudo-problems generated by the realist intuition that true statements stand in a representational relation to the world. Antirepresentationalists, equipped with Wittgenstein's sense of what it is to do philosophy, think that the realist-idealist and skepticism-antiskepticism controversies have been both pointless and undesirable, if only because they see no way of formulating an independent test of accuracy of representation. The notion of such a test implies a standpoint outside our own conceptual scheme for purposes of analyzing and comparing the correspondence of representations with nonlinguistic entities. Rorty proposes a highly influential interpretation of Wittgenstein, defending him from the charge of transcendental idealism levelled by Bernard Williams and Thomas Nagel, by arguing that Wittgenstein was not attempting to answer realist-type questions, that he certainly "was not suggesting that we determine the way reality is," but rather he was abandoning a picture that had held him captive: "He was suggesting that questions which we should have to climb out of our own minds to answer should not be asked. He was suggesting that both realism and idealism share representationalist presuppositions which we would be better off dropping" (Rorty, 1991a, p. 7).

Rorty embraces the work of Donald Davidson as that which lets the fly out of the fly-bottle, yet he does not question whether Davidson's Darwinian antirepresentationalism and causal theory of belief is in any sense Wittgensteinian.[8] If we take Davidson's recommendation seriously and we reject the scheme-content distinction we shall no longer be worried about relativism. If we accept that there is no vantage point for comparison outside our own conceptual scheme we will no longer think of natural science or physics as that privileged part of culture that can provide us with a skyhook for escaping our culturally saturated beliefs and an independent standpoint from which we can view clearly the relations of those beliefs to reality. On this view, there are no interesting epistemological differences between natural science or physics and the rest of culture. The end of metaphysics is "the final stage in the secularisation of culture" (cited in Borradori, 1994, p. 106) and philosophy, radically detranscendentalized and deprofessionalized, becomes just one form of "cultural criticism" among others. Deprived of any privileged status or the definitive vocabulary, philosophy must operate with historical and socially contextual criteria in the same way as the humanities and the social sciences. Rorty's hope is that "English-speaking philosophy in the twenty-first century will have put the representational problematic behind it, as most French- or German-speaking philosophy already has" (Rorty, 1991a, p. 12).

Rorty uses the notion of ethnocentrism as a link between his antirepresentationalism and his political liberalism. Although there is no escape from ethnocentrism or the contingency of our acculturation, especially through the appeal to the truth of representations, Deweyan liberalism is the culture of an *ethnos* that prides itself on the freedom and openness of its encounters with other cultures and, thus, makes this openness central to its own self-image. This Deweyan culture (as opposed to Heideggerian culture based on the onto-theological tradition) no longer has the need for the ideas of objectivity and transcendence as last remnants of metaphysical baggage. It can get along quite happily with the notion of community construed as intersubjective agreement (or solidarity) — one that is, as Dewey dreamed, equally and at the same time, democratic, progressive, and pluralist. By embracing such a notion we will be purged of the attempts either to provide epistemological foundations for our institutions or to ask metaphysical questions about who we are. Rather, we will give up on trying to escape from culture to ask the question of what sort of human being we want to become. This existential question Rorty (1989) divides into two on the basis of a distinction he draws between the public and the private: the first is a question of obligation to others, inquires of the individual's membership in and identification with various communities; the second is motivated by the question "what should I do with my aloneness?" and it concerns one's obligation to "become who you are" (Rorty, 1991a, p. 13). The first concerns the question of ethnocentrism and the development of a culture described as postmodernist bourgeois liberalism, or more simply, bourgeois liberalism; the second involves a lifelong project of self-edification where the most important thing we can do is to redescribe ourselves and our past in ever new and singular terms.

The effect of this analysis is to erase a picture of the self as a natural, ahistorical entity — "the locus of human dignity" and the possessor of inalienable rights — and, in turn, "to break the link between truth and justifiability," thereby polarizing liberal social theory between absolutists and pragmatists (Rorty, 1991a, p. 176). Absolutists, like Ronald Dworkin, identify a transcultural self and insist on talking of human rights in ahistorical terms; pragmatists, like Dewey and John Rawls, substitute the

notion of "our own community" for the Kantian self, "something relatively local and ethnocentric" — the tradition and consensus of a particular culture (Rorty, 1991a, p. 176). Rorty interprets Rawls in Deweyan
terms as "simply trying to systematize the principles and intuitions typical of American liberals" (p. 189) and, indeed, it seems as though Rawls'
(1980, 1985) writings subsequent to *A Theory of Justice* are consistent with
Rorty's interpretation. Rawls' (1980) distinction between a "conception of
a person" and a "theory of human nature" is designed to undermine a
conception of justice that is Kantian in nature, known a priori, and
inferred from a theory of what it is to be human, while at the same time
promoting a conception that is contingent and culturally congruent.[9]

Rorty divides liberal social theory into "Kantians" and "Hegelians,"
where the latter understand humanity as a biological rather than a moral
notion and dignity as something that is conferred by a community. He
calls the Hegelian defense of U.S. democracy postmodernist bourgeois
liberalism, a term that only sounds oxymoronic because of an inherited
but optional political vocabulary used to justify bourgeois liberal institutions and the fact the most "of those who think of themselves as beyond
metaphysics and metanarratives also think of themselves as having opted
out of the bourgeoisie" (Rorty, 1991a, p. 199). Bourgeois liberalism — a set
of cultural practices and institutions prevailing under certain economic
and historical conditions — is contrasted with philosophical liberalism —
a set of Kantian principles. Postmodernist is used simply to mean
"distrust of metanarratives," and although Rorty attributes his use of the
term to Lyotard, it really reflects Rorty's naturalization of Hegel and his
Wittgensteinian anti-foundationalism. The crucial point, in Rorty's view,
is that the moral self is redescribed in Quinean terms "as a network of
beliefs, desires, and emotions with nothing behind it" (Rorty, 1991a, p.
200).

"Cosmopolitanism without emancipation" is the essence of Rorty's
(1991a) approach to the issue of cultural difference given in response to
Lyotard's (1989b, p. 314) question: "can we continue today to organize the
multitude of events . . . by subsuming them beneath the idea of a universal history of humanity?"[10] Invoking Dewey's liberalism Rorty is happy
to drop the philosophical pretense of any metanarrative. At the same time
he wants to spin an edifying first-order utopian liberal narrative about
world history that positions U.S. democracy at the end of a story of world
progress, continuous both with the overthrow of feudalism and the aboli-
tion of slavery. This is a consequence of the inevitable and unobjection-
able ethnocentrism that results from the pragmatists' substitution of a
local, historical, and contingent sense of self for a transhistorical metaphysical subject. Cultural differences "are no more than differences of
opinion" (p. 218) and, like differences between old and new theories
propounded within a single culture or the differences between

discourses, they "are just ways of dividing up the corpus of sentences so far asserted into clusters," (p. 218) which, as it happens, has been organized thus far on the basis of ethnicity. On the Quinean view of language that Rorty holds there are no important linguistic differences that make other languages unlearnable or other cultures incommensurable.

Bourgeois liberals of Rorty's ironic breed pride themselves on the way their culture is free and open: it requires no metaphysical justification and it drops the revolutionary rhetoric of emancipation for a reformist rhetoric of increased tolerance. At the same time there are limits. Rorty (1991a, p. 212) writes: "We cannot leap outside our Western social democratic skins when we encounter another culture, and we should not try. All we should try to do is get inside the inhabitants of that culture long enough to get some idea of how we look to them, and whether they have any ideas we can use." People from other cultures may have suggestions about further reforms that are needed but we will not be inclined to accept them until we manage to integrate them with our own distinctive form of life based upon our social democratic aspirations. This kind of ethnocentrism, Rorty maintains, is both natural and inescapable in the sense that rational change of belief can only occur if most of our beliefs remain firm. Cultural interaction and changes that occur as a result of such interaction are, thus, wholly experimental, piecemeal, and nonprogrammatic. They proceed from the rationality of tolerance and have an aesthetic rather than scientific character.

We transgress the limits of bourgeois liberalism when we take the ethnocentric line of argument too seriously and begin to wonder "whether our own bourgeois liberalism is not just one more example of cultural bias" (Rorty, 1991a, p. 203), thereby placing our culture somehow on a par with other cultures. If we continue this line too far we lose the capacity for moral indignation, "our sense of self dissolves," (p. 203) and we lose "our contingent spatio-temporal affiliations" (p. 208). The postmodernist bourgeois liberal views this as a local psychological problem of "wet liberals" who, as both "connoisseurs of diversity" and Enlightenment rationalists, face a self-referential paradox when they ask whether the Western belief in equality is not simply another case of cultural bias. For postmodernist bourgeois liberals who follow Dewey there is no justification for liberal ideals by appeal to transcultural criteria of rationality: the Western liberal ideal of procedural justice is just what we believe, and all we can do is point out the practical advantages of it "in allowing individuals and cultures to get along together" (p. 209). Pragmatist utopians like Rorty see political liberalism as providing "a rationale for nonideological, compromising, reformist muddling-through" (p. 211) and look forward to a time when every culture "will all be part of the same cosmopolitan social democratic community" (p. 212).

Rorty's postmodernist bourgeois liberalism and in particular his use of the term "ethnocentrism" have engendered an outpouring of criticism from the left.[11] Rorty's response is to admit a "misleading ambiguity" in his original use of the term, which, he says, made him appear as though he was attempting "a transcendental deduction of democratic politics from antirepresentationalism premises" (Rorty, 1991a, p. 15). He then proceeds to distinguish between ethnocentrism "as an inescapable condition," synonymous with "human finitude" on the one hand, and "as a reference to a particular *ethnos*" on the other; that is, as loyalty to the sociopolitical culture of liberalism.[12] Although his critics, he says, are willing to accept the antirepresentationalism, they see themselves as standing outside the culture of liberalism. Rorty, however, does not see them as outsiders but rather as playing a role within this culture, because they have neither developed an alternative culture nor have they a utopian vision to offer. Their rage at the slow extension of freedom to marginal groups is understandable, but the "over-theoretical and over-philosophized" form that it takes is of no practical or political use. This seems to be Rorty's most trenchant criticism of the contemporary post-Marxist left: ideology-critique or deconstruction of existing social practices or liberal institutions have no point unless they point to alternative practices or a new utopia. He writes: "My doubts about the contemporary Foucauldian left concern its failure to offer such visions and such suggestions" (Rorty, 1991a, p. 16). It is a point he again emphasizes in his response to Lyotard ("Cosmopolitanism without Emancipation") when he writes:

Given our noncriterial conception of rationality, we are not inclined to diagnose "irrationalism" [of French thought as does Habermas]; since for us "rational" merely means "persuasive," "irrational" can only mean "invoking force." . . . But we are inclined to worry about their antiutopianism, their apparent loss of faith in liberal democracy. Even those who, like myself, think of France as the source of the most original philosophical thought currently being produced, cannot figure out why French thinkers are so willing to say things like "May 1968 refutes the doctrine of parliamentary liberalism." From our standpoint, nothing could refute that doctrine except some better idea about how to organize society. . . . Only another, more persuasive, utopia can do that. (Rorty, 1991a, p. 220)

He suggests in a conciliatory tone that "the difference between what Lyotard gets out of Wittgenstein and what I get out of him, and also the difference between Lyotard's interpretation of 'postmodernism' as a decisive shift which cuts right across culture and my view of it as merely the gradual encapsulation and forgetting of a certain philosophical tradition, reflect our different notions of how politically conscious intellectuals should spend their time" (Rorty, 1991a, pp. 221–22). Rorty doubts whether there is an identifiable phenomenon called postmodernism because he sees no sharp break in Western political or cultural life since the time of the French Revolution, although he does acknowledge there is "increasingly less respect for the Enlightenment divisions between spheres of culture," a process beginning with Hegel and completed in Dewey. Poststructuralism to him is simply "the latest moment of a historicization of philosophy which has been going on continuously since Hegel" (Rorty, 1990, p. 43).

How Wittgensteinian is Rorty? In terms of his philosophical development, Rorty (1991a, p. 16) acknowledges in the decade since writing *Philosophy and the Mirror of Nature* how, in his imagination, Dewey has gradually eclipsed both Wittgenstein and Heidegger.[13] This may be part of the reason why Rorty differs from Wittgenstein. Although Rorty may share Wittgenstein's antifoundationalism and even his notion of philosophy as a kind of therapy, there is a world of difference between their general philosophical outlooks. There is nothing utopian in Wittgenstein's thought and his assessment of U.S. culture is the antithesis of Rorty's. Where Rorty sees grounds for hope and regards U.S. liberal culture as already having the right institutions and practices in place, Wittgenstein is much more pessimistic. Although he, like Rorty, is skeptical of attempts to justify or provide foundations for Anglo-American institutions and practices by appeal to Enlightenment rationalism, Wittgenstein's counter-Enlightenment outlook exhibits a certain philosophical distaste for the contemporary climate of modernity with its overriding hallmark belief in progress. Rorty's ethnocentrism and loyalty to the North Atlantic liberal bourgeois democracies would be very foreign, even odious, to Wittgenstein. Our guess is that he would not see any grounds for hope in Rorty's redescription of the sociopolitical culture of U.S. liberalism as a global first-order narrative of world progress and freedom, and for a very good reason: Wittgenstein's interpretation of the contemporary West, if anything, is a story of the disappearance or disintegration of culture. Certainly, Rorty's minimalist notion of culture in respect of American liberalism, unified only in terms of a consensual belief in a Rawlsian procedural justice, would not count for Wittgenstein as a culture in any sense of the word. This philosophical difference, we think, bespeaks a more fundamental difference between the cultural affiliations and philosophical outlooks of Rorty and Wittgenstein: Rorty is a philosopher of culture in the narrow sense, that is, a philosopher of the sociopolitical culture of U.S. liberalism, whereas Wittgenstein is a philosopher of culture in the wider sense, strongly influenced by his Viennese background, *fin de siècle* cultural pessimism, and acutely aware of his identity as a European. Let us briefly elaborate this point by focusing once again upon an interpretation of Wittgenstein first put forward by Allan Janik and Stephen Toulmin's (1973) path-breaking *Wittgenstein's Vienna*[14] (see Chapter 2).

Janik and Toulmin's book established for us the inadequacy of the prevailing view structuring university philosophy courses, which saw him as a place-holder in the analytic tradition. Together they demonstrated the importance of the historico-cultural approach to philosophy and established the extent to which Wittgenstein in his early work was addressing problems — in particular the problem of representation — that arose and can only be fully understood against the background of Viennese modernism, involving in one way or another such notable figures as Karl Kraus, Robert Musil, Fritz Mauthner, Adolf Loos, Arnold Schönberg, Johann Nestroy, Ludwig Boltzmann, and Eduard Spranger. Janik and Toulmin viewed Wittgenstein as extending in his own way the critique of language and culture initiated by Kraus. In particular they provided an account of Wittgenstein of the *Tractatus* as using the logical framework he inherited from Frege and Russell only to underscore the ethical point that questions of value lie outside the scope of factual or descriptive language.

They suggested that Wittgenstein in his later work, although still drawn to an "extreme Kierkegaardian individualism," had changed his philosophical method to focus on language as behavior. Wittgenstein's analysis of language games, the pragmatic rules that govern the uses of different expressions, and the broader forms of life that give those games their significance meant that Wittgenstein had to rethink his understanding of the transcendental problem. It was no longer seen "to lie in the formal character of linguistic representations; instead it became an element in 'the natural history of man'" (Janik & Toulmin, 1973, p. 223). They suggested that this change "did not lead him in fact to abandon his long-standing ethical individualism" (p. 235), even though he was "no longer in a position to underpin his own individualistic view of ethics by appeal to a sharp dichotomy between the expressible and the transcendental" (p. 234).[15]

We have subsequently become more confirmed in this Continental repositioning of Wittgenstein on the basis of reading Smith (1978), Haller (1981), and Janik (1981), who explicitly interpret Wittgenstein within the tradition of Austrian philosophy. Janik (1981, p. 85), in particular, identifies Wittgenstein with the spirit of counter-Enlightenment and a focus upon the limits of reason, in the tradition of Lichtenberg, Kraus, Schopenhauer, Kierkegaard, Weininger, and Nietzsche.[16]

Von Wright (1982, p. 116), in an influential essay based upon his intimate knowledge of *Vermischte Bemerkungen*, although acknowledging that Wittgenstein did not develop a philosophy of history, maintains he possessed a Spenglerian attitude to his times: "he *lived the 'Untergang des Abendlandes,'* the decline of the West." On this view, Wittgenstein understood himself to be living in an age without culture, an age where modern philosophy was no longer able to provide the metalanguage (or metanarrative) that united the family resemblances of culture's various manifestations. Von Wright's (1982) interpretation has given considerable weight to Wittgenstein's Spenglerian "rejection of scientific-technological civilization of industrialized societies, which he regarded as the decay of a culture." He remarks upon how Wittgenstein found the spirit of European and American civilization both alien and distasteful and how Wittgenstein "deeply distrusted" its hallmark belief in progress based upon the technological harnessing of science, with its inherent dangers of self-destruction and its capacity to cause "infinite misery." Von Wright (1982, p. 118) suggests that it is this aspect of Wittgenstein's thinking that constitutes a link between "the view that the individual's beliefs, judgements, and thoughts are entrenched in unquestioningly accepted language-games" and "the view that philosophical problems are disquietudes of the mind caused by some malfunctioning in the language-games and hence in the life of the community."

It is a view that von Wright (1993) has returned to recently. In an essay "Analytical Philosophy: A Historico-Critical Survey," von Wright identifies analytic philosophy as that which is "most typical of the spiritual climate of our time" in that it exemplifies the form of rationality represented by science and technology. This form of rationality, he suggests, has become problematic "due to its repercussions on society and the living conditions of men" and analytic philosophy "itself an offspring of belief in progress through science appears incapable of coping with these problems."[17] It is in this context that von Wright (1993, p. 32) raises the question of whether Wittgenstein can be rightly called an analytic philosopher, only to answer it emphatically in the negative.[18] Although he agrees with Janik against Nyiri's (1982) conservative interpretation of Wittgenstein, he disagrees with Janik (1985) that there is no close correspondence between Wittgenstein's philosophy and his cultural pessimism, arguing that Wittgenstein's philosophy was a fight against the dominant climate of modernity with its "euphoric belief in progress" and its "managerial uses of reason in industrialised democratic societies" (von Wright 1993, p. 101).

It was Janik's reading of Wittgenstein initially and von Wright's interpretation above all that encouraged us to view the work of the later Wittgenstein within the intellectual milieu of Continental philosophy and specifically within the counter-Enlightenment tradition of Austrian philosophy (rather than simply and unproblematically as a place-holder in the analytic tradition). It is a reading that has been embraced in novel terms by Stanley Cavell (1988, pp. 261–62), who argues that the *Investigations* "diurnalizes Spengler's vision of the destiny toward exhausted forms," toward the loss of culture and community. Cavell shows how Wittgenstein's uniqueness as a philosopher of culture springs from the way in which Wittgenstein ties the future of philosophy to philosophy of culture or, more broadly, cultural criticism, which calls into question philosophy's claim to a privileged perspective on culture based on reason.

As we remarked in Chapter 2 there is a certain Nietzschean quality in Wittgenstein's remarks on culture in *Culture and Value*. In particular Wittgenstein's view should be compared to Nietzsche's Goethean idea of culture as unity in diversity and Nietzsche's view that modern culture lacks genuine unity and therefore is not a true culture, or is false or counterfeit. Wittgenstein, like Nietzsche, seems to want (as evidenced in the above remarks) to forecast or prophesize a collapse of Western civilization upon the basis of the disintegration or dissolution of culture.[19]

By contrast, philosophy as cultural criticism, radically historicized and democratized vis-à-vis the other disciplines, in Rorty's hands, ends up by embracing, in a sort of neopragmatist Deweyan manner, a core ideological but minimalist commitment to the liberal project. What begins as a Wittgensteinian detranscendentalism and historicization ends up as a Deweyan celebration of the culture of liberalism — a celebration that Wittgenstein would find philosophically distasteful and undesirably utopian.

This kind of reading of Rorty's philosophical development would make sense of the kind of criticism levelled at Rorty by his fellow pragmatist and countryman, Hilary Putnam (1995, pp. 33–34), who suggests that Rorty's interpretation, although undeniably influential, is as much a falsification of Wittgenstein as a clarification. His comments are salutary and worthy of quoting at some length:

The heart of Rorty's reading is his comparison of criteria with "programs." Ever since he published *Philosophy and the Mirror of Nature*, Rorty has seen what he called "normal" discourse in that book, and what he calls by the Wittgensteinian term "language games" in *Contingency, Irony, Solidarity*, as governed by what he calls "algorithms" or "programs." When we are within "normal discourse," when we are "playing the same language game," we follow programs in our brain and we all agree. . . . This picture of language speakers as automata is deeply un-Wittgensteinian. . . . I think it is because Rorty sees language games as virtually automatic performances.

Putnam's (1995, p. 37) argument is that "Rorty's notion of a 'program' is one that leads to identical behavior in all the members of the speech community," which fudges the Wittgensteinian point that there are better and worse performances within a language game. This explains in part Rorty's "cultural imperialism" (the phrase is Haber's, 1994, p. 64): his inability to take his neo- and post-Marxist critics seriously as speaking from an oppositional counter-culture, and his willingness to assimilate other cultures to a sociopolitical culture of liberalism, glossed as "cosmopolitanism without emancipation."

We think that Putnam convincingly demonstrates that, contra Rorty, for Wittgenstein there are not only better and worse performances but also better and worse language games. Wittgenstein, Putnam (1995, p. 37) maintains, finds the games philosophers play as nonsensical (and Wittgenstein distinguishes among different types of nonsense), although he is more generous to other kinds of language games: those of ordinary language and, especially, as Putnam notes, "the language games of 'primitive' people." He ascribes to Rorty what he calls the positivistic interpretation of Wittgenstein — based on the idea that if you know under what conditions a statement is confirmed, you understand the statement — and he differentiates this from the interpretation offered by Peter Winch (1963), which maintains, as Putnam (1995, p. 37) notes, that "the use of the words in a language game cannot be described without using concepts which are related to the concepts employed *in* the game."[20]

It is in regard to the question of other cultures that Putnam offers us a point of reference from which to see the difference between Wittgenstein and Rorty, because Putnam detects not only an emphasis on the primacy of practical reason (the pragmatist strain) in Wittgenstein but also an ethical aim that is clearly evidenced in his discussions of religious language, primitive language games, and differing forms of life. He takes Wittgenstein as demonstrating a moral purpose, "a kind of empathetic understanding," when Wittgenstein suggests that the possibilities for an external understanding of cultures different from our own are extremely limited: "Wittgenstein thinks that secular Europeans see all other forms of life as 'pre-scientific' or 'unscientific' and that this is a vulgar refusal to appreciate difference. . . . The question, the one we are faced with over and over again, is whether a form of life has practical or spiritual value. But the value of a form of life is not, in general, something one can express in the language games of those who are unable to share its evaluative interests" (Putnam, 1995, p. 51).[21]

Certainly, we take Putnam's comments to be centrally in place when Wittgenstein (1979) is given to understand how Frazer's remarks (in *The Golden Bough*) make magical and religious notions from other cultures appear as mistakes: such notions are mistakes only if they are put forward as hypotheses or as scientific theories. As Wittgenstein says, "All that Frazer does is to make this practice plausible to people who thinks as he does" (p. 1e), and he admonishes him: "What narrowness of spiritual life we find in Frazer! And as a result; how impossible for him to understand a different way of life from the English one of his time!" (p. 5e); "Frazer is much more savage than most of his savages, for these savages will not be so far from any understanding of spiritual matters as an Englishman of the twentieth century."

Under the influence of a second phase of U.S. analytics (merged with a utopian Deweyan pragmatism) Rorty assimilates different language games within the same culture to an algorithmic sameness and his neopositivistic interpretation of Wittgenstein drives him to elide and gloss differences between cultures. This means that Rorty, having taken the historicist and given up on universal narratives where we identify ourselves with humanity, cannot recognize or appreciate the multiple and conflicting voices that constitute the democratic interpretive horizon or present historical context within which we have no choice but to "work through the status of the *we* and the question of the subject" (Lyotard, 1989b, p. 317).[22]

NOTES

1. A version of this paper was presented to the conference, "The Democratic State: Individuals and Community," Political Studies Department, University of Auckland, July 8–10, 1996.

2. We outline the themes of individualism and community in relation to questions of education and social policy in Aotearoa/New Zealand in *Individualism and Community: Education and Social Policy in the Postmodern Condition* (Peters & Marshall, 1996). We critique both neoliberalism individualism and romantic, utopian forms of communitarianism from a poststructuralist perspective.

3. In this respect it is interesting to consider the claims of Joseph Margolis (1995), who, in taking a biopsy of recent analytic philosophy, concludes that it is a muddle. Drawing upon the work of recent heirs of the analytic movement — Quine, Davidson, Kim, Rorty, and Churchland — he concludes that the movement can be reduced to three contemporary variants, which he calls naturalism, postmodernism, and physicalism. These variants comprise "the most salient strategies of current analytic philosophy" and together constitute "an inexplicit generic philosophical policy at the heart of the 'analytic' orientation" (p. 162). Such an enterprise, he suggests, is careless about its largest premises; it speaks only to its own cohort and ignores for the most part any sustained reference to philosophers who challenge its fundamental premises. What is philosophically interesting to me about Margolis's claim is that Rorty, who purports to walk in Wittgenstein's shoes, is classified as a postmodernist and yet also is seen as an integral part of the analytic project, demonstrating its inherent weakness. Rorty is a philosopher who champions the "most extreme version of recent analytic 'naturalism,'" which leads to the ultimate repudiation of philosophy. Margolis, in a roundabout way, denies (correctly in my opinion) that Rorty is Wittgensteinian.

4. He writes:

I have sometimes used "postmodern" myself, in the rather narrow sense defined by Lyotard as "distrust of metanarratives." But I wish that I had not. The term has been so over-used that it is causing more trouble than it is worth. I have given up on the attempt to find something common to Michael Graves' buildings, Pynchon's and Rushdie's novels, Ashberry's poems, various sorts of popular music, and the writings of Heidegger and Derrida. I have become more hesitant about attempts to periodise culture . . . it seems safer and more useful to periodise and dramatise each discipline or genre separately, rather than trying to think of them all as swept up together in massive sea changes. (Rorty, 1991b, p. 1)

5. For examples of these left wing criticisms see, for example, Bernstein (1987), Burrows (1990), and Fraser (1990). In reply see Rorty's introduction to *Objectivity, Relativism, and Truth* (1991a) and the essay "De Man and the American Cultural Left" in *Essays on Heidegger and Others* (1991b).

6. Davidson, for instance, asked whether he considers himself a pragmatist, responds:

No, I don't believe in it, but I don't particularly understand what Rorty means by that, because for him that's a special kind of anti-metaphysical attitude. At one time, he actually had a pragmatic theory of truth, and then dropped it. I remember one of his articles, called "Truth, Pragmatism, and Davidson," in which he explains what he means by calling me a pragmatist. But part of what he has in mind is just that I seem to have dropped the attempt to get a certain definition of the notion of truth. I've certainly dropped the idea that philosophers are in charge of a special sort of truth. But I don't think of that as being any more pragmatic than a lot of other positions. (Borradori, 1994, p. 44)

7. We take this suggestion from Jean-François Lyotard (1984, p. 41) who, in discussing the present situation of delegitimation that has come about through the loss of faith in metanarratives, views Wittgenstein's later work as a philosophical response to this cultural crisis. The classic texts on European pessimism are, of course, Nietzsche's Book 1 (European Nihilism) of *The Will to Power* (1968) and Heidegger's commentary in Volume 4 of his *Nietzsche* (1991). See also Karl Löwith's *Martin Heidegger and European Nihilism* (1995) and Maurice Blanchot's (1987, p. 36) essay, in which he writes:

In short, it [nihilism] stands like an extreme that cannot be gotten beyond, and yet it is the only true path of going beyond; it is the principle of a new beginning. . . . God is dead. God: this means God, but also everything else that, in rapid succession, has tried to take its place — e.g., the ideal, consciousness, reason, the certainty of progress, the happiness of the masses, culture etc. Everything not without value nevertheless has no *absolute* value of its own — there is nothing man can rely on, nothing of any value other than the meaning given to it in an endless process.

8. Rorty provides a neopragmatist reading of Davidson's work, which Davidson himself rejects. See Giovanna Borradori's (1994, p. 47, 49) interview with Davidson.

9. In "Priority of Democracy to Philosophy" Rorty (1991a) discusses communitarianism as a third type of social theory. He distinguishes between three strands of communitarianism (attributed, respectively, to Horkheimer and Adorno, Alastair MacIntryre, and Charles Taylor) that share the Heideggerian belief that liberal culture "cannot survive the collapse of the philosophical justification that the Enlightenment provided for them" (p. 177).

10. Lyotard (1989b) is pointing out to Rorty that, given suspicion of metanarratives, there is no unifying framework that we can appeal to in order to ground or celebrate the democratic sense of identity of a historically situated community. As Hendley (1995, p. 242) notes, "the postmodern rejection of the voice of humanity entails . . . the problematization of the 'we' that must come to terms with the loss of that voice."

11.   See note 4 and Rorty's (1991a, p. 15) footnote 28 for further examples of such criticisms.

12.   Rorty (1991a, p. 15 n.29) does indicate that his loyalty might be severely tested if those who are presently in control — "an increasingly greedy and selfish middle class" — continue the process for another generation of depriving the weak in order to reward the rich through tax cuts. If this happens the North Atlantic democracies will become "barbarized" and under those conditions "it may be silly to hope for reform, and sensible to hope for revolution."

13.   Rorty says that he differs from Dewey mainly in terms of the account he offers of the relation of natural science to the rest of culture and in stating the problematic of representationalism versus antirepresentationalism in terms of words and sentences rather than in terms of ideas and experiences.

14.   We wish to reiterate that, curiously, nowhere in *Wittgenstein's Vienna* do Janik and Toulmin mention Nietzsche or his influence.

15.   Jacques Le Rider's (1993, p. 1) work provides an endorsement of Janik and Toulmin's view, although he sees Nietzsche as the common starting point for most Viennese modernists, arguing that "The crisis of the individual, experienced as an identity crisis, is at the heart of all questions we find in literature and the humane sciences." He remarks how Wittgenstein found his Jewish identity a problem and the way in which Wittgenstein experienced a crisis of sexual identity, when, at least at some points in his life, he sought refuge from his homosexual tendencies in a kind of Tolstoyan asceticism. He argues that this double crisis of identity, much more than is commonly accepted, is intimately tied up with the fundamentals of his thought and with a number of his intellectual preoccupations: his interest in Weininger and in psychoanalysis, his mystical tendencies, but also his reflections on genius, on the self, and on ethics" (p. 296).

16.   See also recent works by Janik (1985, 1989) and Haller (1988). Haller (1988, p. 76) demonstrates sympathy for von Wright's Spenglerian view of Wittgenstein when he remarks that Wittgenstein, in the sketch of a preface to *Philosophical Remarks*, saw himself as a critic of culture in Spengler's sense.

17.   Von Wright (1993) continues: "The task lies rather with other types of philosophy, different from and often critical of the analytic current."

18.   Von Wright (1993, p. 86), in his essay "Wittgenstein and the Twentieth Century," writes: "If Wittgenstein is not an analytic philosopher, what kind of philosopher is he then? This question certainly cannot be answered in the terms of current classifications. He is not a phenomenologist or hermeneuticist, nor an existentialist or hegelian, least of all is he a marxist."

19.   See the excellent selection from Nietzsche's notebooks of the early 1870s and the introduction by Daniel Breazeale in *Philosophy and Truth* (1979). We found Nietzsche's notion of "The Philosopher as Cultural Physician" (pp. 69–76) particularly helpful and suggestive.

20.   Note that Putnam warns us against Winch's tendency to regard language games of primitive peoples as incommensurable with ours. In his view such incommensurability was never a part of Wittgenstein's thinking.

21.   These remarks by Putnam, especially the reference to difference, should not obscure Putnam's opposition to what he regards as a nihilistic tendency in French poststructuralism. His early political militancy, his recovery of theological Judaism, and the consequent importance he confers on the moral order, distances

him from the bourgeois liberalism of Rorty in favor of the redemptive philosophy of Habermas. His remark, in the interview with Borradori (1994, p. 67), that there are at least two ways of reading Wittgenstein, is interesting in this context: "The first is that one can read Wittgenstein as simply a voice of despair, a voice saying that philosophy is over. The second way is much more tentative and much more difficult, but I feel it's what I would like to do and it's what I think Stanley Cavell is doing. That is to say that Wittgenstein wants to shut down or disabuse us, or better yet, to disabuse something which has been called philosophy, in order to make room for something else, something that is very hard to characterize." Also note Cavell's remark (in Borradori 1994, p. 129) "when I came to the *Investigations,* I felt, here is a refusal of philosophy that *is* philosophy. This is the tone in which philosophy can refuse philosophy." Elsewhere Cavell (1995, p. 184) suggests that "the theme of the coming to an end of philosophy contained perhaps the most telling contrast between the traditions of philosophizing represented by Heidegger and by the late Wittgenstein." For Derrida, it is the whole metaphysical tradition and its "powerfully protected" institutionalization "in or by Western culture, in its pedagogy, its sciences, its writing" that is the object of deconstruction; for Wittgenstein, what he wishes to destroy in philosophy is "a house of cards, something that will collapse of its own weight" (p. 77). See also Cavell (1994, pp. 62–63).

22.   Steven Hendley (1995) argues that only by keeping the question of who we are radically open ended can we approach the kind of inclusive and cosmopolitan community that Rorty envisages. In a sense this position follows from and takes more seriously than Rorty does himself, Rorty's comment that the distinguishing feature of our *ethnos* is the distrust of ethnocentrism. Hendley (1995, p. 251) writes: "We must get used to thinking of a democratic justification of democracy as an inherently multiple and contested process that is without guarantee and that can know no end; as, in short, a process identical to the unpredictable adventure of democracy itself in which the question of who we are and what we ought to be is never finally answered but kept permanently up for question."

9

Wittgenstein, Styles, and Pedagogy

I think I summed up my attitude to philosophy when I said: Philosophy ought really to be written only as *poetic composition*. It must, as it seems to me, be possible to gather from this how far my thinking belongs to the present, future or past. For I was thereby revealing myself as someone who cannot do what he would like to be able to do.

— Wittgenstein, 1980, p. 24e

I don't believe that there is "a specifically philosophical writing," a sole philosophical writing whose purity is always the same and out of reach of all sorts of contaminations. And first of all for this overwhelming reason: philosophy is spoken and written in a natural language, not in an absolutely formalizable and universal language. That said, within this natural language and its uses, certain modes have been forcibly imposed (and there is a relation of force) as philosophical. The modes are multiple, conflictual, inseparable from the philosophical content itself and from its "theses." A philosophical debate is also a combat in view of imposing discursive modes, demonstrative procedures, rhetorical and pedagogical techniques. Each time philosophy has been opposed, it was also, although not only, by contesting the properly, authentically philosophical character of the other's discourse.

— Derrida, 1995, p. 219

PHILOSOPHY AND THE QUESTION OF STYLE

In May 1992 some 20 analytic philosophers from ten countries wrote a letter to the editor of *The Times* (May 9) to protest and to intervene in a debate that occurred at Cambridge University over whether Jacques Derrida should be allowed to receive an honorary degree.[1] The signatories, none of whom were faculty at Cambridge, laid two very serious charges against Derrida: that his work "does not meet accepted standards of clarity and rigour" and that he is not a philosopher. In elaborating these two charges, they argued, first, that although Derrida has shown "considerable originality" (based upon a number of tricks and gimmicks) he has, at the same time, stretched "the normal forms of academic scholarship beyond recognition," employed "a written style that defies comprehension," brought contemporary French philosophy into disrepute, and offered nothing but assertions that are either "false or trivial" in a series of "attacks upon the values of reason, truth and scholarship."[2] Second, they submitted, the fact that the influence of his work has been "almost entirely in fields outside philosophy" was sufficient grounds for casting doubt on his suitability as a candidate for an honorary degree in philosophy. This affair constitutes an event of some significance because, to our knowledge, it is unprecedented for philosophers to organize an opposition to the granting of an honorary degree.

What Derrida calls "the Cambridge Affair" clearly demonstrates the extent to which questions of style are at center stage in contemporary philosophy and how battle lines have been drawn over the issue of philosophy as both a form of discourse and a kind of writing.[3] On one side are a group of prominent and, indeed, internationally well respected analytic philosophers who, in their joint attack upon Derrida, want to occlude questions of style. Driven by a conception of scientific philosophy wedded to a distinct method of analysis, they are deeply concerned for the future of their discipline. The possibility that the institution of modern philosophy might come to accept as important the notion of style in philosophical writing, for them, leaves open the door to the enemies of rigor and clarity: persuasion, rhetoric, and metaphor.

Derrida's (1992, p. 134) response to "the Cambridge Affair" has been to focus upon the journalistic style of the letter itself and to understand it as "another demonstration of [philosophical] nationalism," which violates the very principles of "reason, truth and scholarship" that it claims to represent. He suggests that his inquisitors "confuse philosophy with what they have been taught to *reproduce* in the tradition and style of a particular institution" (p. 135), and in response to a question concerning the Parisian location of his own work, he comments: "One never writes just anywhere, out of a context and without trying to aim or privilege a certain readership, even if one can't and shouldn't limit oneself to this" (p. 137). Perhaps more than any philosopher before him and from his earliest beginnings,[4] Derrida (1995, p. 218) has called attention to the form of philosophical discourse — its "modes of composition, its rhetoric, its metaphors, its language, its fictions" — not in order to assimilate philosophy to literature but rather to recognize the complex links between the two and to investigate the ways in which the institutional authority of academic philosophy and the autonomy it claims rests upon a "disavowal with relation to its own language." The question of philosophical styles, he maintains, is itself a philosophical question.

Although we do not engage the polemics of the debate between Derrida and his detractors, it is clear that "the Cambridge Affair" and its continuing aftermath[5] have given fresh impetus to the question of style in philosophy.[6] An important recent collection of essays, for instance, takes the question of style in philosophy and arts as central. The editors boldly proclaim "Philosophers can no longer consider the question of style a mere artistic or literary question" and, drawing upon Berel Lang's (1995)[7] opening chapter, they suggest that "the question of style is inescapable, even for those philosophical writings that profess to be style-less" (Van Eck, McAllister, & Van de Vall, 1995, p. 1). Lang's (1995, p. 24) diagnosis is that the relation between method and style in philosophical discourse has been repressed. Philosophy has denied any role for style except in a merely ornamental sense and this denial is part of "a more inclusive repression — the tendency of philosophers to decontextualise or dehistoricise their own discourse." Although Lang does not direct his criticisms at contemporary analytic philosophy, focusing rather upon Descartes, Locke, and Kant, it is clear that his diagnosis also embraces it.

For Lang and others any choice of style — whether conscious or not, whether defined in terms of the individual or by a particular tradition — will involve a commitment to certain metaphors and modes of representation (Norris, 1984). We would argue that the issue is not that analytic philosophers do not want to admit the question of style as a philosophical issue; rather, they want to impose one style over all others. This deepseated preference for a particular style, based on appeals to logical structure, rigor, and clarity, has its roots not only in the self-image of philosophy going back, at least, to Plato (who sought to ban poetry from The Republic[8]) but also in the nineteenth century, with the scientization of philosophy and the rise of a kind of linguistic nationalism, where English — as an emerging metropolitan language — was seen as the most appropriate and transparent medium for the expression of thought.

Van Eck and others (1995, p. 1) suggest that style has "invaded" philosophy: "One of the consequences of what could be called postmodern pluralism in philosophy is that philosophy as a whole — whether it accepts a postmodern stance or opposes it — has grown more conscious of the importance of its medium, which is generally the written text, and

as a consequence of its own hidden aesthetics." They attribute this awareness to philosophers such as Nietzsche and Wittgenstein "who write in a
distinctive . . . literary style, and who, moreover, attach a particular
importance to style in philosophical thinking, knowledge, or life in
general" (p. 1).[9] They claim that Nietzsche and Wittgenstein were instrumental in eroding a stylistic monism and relaxing what counts as philosophical reasoning. Their stylistic diversity redefined and contributed to
the acceptance of a greater range of works and styles as belonging to
philosophy.

The purpose of this chapter is to explore the importance of style to
philosophy through a close study of the writings of Wittgenstein. In
particular, we argue that the question of style remained an obsession of
Wittgenstein's throughout his career and that it is inseparable from his
practice of philosophy. Finally, we suggest, in terms to be fully explored
in the following chapter, that Wittgenstein's style is, in a crucial sense,
pedagogical; that appreciating his style is essential to understanding the
purpose and intent of his philosophy, especially his later philosophy. The
first section of the chapter seeks to understand Wittgenstein's concern for
style as originating within the intellectual milieu of Viennese modernism
(see Chapter 2). On this basis we interpret Wittgenstein's philosophical
style as related to his double crisis of identity concerning his Jewish
origins and his sexuality, both inseparable from his concern for ethics and
aesthetics (which are, he said, one) and from his personal life. In the
second section of the chapter, we explore how these concerns are manifested in his work and his way of doing philosophy. In the last section we
try to show how Wittgenstein's style may be seen as deeply pedagogical.

WITTGENSTEIN AND VIENNESE MODERNISM

> Lying to oneself about oneself, deceiving yourself about the pretence
> in your own state of will, must have a harmful influence on [one's]
> style; for the result will be that you cannot tell what is genuine in style
> and what is false . . . If I perform to myself, then it's this that the style
> expresses. And then the style cannot be my own. If you are unwilling
> to know what you are, your writing is a form of deceit.
>   — Wittgenstein, cited in Monk (1991, pp. 366–67)

> "Le style c'est l'homme," "Le style c'est l'homme meme." The first
> expression has cheap epigrammatic brevity. The second, correct
> version opens up quite a different perspective. It says that a man's
> style is a picture [image] of him.
>   —Wittgenstein, 1980a, p. 78e

> Ethics and aesthetics are one and the same.
>   — Wittgenstein, 1971, #6.421

Janik and Toulmin's (1973) path-breaking book *Wittgenstein's Vienna* established the inadequacy of the prevailing view of Wittgenstein as a place holder in the analytic tradition. They demonstrated the importance of a historico-cultural approach to philosophy; for them, Wittgenstein, in his early work, was addressing problems — in particular, the problem of representation — that arose within and can only be fully understood against the background of Viennese modernism, involving in one way or another such notable figures as Karl Kraus, Robert Musil, Fritz Mauthner, Adolf Loos, Arnold Schöenberg, Johann Nestroy, Ludwig Boltzmann, and Eduard Spranger. Janik and Toulmin viewed Wittgenstein as extending in his own way the critique of language and culture initiated by Kraus. In particular, they provided an account of Wittgenstein in the *Tractatus* as using the logical framework he inherited from Frege and Russell only to underscore the ethical point that questions of value lie outside the scope of factual or descriptive language: "On this interpretation, the *Tractatus* becomes an expression of a certain type of language mysticism that assigns a central importance in human life to art, on the ground that art alone can express the meaning of life. Only art can express moral truth, and only the artist can teach the things that matter most in life" (Janik & Toulmin, 1973, p. 197).

In his later work they suggested that Wittgenstein, although still drawn to an extreme Kierkegaardian individualism, had changed his philosophical method to focus his attention on language as behavior. Wittgenstein's analysis of language games, of the pragmatic rules that govern the uses of different expressions, and of the broader forms of life that ultimately give those language games their significance meant that Wittgenstein had to revise his understanding of the transcendental problem. It was no longer seen "to lie in the formal character of linguistic representations; instead, it became an element in 'the natural history of man'" (Janik & Toulmin, 1973, p. 223). They suggested that this change "did not lead him in fact to abandon his long-standing ethical individualism" (p. 235), even though he was "no longer in a position to underpin his own individualistic view of ethics by appeal to a sharp dichotomy between the expressible and the transcendental" (p. 234). In retrospect, it is remarkable that Janik and Toulmin's interpretation neither mentions nor makes anything of Nietzsche's influence on *fin de siècle* Vienna or upon many of Wittgenstein's intellectual contemporaries and forbears.

In the previous chapter we commented on the way in which several authors had repositioned Wittgenstein within the broad Continental tradition and, specifically, within the Austrian counter-Enlightenment tradition. In particular, drawing on the work of von Wright (1982, 1993), we emphasized Wittgenstein's Spenglerian rejection of the technoscientific civilization of advanced industrial societies. Wittgenstein clearly found contemporary Western societies odious and he was very skeptical of their underlying belief in progress, in modernity, and in the expected positive benefits to flow from technoscience. In this sense, Wittgenstein, it might be argued, shared a similar suspicion with Martin Heidegger of claims made on behalf of technology although, unlike Heidegger, his views did not spring from any systematic view on the nature of technology or from questions concerning the interpretation of being.[10]

Certainly, von Wright's (1993) analysis that Wittgenstein is not to be regarded as an analytical philosopher, insofar as analytic philosophy pictures itself as the handmaiden to science, ought to be understood more widely. On this basis, von Wright, rightly in our opinion, concludes that there is a strong connection between Wittgenstein's philosophy and his cultural pessimism.

Jacques Le Rider's (1993) reading of Wittgenstein locates him in the context of Viennese modernism. He sees Nietzsche as the common starting point for most Viennese modernists, arguing that "The crisis of the individual, experienced as an identity crisis, is at the heart of all questions we find in literature and the human sciences" (p. 1) and he remarks that "Viennese modernism can be interpreted as an anticipation of certain important 'postmodern' themes" (p. 6). Le Rider has in mind, for instance, the way in which Wittgenstein's philosophy of language "deconstructs the subject as author and judge of his own semantic intentions" (p. 28). He remarks in terms of the crisis of identity how Wittgenstein, "like all assimilated Jewish intellectuals, found his Jewish identity a problem" and the problem of his Jewish identity was coupled with a crisis of sexual identity, when at least during some periods of his life he sought refuge from his homosexual tendencies in a kind of Tolstoyan asceticism (p. 295). He suggests:

Wittgenstein, who . . . looked back nostalgically on a well-ordered world where everyone had his place, found modernity uncultured because it had lost its power to integrate, and left individuals in a state of confusion. The only ones who can keep their balance and personal creativity are those whom Nietzsche calls the strong men, that is the most moderate, who need neither convictions nor religion, who are able not only to endure, but to accept a fair amount of chance and absurdity, and are capable of thinking in a broadly disillusioned and negative way without feeling either diminished or discouraged. (p. 296)

He argues that the consequences of this double crisis of identity, much more than is commonly accepted, were intimately tied up with the fundamentals of his thought and with a number of his intellectual preoccupations: "his interest in Weininger and in psychoanalysis, his mystical tendencies, but also his reflections on genius, on the self, and on ethics" (p. 296).

Many of these intellectual concerns came together in a confessional autobiography that Wittgenstein planned to write. Ray Monk's (1991, p. 312) biography notes that it was 1931, "the year in which the autobiography received its greatest attention, that Weininger and Weiningerian reflections abound in Wittgenstein's notebooks and conversations." Indeed, Monk's (1991) study, subtitled "The Duty of Genius," begins with a guiding motif for the biography as a whole taken from Weininger's *Sex and Character*: "Logic and ethics are fundamentally the same, they are no more than duty to oneself." Wittgenstein's anti-Semitism and his related remarks on the distinction between genius and talent owe much to the influence of Weininger and, of course, Schopenhauer, who influenced them both. Weininger coopted Schopenhauer's distinction between genius and talent, paralleling it with a masculine Aryan creativity on the one hand, and a feminine Judaic reproductiveness on the other.[11] Such comments found fertile ground in Wittgenstein's ambivalent feelings about his own Jewish origins and his sexual identity. Wittgenstein (1980a, pp. 18e, 19e) echoes Weininger in a remark of Jewish self-hatred written in 1931:

Amongst Jews "genius" is found only in the holy man. Even the greatest of Jewish thinkers is no more than talented. (Myself for instance.) . . . I think there is some truth in my idea that I really only think reproductively. I don't believe I have ever *invented* a line of thinking, I have always taken one over from someone else. I have simply straightaway seized on it with enthusiasm for my work of clarity. That is how Bolzmann, Hertz, Schopenhauer, Frege, Russell, Kraus, Loos, Weininger, Spengler, Sraffa have influenced me. . . . What I *invent* are new similes.

Jews are untragic, and Mendelssohn, as a Jewish composer, for example, is "the most untragic of composers" (Wittgenstein, 1980a, p. 1e). His music lacks a certain rigor (p. 16e); it lacks integrity (p. 2e) and courage (p. 35e). He "wrote no music that is hard to understand" (p. 23e). Mendelssohn's music cannot be classified as "great art" because it lacks the power and depth that comes from "man's primitive drives"; "in *this* sense Mendelssohn can be called a *'reproductive'* artist" (p. 38e).

For Wittgenstein, genius is intimately related to strength of character and courage, (and courage with originality): "Genius is *talent exercised with courage*" (Wittgenstein, 1980a, p. 38e), or, "Genius is talent in which character makes itself heard" (p. 65e). Wittgenstein was haunted by the question of his own philosophical originality. As Weiner (1992, p. 19) explains: "Wittgenstein was anxious, indeed obsessed, about his relations to other philosophers. He was plagued by the notion that he was only a reproductive, talented thinker not a creative, original genius like Schopenhauer."[12] In *Culture and Value*, for instance, there are a set of highly revealing remarks that Wittgenstein makes about himself, linking

once again questions of creativity and identity: "I believe that my originality (if that is the right word) is an originality belonging to the soil
rather than to the seed. (Perhaps I have no seed of my own)" (Wittgenstein, 1980a, p. 36e). He suggests that Freud's originality is similar (that
the real germ of psychoanalysis came from Breuer). He wonders on occasions whether he brings to life "new movements of thought" or whether
he simply applies old ones (p. 20e); he puzzles over his ability to write
prose and concludes that his ability has limits that are part of his nature:
"In this game I can only attain *such and such* a degree of perfection, I can't
go *beyond* it" (p. 59e). He suggests: "One's style of writing may be unoriginal in form — like mine — and yet one's words may be well chosen; or,
on the other hand, one may have a style that's original in *form*, one that is
freshly grown from deep within oneself" (p. 53e).

Wittgenstein believes that "the greatness of what a man writes
depends on everything else he writes and does" (1980a, p. 65e). There is a
close link between ethics and style because the mark of great style is originality, and originality is a moral attribute. Speaking or expressing the
truth is not a matter of cleverness: "No one *can* speak the truth; if he has
still not mastered himself. . . . The truth can be spoken only by someone
who is already *at home* in it" (p. 35e). Wittgenstein, in these passages, is
not simply reflecting on the nature of originality, genius, and greatness;
he is agonizing over himself, expressing doubts concerning his own moral
character and whether he has the strength, depth, and courage required to
achieve greatness (compare p. 47e). He raises doubts in the most intense
self-scrutiny: "I am too soft, too weak, and so too lazy to achieve anything
significant" (p. 72e).

Greatness, genius, and originality critically depend upon insight and
accurate judgment of oneself — "a man will never be great if he misjudges
himself: if he throws dust in his own eyes" (Wittgenstein, 1980a, p. 49e) —
yet "Understanding oneself properly is difficult" (p. 48e) because good
action might be equally prompted by cowardice and indifference as much
as generous motives. Acting in a particular way may be motivated as
much by love as by deceitfulness. Philosophy is not only a battle against
the bewitchment of language, an investigation of the ordinary and familiar with the aim of showing "the fly the way out of the fly-bottle" (1953,
#309), it also necessarily involves work on the self (1980a, p. 16e). In his
often quoted comment to Norman Malcolm: "What is the use of studying
philosophy if all that it does for you is enable you to talk with some plau-
sibility about some abstruse questions of logic, etc., and if it does not
improve your thinking about the important questions of everyday life? . . .
You see, I know that it is difficult to think well about 'certainty,' 'proba-
bility,' 'perception,' etc. But it is, if possible, still more difficult to think, or
try to think, really honestly about your life and other people's lives."

It is no accident that Wittgenstein begins the *Investigations* with a quotation from Saint Augustine's *Confessions*, or that many of his writings have a confessional tone: "A man can bare himself before others only out of a particular kind of love. A love which acknowledges, as it were, that we are all wicked children" (1980a, p. 46e), yet "A confession has to be part of your new life" (p. 18e). Wittgenstein was, at many points in his life, preoccupied with what he thought was his own deceit: "Nothing is so difficult as not deceiving oneself" (p. 34e). Yet confession and confessional forms of writing such as autobiography depend upon the spirit in which one can write the truth about oneself. These confessional forms are, perhaps, the most direct forms of writing the truth about oneself, and yet Wittgenstein would maintain that the truth about oneself can only be shown in one's style; the style of one's works considered as a whole. It is, accordingly, only in the prefaces and forewords to his works, and in *Culture and Value*, along with his correspondence, that Wittgenstein directly approaches such questions.[13]

Monk (1991, p. 364ff) also makes much of Wittgenstein's quoting Saint Augustine. The *Confessions* is, he points out, a religious autobiography rather than a philosophical work, and Augustine is not theorizing, he is simply describing how he learned to talk.[14] What is contained in the quote from Augustine, Monk maintains, is a picture, which must be overcome, but only through the introduction of another picture or metaphor. There is another reason, Monk (1991, p. 366) asserts, that Wittgenstein begins with Augustine: "for Wittgenstein, *all* philosophy, in so far as it is pursued honestly and decently, begins with a confession."[15] It sets the tone for the *Investigations* and indicates the serious demands it places upon the reader, because Wittgenstein cannot be read as one might read other philosophers — to find out what they said or for interest and entertainment. The *Investigations*, by contrast, requires a personal involvement on the part of the reader; it requires one to make Wittgenstein's confusions and problems one's own.

Indeed, there is ample evidence to support Monk's view from Wittgenstein's own concerns about who would read his works and how they might read them. He entertained doubts about whether his work would be read in the right spirit. As he says in the foreword to *Philosophical Remarks*: "This book is written for such men as are in sympathy with its spirit." His earlier drafts of the foreword (1980a, pp. 6e, 7e) reveal that Wittgenstein believed he would be misunderstood because he wrote in a spirit out of sympathy with the prevailing spirit of the age. It is a concern Wittgenstein has in the *Tractatus* as well; the preface begins, "Perhaps this book will be understood only by someone who has already had the thoughts that are expressed in it — or at least similar thoughts." Only a "few friends" may understand him, because the reader must make Wittgenstein's style of thinking and his problems his or her own.

WITTGENSTEIN'S PHILOSOPHICAL STYLE

> We speak of understanding a sentence in the sense in which it can be replaced by another which says the same; but also in the sense in which it cannot be replaced by any other. (Any more than one musical theme can be replaced by another.) In the one case the thought in the sentence is common to different sentences; in the other, something that is expressed only by these words in these positions. (Understanding a poem.)
>
> — Wittgenstein, 1953, #531

Of the many hundreds of books and articles written on Wittgenstein and his work only a very tiny proportion deal with the question of Wittgenstein's style.[16] Few philosophers have approached Wittgenstein centrally through an examination of his style or considered the question of his style as important or interesting in a philosophical sense.[17] Von Wright (1982, pp. 33–34) perhaps came closest when he wrote:

An aspect of Wittgenstein's work which is certain to attract growing attention is its language. It would be surprising if he were not one day ranked among the classic writers of German prose. The literary merits of the *Tractatus* have not gone unnoticed. The language of the *Investigations* is equally remarkable. The style is simple and perspicuous, the construction of sentences firm and free, the rhythm flows easily. The form is sometimes that of dialogue, with questions and replies; sometimes, as in the *Tractatus*, it condenses to aphorisms. There is a striking absence of all literary ornamentation and of technical jargon or terminology. The union of measured moderation with richest imagination, the simultaneous impression of natural continuation and surprising turns, leads us to think of some other great productions of the genius of Vienna. (Schubert was Wittgenstein's favorite composer.)

We shall briefly mention three scholars who do highlight Wittgenstein's style and investigate through these authors why analytic philosophers have tended to ignore it. Charles Altieri (1994, 1995), rather than directly commenting upon Wittgenstein's style, uses what he calls a "Wittgensteinian phenomenology" to provide an expressivist account of subjective agency — an intentionality without interiority — and its relations to communities. He develops this account through a discussion of "personal style," which he defines at one point as "that dimension of stylistic analysis which attributes responsibility and expressivity to particular agents" (1994, p. 255).

Allan Janik (1989, p. ix) approaches the question of Wittgenstein's style more directly. He asks why Wittgenstein (and Heidegger) wrote "in such a curious fashion" and whether such "curious writing strategies have a philosophical significance." He suggests that Wittgenstein is an "astonishingly difficult thinker to approach" precisely because of "his typical modes of expression, unanswered questions, analogies, aphorisms, and curious examples" (p. x) which, when contrasted with Carnap or Quine, seem to the uninitiated as obscurantist. Janik suggests that consequently some branded him an "outright charlatan," while others wrote "not about what he said . . . but what they think he said," thereby "eliminating just what he took to be most important in his work" (p. x). In particular, Janik describes a common analytic interpretative strategy in reconstructing his thought: "Wittgenstein wrote the way he did out of necessity rather than choice, capable of brilliant intuition but unable to express himself in clear and distinct arguments in the way a philosopher should" (p. x). A recent example of this attitude is Hans-Johann Glock's (1996, p. 28) comment in *A Wittgenstein Dictionary*:

In their different ways, both the *Tractatus* and the *Investigations* are among the few highlights of German philosophical prose. But there are also serious flaws. Because of his aesthetic aspirations Wittgenstein often condensed his insights to the point of impenetrability, and failed to spell out the arguments in support of his claims. . . . As a result, his work often pursues conceptual clarity in an obscure fashion, and constitutes a formidable challenge to readers. Some analytic philosophers simply condemn it out of hand, while others, in the belief that interpretation is an integral part of philosophy, welcome it, even if it occasionally makes them feel like slaves. In any event, Wittgenstein's work possesses a scintillating beauty lacking in other analytic philosophers.

In this passage Glock repeats the kind of interpretation that Janik asserts is true of some analytic philosophers. Glock seems perilously close to endorsing such a view and suggesting that aesthetics and philosophy are quite separate realms. Against this common interpretation Janik reaches two dissenting conclusions:

First, Wittgenstein's conception of philosophy was thought out in full awareness of the alternatives. Second, his style reflects the results of that remarkable confrontation with the western philosophical tradition from Socrates onwards according to which the philosopher's task has been transformed from resolving problems on the basis of a theory to that of dissolving them in tortuous reflections on the nature of practice, which can only be accomplished through a certain linguistic *gesturing*. (p. xi)

He claims, correctly in our view, that Wittgenstein's style of philosophizing is "rooted in dissatisfaction with traditional ways of philosophising" (p. xi) and he sees in Wittgenstein a third way, between critical theory and deconstructionism, of regarding morality and rationality as immanent in our practices.[18]

Most revealing is Jan Zwicky's (1992) *Lyric Philosophy*, which is referred to little in the literature on Wittgenstein, perhaps because of its unusual form. It consists of a series of epigrammatic and aphoristic comments organized in terms of a musical composition with both a left-hand and a right-hand text; the first, "organisationally dominant" (thematically arranged comments of the author), the second, a kind of scrapbook with suggestions for further reading and the relation between the two "somewhere between counterpoint and harmony" (pp. ix–x). The book is "a new *sort* of overview" of Wittgenstein's work and the format is a response to philosophical analysis as a form of thought that sets "unintuitive limits to what can be meant and understood by human beings" (p. ix). Zwicky's work is performatively consistent; it emulates Wittgenstein's styles and strategies as the means by which to prompt attention to those elements in his work "which have generally been regarded as subsidiary to the main enterprise" (p. ix). For instance, she engages in a dialogue with an imaginary interlocutor in the same way as Wittgenstein does in the *Investigations*. She suggests that "Wittgenstein was driven by a desire for clarity which matches the best Anglo-American analytic philosophy; but his work embodies a notion of clarity which is more complex" (p. x).

All students of Wittgenstein who have grown up with the Wittgenstein mythology know certain fundamental things about him and his work: that although Wittgenstein wrote a great deal he published very little in his own lifetime; that everything he wrote became part of a complex process of composition, passing from first or early drafts to finished work, through a number of phases; that what he wrote is difficult, if not impossible, to distinguish from what he said; and that what he did not write or say — what could only be shown — was at least as important as what he said and wrote. Each of these features, although perhaps obvious and familiar, requires further elucidation for the light they shine on Wittgenstein's styles.

The scope and character of Wittgenstein's literary *Nachlass*, the so-called "Wittgenstein Papers," fall into three main groups: (a) the manuscripts (78), consisting of two strata of writings: "first drafts" and "more finished versions"; (b) the typescripts (34), which were dictated or prepared by Wittgenstein himself; and (c) verbatim records of dictations (8) to colleagues or pupils (von Wright, 1969, pp. 485–86). In addition, von Wright mentions two further groups: the notes, more or less verbatim, of Wittgenstein's conversations and lectures and his correspondence. Already, one might note that there is something extraordinary about the amount he wrote, most of which was never published in his lifetime.[19] He agonized over the form and composition of his work and he developed very complex methods of composition. He comments in *Culture and Value* that when he is thinking about a topic he "jump[s] about all round it": "Forcing my thoughts into an ordered sequence is a torment for me. . . . I squander an unspeakable amount of effort making an arrangement of my thoughts which may have no value at all" (Wittgenstein, 1980a, p. 28e).

Von Wright (1969, p. 503) refers to the "layers of composition" of his work and describes the process of composition in the following manner: "From the manuscripts of a more finished character Wittgenstein dictated to typists. In the course of dictation he evidently often altered the sentences, adding new ones, and changed the order of the remarks in the manuscripts. Usually he continued to work with the typescripts. A method which he often used was to cut up the typed text into fragments (*Zettel*) and to rearrange the order of the remarks. . . . A further stage was the production of a new typescript on the basis of a collection of cuttings."

Wittgenstein often wrote philosophical remarks or fragments (for example, *Zettel*). It was this characteristic method of composition that he followed in composing the first part of the *Investigations*.[20] As he himself says in its preface: "I have written down these thoughts as *remarks*, short paragraphs, of which there is sometimes a fairly long chain about the same subject, while I sometimes make a sudden change, jumping from one topic to another. — It was my intention at first to bring all this together in a book whose form I pictured differently at different times. But the essential thing was that the thoughts should proceed from one topic to another in a natural order and without breaks" (1953, p. vii).

The questions of form, style, and the method of composition are central to the *Investigations*, as Wittgenstein's own testimony makes clear.[21] Sometimes he referred to his procedure of composition as one of assemblage[22] — philosophy "consists in assembling reminders for a particular purpose" (1953, #127); his style of philosophizing and composition can be likened to the composition of poetry, music, or painting. Language and sentences have rhythm (1980a, p. 52e), the sounds of words are important, as is their position; their "temporality is embedded in their grammar" (p. 22e). As Wittgenstein says, invoking an analogy with music: "Sometimes a sentence can be understood only if it is read at the *right tempo*. My sentences are all supposed to be read *slowly*" (p. 57e).[23] He sees himself as bringing "to life new *movements* in thinking" (p. 20e, emphasis added); often, he makes reference to music in order to understand or throw light on the question of meaning[24] and sometimes, as in *Culture and Value*, Wittgenstein includes an actual phrase or theme in musical notation.[25] He said in 1941: "My style is like bad musical composition" (p. 39e). His work has been described as variations on a theme and Wittgenstein's comments in the preface to the *Investigations* offer some confirmation of this view: there is a *natural* order to (his) ideas. He says that the best he could write would never be more than philosophical remarks and adds: "my thoughts were soon crippled if I tried to force them in any single direction against their natural inclination" (1953, p. vii). The analogy with musical composition is strong here, and it suggests that when composing his thoughts Wittgenstein self-consciously understood the process as akin to arranging a musical work.

Wittgenstein's (1980a, p. 24e) comment regarding his attitude to philosophy that "Philosophy ought really to be written only as *poetic composition*" (the motif we chose as our opening quotation) is a revealing remark. What does it mean? That philosophy at its best would recognize the lyrical resources of language — cadence, meter, and simile? (Does this amount to a consideration of style?) Or that philosophy as poetry, as an elevated form of expression, comes closest to capturing the truth of human experience and transmuting that experience into feelings? Certainly, Wittgenstein's aestheticism might lead one to guess that philosophy written as poetry would combine elements of simplicity, elegance, clarity, and order in a form in which aesthetics and ethics are one and the same.

Paradoxically, especially given the poetic quality of the *Tractatus* and his penchant for simile and metaphor, Wittgenstein believed that he was unable to write verse and that his ability to write prose extended only so far; limitations that were inherent in the "nature of my equipment" (1980b, p. 59e). As his friend Paul Engelmann (1967, pp. 89–90) tells us, Wittgenstein never wrote poetry or played a musical instrument.[26] Yet he talked of experiencing a "poetic mood," like Schiller, where thoughts take on a luster as vivid as nature itself (Wittgenstein, 1980b, p. 66e), and he assessed his own style of philosophizing, in a characteristic anguished moment of self-reflection, as inventing new similes rather than a line of thinking (1980a, p. 19e). Yet "A good simile refreshes the intellect" (p. 1e) and "a man's philosophy" might be seen to rest on a preference for certain similes (p. 20e). He muses upon the way in which a philosophical investigation resembles an aesthetic one (p. 25e) and indicates that although he finds scientific questions interesting they never really grip him in the way that aesthetic and conceptual questions do (p. 79e).

Wittgenstein's use of the word "picture" is extremely complex as he uses this word both in the sense of a mental picture, that is, an image, and in the related sense of a conception or model. In these uses Wittgenstein in the *Investigations* is, in part, combating his earlier Tractarian view that a sentence, proposition, or fact-stating *satze* is a picture of reality. Speaking of the picture theory of the *Tractatus* he says in the *Investigations*: "A picture held us captive. And we could not get outside it, for it lay in our language and language seemed to repeat it to us inexorably" (1953, #115). The relation of images to imagination and the relations between pictures and images is a complex matter and well beyond the scope this chapter.[27] To make matters more complex Wittgenstein uses picture (*Bild*) in the ordinary sense of the word to mean illustration, landscape, photograph, projection, and representation.

The *Investigations* and later works are interspersed with remarks that begin with asking us to imagine: "Let us imagine a language" (Wittgenstein, 1953, #2); "Imagine a script" (#4); "We could imagine that the language" (#6); "I can imagine such a use of words" (#6); "Imagine some-one's saying" (#14); "it is easy to imagine a language" (#19), and so on. Wittgenstein says: "The 'philosophy of as if' itself rests wholly on this shifting between simile and reality" (1981, #261), and he explicitly acknowledges: "One of the most important methods I use is to imagine a historical development for our ideas from what actually occurred. If we do this we see the problem from a completely new angle" (1980a, p. 37e). Establishing a new way of thinking is difficult, and yet: "Once the new way of thinking has been established, the old problems vanish; indeed they become hard to recapture. For they go with our way of expressing ourselves and, if we clothe ourselves in a new form of expression, the old problems are discarded along with the old garment" (p. 48e).

At one point in *Culture and Value*, discussing Bacon's philosophical work, Wittgenstein talks of inventing a style of painting capable of depicting what is "fuzzy" (1980a, p. 68e). In the *Investigations* he compares a concept with a style of painting and asks whether it is arbitrary, something we might choose at our pleasure (1953, p. 230). "A thinker is very much like a draftsman whose aim it is to represent all the interrelations between things"(1980a, p. 12e). Wittgenstein himself consistently incorporated diagrams, little drawings, and geometrical figures into his work.[28] He also made frequent allusions to architecture and employed analogies, metaphors, and examples from building and architecture. He was for years registered as an architect, with Paul Engelmann, in the Vienna city directory and assumed sole responsibility for the design and building of a new residence for his sister, Margarethe Stonborough-Wittgenstein.[29] He writes: "Working in philosophy — like work in architecture in many respects — is really more a working on oneself. One's own interpretation. On one's way of seeing things. (And what one expects of them)" (p. 16e).

Perhaps most difficult to interpret are the remarks that Wittgenstein makes relating the notion of style to that of spirit. For instance, he describes the technical improvements that had occurred in film-making and modern dance music (meaning jazz) and asserts that these technical improvements could not be compared with the improvement of an artistic style: "What distinguishes all these developments from the formation of a *style* is that spirit plays no part in them" (1980a, p. 3e). Style, then, is not a technical accomplishment. In the same way that "The human being is the best picture of the human soul" (p. 49e), so "a man's style is a *picture* of him" (p. 79e). A work of "supreme art" has something that can be called "style" (p. 37e), and we can talk of a "style of writing" that can be great (Frege's writing is sometimes great but Freud's, although excellent, is never great) (Wittgenstein, 1980a, p. 87e).

One can reproduce an old style, that is, translate it into a newer language, which is how Wittgenstein characterizes his own "building work" (1980a, p. 60e). His words, he says, are well chosen but the form of his work (construed as a question of style) he considers to be unoriginal. A style that is original in form is "freshly grown from deep within oneself" (p. 53e). Great style is original in form; originality in this sense cannot be a "clever trick," simply the use of "stylistic devices" (p. 71e), or a "personal peculiarity": "the beginnings of good originality are already there if you do not want to be something you are not" (p. 60e). Style is an expression of human value.

In "Sketch for a Foreword" (Wittgenstein, 1980a, p. 6e), an early draft of the printed foreword to *Philosophical Remarks*, Wittgenstein writes: "This book is written for those who are in sympathy with the *spirit* in which it is written" (emphasis added). It is a spirit that expresses an certain "cultural ideal"[30] (p. 2e); one that would not be understood by the typical Western scientist who, imbued with the spirit of contemporary European and American civilization, is committed to the form of progress and "building an ever more complicated structure." In this age even clarity is sought only as a means to this end. Wittgenstein finds the spirit of this age both alien and uncongenial. His way of thinking is different: for him "clarity, perspicuity are valuable in themselves" (p. 7e). Clarity is an aesthetic and ethical ideal; the work of clarification requires courage; it is not "just a clever game" (p. 19e). The clarity that Wittgenstein is aiming at is, as he says, "*complete* clarity," which means that "philosophical problems should *completely* disappear." He goes on to say "There is not *a* philosophical method, though there are indeed methods, like different therapies" (1953, #133).[31] Wittgenstein's style of philosophizing and the stylistic devices he innovates are designed to command a clear view of the use of words (#5, #122).

Hence, Wittgenstein's notion of clarity is more complex than that employed by analytic philosophers. In the *Tractatus*, Wittgenstein claims that "Philosophy aims at the logical clarification of thoughts" consisting of elucidations (1971, #4.112); but in the *Investigations*, the notion of clarity has become more complex. It retains its aesthetic value but the method of logical clarification has given way to a style that aims at commanding a clear view of the use of words, where speaking and writing are regarded as activities and parts of a form of life. Commanding a clear view establishes "an order in our knowledge of the use of language" but it is "an order with a particular end in view; one out of many possible orders; not *the* order" (1953, #132).

There is for Wittgenstein a family resemblance among the terms "spirit," "form," and "style." In terms of the doctrine of saying and showing, form or style, like spirit, can only be shown or exhibited, as he says: "the spirit of a book has to be evident in the book itself and cannot be described" (1980a, p. 7e).[32] This cultural ideal, it might be argued, is closely tied to Viennese modernism and to modernism in general — to present the unpresentable, as Lyotard (1984, p. 78) describes it, explaining it in terms of the Kantian sublime, or to express the inexpressible, where the inexpressible can only be shown. (Perhaps, this may be expressed as a feature marking the limits of modernism.) Wittgenstein remarks: "In art it is hard to say anything as good as saying nothing" (p. 23e).[33]

In Wittgenstein's writing throughout his career, but especially in his later works, one finds a preoccupation with composition and form; with analogies to music and poetry; with the use of pictures and word pictures (thought experiments and imaginings); and, throughout, with a conception of style that is at once conceptual and aesthetic. Style, for Wittgenstein, was not a literary extravagance that threatened philosophical clarity, but a means to it: "writing in the right style is setting the carriage straight on the rails" (1980a, p. 39). Style is necessary to achieve clarity. It is crucial to see here that clarity meant something different for Wittgenstein: not a transparency of language that allowed something else (meaning) to shine through, but a manifestation of style, an effect of arranging a text in just one way rather than another. Clarity is produced not out of a linear narrative, but in the criss-cross of different ways of approaching a problem, a pattern designed and balanced with the care of a poetic (or musical) composition.

WITTGENSTEIN'S PHILOSOPHICAL
STYLE AS A FORM OF PEDAGOGY

Engelmann (1967, p. 114), in his memoir of Wittgenstein, warns us not to underestimate the influence of Wittgenstein's teaching experience on his philosophical works. Wittgenstein, Engelmann maintains, "used the acquired art of asking questions with consummate skill, and the crucial simplicity with which he accomplished this in his most profound mental probings constitutes his great new philosophical achievement" (p. 115). Engelmann suggests that Wittgenstein moved to the Socratic form of questions in his later work in order to correct the reflective monologue of the *Tractatus* that was written in the form of categorical propositions.

There is something fundamentally correct about Engelmann's description. Wittgenstein himself writes "Nearly all my writings are private conversations with myself. Things that I say to myself tête-à-tête" (1980a, p. 77e). Terry Eagleton (1993, p. 9) also makes the observation that the *Investigations* "is a thoroughly dialogical work, in which the author wonders out loud, imagines an interlocutor, asks us questions which may or may not be on the level . . . forcing the reader into the work of self-demystification, genially engaging our participation by his deliberately undaunting style."

Yet there is also something awry for Wittgenstein in the dialogue form, at least as it was practiced by Socrates. He says, "Reading the Socratic dialogues one has the feeling: what a frightful waste of time! What's the point of these arguments that prove nothing and clarify nothing?" (1980a, p. 14e). Socrates gets into difficulty in trying to give the definition of a concept because "again and again a use of the word emerges that seems not to be compatible with the concept that other uses have led us to form" (p. 30e). On this basis Wittgenstein questions Socrates's right to keep on reducing the sophist to silence (p. 56e).

Wittgenstein's later writing is dialogical, but not in the Socratic sense: the aim is not the search for an adequate definition of a concept. Indeed, if we keep in mind the multiplicity of language games we will not be inclined to ask questions like "What is the meaning of . . . ?" (1953, #24). Moreover, the kind of questions Wittgenstein asks, and the way he asks them, is different from those of Socrates. Fann (1967, p. 109) notes that Wittgenstein asks himself (and his readers) on the order of 800 questions in the *Investigations*, but he only answers 100 of them and of these the majority (some 70) wrongly. If a dialogical work the *Investigations* is unconventional because Wittgenstein, by asking questions and answering them wrongly (deliberately) wants to stop us from asking certain kinds of questions: the sort of philosophical questions that require that we provide a theoretical answer abstracted from the context of use and social practice. Philosophy does not make progress because "our language has remained the same and keeps seducing us into asking the same questions" (1980a, p. 15e). Moreover, the questions Wittgenstein poses are frequently posed by an imaginary interlocutor to himself — linking his approach again with a confessional mode in which the primary dynamic is of an inner dialogue (Finch, 1995, p. 76).

This mode of dialogue is not one of demonstration (as it often was for Plato) but of investigation. Wittgenstein's use of imagined interchanges, thought experiments, and frequently cryptic aphorisms was meant to engage the reader in a process that was, in Wittgenstein's actual teaching as well as in his writing, the externalization of his own doubts, questions, and thought processes. Hence, his philosophical purpose was manifested in how he pursued a question; his style was his method, and his writings sought to exemplify how it worked. His concern with matters of composition and form were not only about the presentation of an argument but also about the juxtaposition that would best draw the reader into the very state of puzzlement he himself felt. Therefore, an appreciation of Wittgenstein's style leads us directly to an understanding of the fundamentally pedagogical dimension of his philosophy.

NOTES

1. Barry Smith (editor, *The Monist*) instigated the letter. The signatories were: Hans Albert, David Armstrong, Ruth Barcan Marcus, Keith Campbell,

Richard Glauser, Rudolf Haller, Massimo Mugnai, Kevin Mulligan, Lorenzo Pena, Willard van Orman Quine, Wolfgang Rod, Edmund Ruggaldier, Karl Schuhmann, Daniel Schulthess, Peter Simons, Rene Thom, Dallas Willard, and Jan Wolenski.

2.   In this context it is interesting to note that Ruth Barcan Marcus, the Halleck Professor of Philosophy at Yale, wrote to the French government (Ministry of Research and Technology) on March 12, 1984, to protest Derrida's nomination to the position of Director of the International College of Philosophy, citing Foucault's alleged description of Derrida as practicing *"obscurantisme terroriste."* Derrida was teaching at Yale at the time. He remarks upon this affair in a footnote to "Afterword: Toward an Ethic of Discussion" in *Limited Inc* (Derrida, 1988, pp. 158–59) in relation to the exchange with John Searle, who used the same epithet as Marcus in an article published in the *New York Review of Books.* In relation to Searle's usage, Derrida remarks: "I just want to raise the question of what precisely a philosopher is doing when, in a newspaper with a large circulation, he finds himself compelled to cite private and unverifiable insults of another philosopher in order to authorise himself to insult in turn and to practice what in French is called a *jugement d'autorite,* that is, the method and preferred practice of all dogmatism" (p. 158). He comments upon the Marcus affair in the same footnote in the following terms: "I have cited these facts in order better to delimit certain concepts: in such cases, we are certainly confronted with chains of repressive practices and with the police in its basest form, on the border between alleged academic freedom, the press, and state power" (p. 159).

3.   "Philosophy as a Kind of Writing" is the title of an essay by Richard Rorty that appears in his *Consequences of Pragmatism* (1982, pp. 90–109).

4.   See Derrida's essay "The Time of the Thesis: Punctuations" (1983) where he reflects upon his preoccupations of (at that point) the past 25 years of scholarship, beginning with his 1957 thesis "The Ideality of the Literary Object." The essay itself is a reflection upon the philosophical form of the thesis.

5.   See the recent collection of essays edited by Barry Smith (1994). In his brief foreword Smith clearly holds Derrida (along with Foucault and Lyotard) largely responsible for the current ills of the American academy: "Many current developments in American academic life — multiculturalism, 'political correctness,' the growth of critical theory, rhetoric and hermeneutics, the crisis of scholarship in the humanities departments — have been closely associated with, and indeed inspired by, the work of European philosophers such as Foucault, Derrida, Lyotard and others" (p. i).

6.   For an account of the relations between analytic philosophy, deconstruction, and literary theory see Dasenbrock's (1989) introduction to the edited collection *Redrawing the Lines: Analytic Philosophy, Deconstruction, and Literary Theory.* Wittgenstein is a favored bridge for those who wish to redraw the boundaries. See the essays in the collection mentioned earlier by Law and Winspur.

7.   See also Lang (1980, 1990).

8.   Here "poetry" included drama; an astonishing proposal, because Plato himself drew heavily from dramatic forms in his dialogues, which can always be read as literary works as well as philosophical investigations.

9.   There is an irony in the fact that the reception of Nietzsche in the last decade of the nineteenth century and the first half of the twentieth century was

primarily and overwhelmingly literary. It was only after 1945 that Nietzsche's work received a more philosophical reception (see Behler, 1996, pp. 282–83). The reverse can be said of Wittgenstein, with some reservations: the initial reception of his work was primarily philosophical and only recently has the literary character of his work and its central importance to his way of philosophizing begun to be recognized.

10.   It is little known that Wittgenstein did engage in sustained conversation with Alan Turing from 1946 to 1948 when Wittgenstein was involved in reexamining the aguments that mathematics required philosophical foundations. It may be said also that Wittgenstein was never a member of the Vienna Circle — a circle that, perhaps more than any other, represented a scientism of Viennese modernism — although he attended some meetings.

11.   On Schopenhauer's influence on Wittgenstein's early philosophy see Weiner (1992). See also his comments on Wittgenstein's remarks on genius and talent, and Weininger's influence (pp. 18–21).

12.   Weiner (1992) interprets Wittgenstein's personal doubts over his own originality and philosophical style in terms of what Harold Bloom calls "the anxiety of influence," which is portrayed as an agonistic struggle between two poetic geniuses: the strong poets who struggle with their precursors and the weaker talents who idealize.

13.   It is difficult on these grounds to understand why von Wright in the preface to *Culture and Value* decided to exclude "notes of a purely 'personal' sort — i.e., notes in which Wittgenstein is commenting on the external circumstances of his life, his state of mind and relations with other people — some of whom are still living."

14.   Von Wright (1982, p. 33) notes the particular influence on Wittgenstein of Augustine, Kierkegaard, Dostoyevsky, Tolstoy, and others in the "borderland between philosophy, religion, and poetry."

15.   See also Monk's (1991, p. 369ff) account of Wittgenstein's confession concerning two major sins: his deception concerning his Jewish background and his denial (lie) to his headmaster of striking a little girl in his class.

16.   A search of *The Philosopher's Index* based on "Wittgenstein and style" turned up 37 items out of more than 1,500 entries. Most of these dealt with style in a peripheral way.

17.   Brief comments on this subject can be found, for example, in Cavell (1976, pp. 70–72); Levi (1967, p. 376); McGuinness (1988, pp. 37–38); and Tilghman (1991). See also the special issue of *New Literary History* (2, 1988) devoted to "Wittgenstein and Literary History," particularly the essays by Quigley and Barrett. In addition, see Perloff (1992).

18.   Janik's (1989) description of Wittgenstein's "philosophical tools" in his critique of Rorty (chap. IV) is enormously helpful, particularly on Wittgenstein's use of aphorisms — "to tease from language that which cannot be expressed in the form of a definite description" (p. 85). See also his essay on Lichtenberg and Wittgenstein's mode of composing his works (pp. 204–5).

19.   Compare Wittgenstein's remarks: "This is how philosophers should salute each other: 'Take your time!'" and "To say, when they are at work, 'Let's have done with it now,' is a *physical* need for human beings; it is the constant

necessity when you are philosophising to go on thinking in face of this need that makes this such strenuous work" (1980a, pp. 75e–76e, 80e).

20. See von Wright (1969, p. 488).

21. This was not a recent preoccupation of Wittgenstein's. In submitting the manuscript of the *Tractatus* to a prospective publisher (Ficker), he described the work as "strictly philosophical and at the same time literary" (Monk 1991, p. 177).

22. See Wittgenstein's comment: "Yes, you have got to assemble bits of old material. But into a *building*. —" (1980a, p. 40e).

23. Compare "I really want my copious punctuation marks to slow down the speed of reading. Because I should like to be read slowly. (As I myself read)" (Wittgenstein, 1980a, p. 68e).

24. For example, "Speech with and without thought is to be compared with the playing of a piece of music with and without thought" (Wittgenstein, 1953, #341); "Understanding a sentence is much more akin to understanding a theme in music than one may think" (#527); and (#22, #523, #531, #536). Compare from the *Tractatus*: "A proposition is not a blend of words. — (Just as a theme in music is not a blend of notes.)" (1971, #3.142; see also, #4.011, #4014). See also *Culture and Value*, particularly the discussion of what it is to understand a musical theme or phrase (1980a, pp. 51e, 69e–73e).

25. See, for example, Wittgenstein (1980a, p. 21e).

26. He could whistle "beautifully," mimicking the most complex musical passages — was this, too, an "imitative" talent?

27. See Hacker (1990, pp. 392–422).

28. See, for example, Wittgenstein (1953): the arrangement of squares (#48); the schema of horizontal lines (#86); the mark (#166); the arrow (#454); the illustration (p. 193); the famous Jastrow "duck-rabbit" (p. 194); the "picture-face" (p. 194); the figures (p. 198); the triangle (p. 200); the figure (p, 203); the "face" (p. 204); the triangle (p. 206); the "double cross" figure (p. 207); and the arbitrary cipher (p. 210). Wittgenstein also makes extensive use of mathematical constructions and equations in his work.

29. Berhard Leibner (1995, p. 11), writing in 1972, indicated how the building's exterior is reminiscent of Adolf Loos' architecture. The interior, he maintains, "is unique in the history of twentieth-century architecture. Everything has been re-thought. Nothing in it has been directly borrowed, neither from any building practice nor from any architectural avant-garde thinking." Hermine Wittgenstein referred to it as the "house turned logic" and wrote that she could not live in it herself because it seemed much more "a dwelling for the gods than for a small mortal like me" (in Leibner, p. 23). She also describes the symmetry and precision that Wittgenstein demanded of his work (radiators, doors, and windows). Von Wright, referring to Wittgenstein's architecture, suggests that it "is of the same simple and static kind that belongs to a sentence of the Tractatus" (cited in Leibner, p. 50). Wittgenstein himself, in a letter (reproduced in Leibner, p. 124) to a firm of metalwork contractors, writes: "it would be impossible without your work to erect the building with the *precision and objectivity* necessary for this kind of construction" (emphasis added). Clearly, the question of style in Wittgenstein's architecture is reminiscent of his style in the *Tractatus*: both have a stark beauty and unadorned simplicity embodyi ₃ values of objectivity and precision. See also Wijdeveld (1994).

30. Compare: "My ideal is a certain coolness. A temple providing a setting for the passions without meddling with them" (Wittgenstein, 1980a, p. 2e).

31. Wittgenstein's view of philosophy as a kind of therapy is well known, as is also the fact that he regarded himself as a disciple of Freud: "The philosopher's treatment of a question is like the treatment of an illness" (1953, #255). See Brian McGuinness (1982) "Freud and Wittgenstein."

32. Compare: "It is a great temptation to try to make the spirit explicit" (Wittgenstein, 1980a, p. 8e).

33. Compare: "I never more than half succeed in expressing what I want to express. Actually not as much as that, but no more than a tenth. That is still worth something. Often my writing is nothing but 'stuttering'" (Wittgenstein, 1980a, p. 18e).

10

Philosophy as Pedagogy: Wittgenstein's Styles of Thinking

> I ought to be no more than a mirror, in which my reader can see his own thinking with all its deformities so that, helped in this way, he can put it right.
>
> — Wittgenstein, 1980a, p.18e

> How much we are doing is changing the style of thinking and how much I'm doing is changing the style of thinking and how much I'm doing is persuading people to change their style of thinking.
>
> — Wittgenstein, 1967, p. 28

In this chapter we maintain that Wittgenstein's work may be given, broadly speaking, a cultural and literary reading that focuses upon his styles.[1] Such a reading legitimates both the importance of Wittgenstein, the person, and the significance of his (auto)biography in a way that analytic philosophers might find hard to accept.[2] In particular, we maintain the question of style is a question inseparable from the reality of his life and the corpus of his work; indeed, we maintain further that Wittgenstein himself actively thought this to be the case and that this belief is shown in his work. This reading also throws into relief questions concerning his appropriation as a philosopher who had something to contribute to education: Wittgenstein not as a philosopher who provides a method for analyzing educational concepts but rather as one who approaches philosophical questions from a pedagogical point of view. One might say, in line with this interpretation, that Wittgenstein's style of doing philosophy is pedagogical. We believe, with many others who have made the point better than we, that the analytic impulse to want to extract a theory or method from Wittgenstein is wrong headed and that to interpret him as offering a systematic philosophy is to miss the point of his philosophizing entirely. His styles are, we will argue, essentially pedagogical; he provides a teaming variety and vital repertoire of non-argumentational discursive forms — pictures, drawings, analogies, similes, jokes, equations, dialogues with himself, little narratives, questions and wrong answers, thought experiments, gnomic aphorisms, and so on — as a means primarily to shift our thinking, to help us escape the picture that holds us captive. It is this notion of philosophy as pedagogy that is, we shall argue, a defining feature of Wittgenstein's later thought.

In terms of this reading it is also possible to see the connections between other aspects of Wittgenstein's life — his cultural background and preferences — and his styles of philosophizing. For example, his architecture and his preference for certain musical and poetic styles and forms: it has only recently become known the extent to which Wittgenstein's style of composition was directly influenced by certain poetic-musical forms. Michael Nedo, the director of the Wittgenstein Archives, makes the point:

> The structure of the manuscripts themselves was especially complicated because Wittgenstein's thinking and writing were very musical, so you have structures and forms that are more common to music than to texts. When he comes to the borderline of his language, his sentences often break apart; one sentence ends and he produces a parallel second sentence that somehow oscillates around the idea of the first. These sets of sentences remind one of a partita where, in order to express something, one has to use different tunes. (cited in Toynton, 1997, p. 32)

Nedo's point is not the scholarly point that Wittgenstein used music as a paradigm for understanding in general (Worth, 1997) — Wittgenstein frequently compared understanding a musical theme to understanding a sentence — but that his intense interest in music resulted in the conscious adoption of musical forms for his writing; that there is a musical aspect to his philosophical style (Zwicky, 1992).

In this regard, perhaps, Wittgenstein could be regarded in terms similar to Nietzsche not only in that Nietzsche gave music a privileged cultural status — the artist-philosopher who is able to create values is the philosopher of the future — but also in that Nietzsche himself emulated musical forms in his writing.[3] (The crystalline, pure structure of the *Tractatus* is so logical in its branching, tree-like form that it has been scored as a motet and put to music by Elizabeth Lutyens.) The question of whether Wittgenstein, in like terms, self-consciously regarded himself as a cultural physician or philosopher of the future, able to cure both himself and his readers of deep disquietudes in the forms of our language and culture, is not to be dismissed too easily.

There are at least three ways that might demonstrate more robustly the pedagogical styles of his thinking. First, we may seek to investigate historically and biographically the connections between his styles of teaching philosophy, relying on accounts and reminiscences of his former students, and his styles of thinking. Second, we can also investigate historical accounts of his experiences as a primary and secondary school teacher in Austria during the crucial period from 1919 to 1929 and the influences upon his thinking during this period. Third, we can look directly at his writings to observe and document these effects on style. This chapter is structured accordingly. In relation to the third section we will concentrate on the pedagogical elements of the dialogue form adopted by Wittgenstein in the *Investigations*.

WITTGENSTEIN AS PHILOSOPHY TEACHER

There is more than a family resemblance between Wittgenstein's styles of teaching at Cambridge and his styles of philosophizing. They represent to all intents and purposes a profound and complex continuity: the dividing line between Wittgenstein's teachings and his posthumously collected and edited works is blurred to say the least. The oral performance runs into and sometimes constitutes the written corpus. Many of his works are transcriptions, discussions, notes, or lectures recorded by his students and colleagues. His notes, at another level of composition, are sometimes reworked even in the process of dictation. His styles of teaching and thinking in performance, therefore, comprise, perhaps more than any modern philosopher, a significant proportion of his extant works.

The accounts of his teaching by his students confirm an intensity of thinking that shows itself in his writings; this intensity is driven, in large part, by the ethical and aesthetic requirements of arranging or composing his thoughts. His writings mirror his approach to teaching philosophy and vice versa. Above all they reflect his honesty as a thinker and teacher. If he was unforgiving in his treatment of his students, it is because he was unforgiving with himself. The long painful silences that interspersed his classes, his disregard for institutional conventions in pedagogy at the time, and his relentless (self) criticism were an essential part of his style as a great educator (in Nietzsche's sense).

Accounts of Wittgenstein as a teacher of philosophy are now legendary. D.A.T. Gasking and A. C. Jackson (1967, p. 51) report the following description Wittgenstein gave of his own teaching:

In teaching you philosophy I'm like a guide showing you how to find your way round London. I have to take you through the city from north to south, from east to west, from Euston to the embankment and from Piccadilly to the Marble Arch. After I have taken you many journeys through the city, in all sorts of directions, we shall have passed through any given street a number of times — each time traversing the street as part of a different journey. At the end of this you will know London; you will be able to find your way about like a Londoner. Of course, a good guide will take you through the more important streets more often than he takes you down side streets; a bad guide will do the opposite. In philosophy I'm a rather bad guide.

This passage indicates Wittgenstein's penchant for comparing doing philosophy with making a journey. It belongs to a characteristic set of spatial metaphors we find in the *Investigations*. Wittgenstein (1953) explains in the preface how he tried to weld his thoughts together into a whole but never succeeded. What was to him essential was that "the thoughts should proceed from one subject to another in a *natural* order and without breaks" (our emphasis). He remarks how his "thoughts were soon crippled if I tried to force them on in any single direction against their *natural* inclination" (our emphasis). The naturalness Wittgenstein refers to here is the process of thought itself, of having the thought and of emulating in the text the very processes by which he arrived at a particular thought. This naturalness is the naturalness of thinking and thinking aloud. He then comments: "The philosophical remarks in this book are, as it were, a number of sketches of landscapes which were made in the course of these long and involved journeyings." He suggests that the book is "only an album," a series of sketches that together might give one a picture of the landscape.

   Later Wittgenstein (1953, #18) uses another spatial metaphor based upon the city, asking whether our language is complete and suggesting that the symbolism of chemistry and the notation of infinitesimal calculus have been added to language like new suburbs to a town: "Our language can be seen as an ancient city: a maze of little streets and squares, of old and new houses with additions from various periods; and this surrounded by a multitude of new boroughs with straight regular streets and uniform houses." He also describes the thoughts of the *Investigations* as a series of written remarks or short paragraphs — "of which there is sometimes a fairly long chain about the same subject, while I sometimes make a sudden change, jumping from one topic to another" (p. vii). One might argue that Wittgenstein's innovative method of composition here is more like a musical score — expressing themes and refrains — than a conventional philosophical genre. It is clearly influenced by the form of the aphorism, a favored poetical-philosophical form adopted by Lichtenberg, Schopenhauer, and Nietzsche.

   Gasking and Jackson (1967, p. 50) focus on the "technique of oral discussion" Wittgenstein utilizes, a technique they describe as, at first, bewildering: "Example was piled up on example. Sometimes the examples were fantastic, as when one was invited to consider the very odd linguistic or other behavior of an imaginary tribe. . . . Sometimes the example was just a reminder of some well-known homely fact. Always the case was given in concrete detail, described in down-to-earth everyday language. Nearly every single thing said was easy to follow and was usually not the sort of thing anyone would wish to dispute." The difficulty came from seeing where this "repetitive concrete" talk was leading. He lectured without notes but each session was, nevertheless, carefully planned. Sometimes he "would break off, saying 'Just a minute, let me think!' . . . or he would exclaim 'This is as difficult as *hell*'" (p. 52). Sometimes the point of the many examples became suddenly clear as though the solution was obvious and simple. They report Wittgenstein as saying that he wanted to show his students that they had confusions that they never thought they could have and admonished them by saying: "You must say what you really think as though noone, not even you, could overhear it" (p. 53). And they make the enormously important remark: "Whether this ideal is realizable in the form of a book is, in the opinion of many, not yet known; whether, if it were, the book would look much like what we think of as a philosophy book is discussable" (p. 53). Wittgenstein was clearly experimenting with the form his remarks should take: he is to be distinguished as a great philosopher not only for his thinking, or for his styles of philosophizing, but also for his deliberate attention to and constant (perhaps, obsessive) experimentation with philosophical form and genre.

G. E. Moore (1967, p. 44) in his memory of Wittgenstein's lectures during the period 1930–33, writes:

I was a good deal surprised by some of the things he [Wittgenstein] said about the difference between "philosophy" in the sense in which what he was doing might be called "philosophy" (he called this "modern philosophy"), and what has traditionally been called 'philosophy'. He said what he was doing was a "new subject" which Wittgenstein said did resemble traditional philosophy in three respects: in its generality, in the fact that it was fundamental to both ordinary life and the sciences, and in that it was independent of the results of science.

Moore confirms the picture of Wittgenstein as the stylist and innovator when it came to doing philosophy. Wittgenstein is to be construed as doing philosophy equally when he is teaching as when he is writing, and Wittgenstein went to great pains to develop a style in the form of his philosophical investigations that enables the readers to think for themselves.

Karl Britton (Drury, 1967, p. 61) reports that Wittgenstein thought there was no test one could apply to discover whether a philosopher was teaching properly: "He said that many of his pupils merely put forward his own ideas: and that many of them imitated his voice and manner; but that he could easily distinguish those who really understood." Wittgenstein urged his students not to become philosophers or to take up academic posts first because he had scant regard for professional philosophers and because philosophical thinking is strenuous with "long periods of darkness and confusion" (Drury, 1967, p. 69).

There are many other recollections of Wittgenstein as a teacher that testify to the way his style of thinking and teaching had dramatically changed in the last 20 years of his life and how his teaching was mirrored or embodied in his work (see, in particular, the contributions of Malcolm and Rhees in Fann's 1967 collection). They call into question our traditional notion of a work in the same way that Michel Foucault and Roland Barthes question the notion of an author. Doing philosophy always took priority for Wittgenstein whether this was in oral or written form: it was important to show the deep puzzles in our language (and our culture and thinking) as well as dissolving them by doing. Doing philosophy let the fly out of the fly-bottle: it cured our buzzing confusion and allowed us to lead useful and practical lives.

Wittgenstein said "a philosophical problem has the form 'I don't know my way about'" (1953, #49) and "A main source of our failure is that we do not *command a clear view* of our use of words — our grammar is lacking in this sort of perspicuity" (p. 49). His style of teaching philosophy was designed to enable us to shift our thinking, to untie the knots in our thinking, to overcome our "mental cramps" by "clearing up the ground of language," but in the end by employing this style we are "destroying nothing but a house of cards."

Although we believe that there are significant resemblances one can mark out in terms of his method of composition and his style of teaching — notes, discussions, confessions, meditations, dialogues, and conversations were as much a part of his repertoire for thinking as they were chosen philosophical genres — there is also an effective biographical element that closely ties in with the pedagogical style of his philosophizing.

WITTGENSTEIN, TEACHING, AND PHILOSOPHY

The years 1919–29 are traditionally seen as years of dormancy for Wittgenstein's philosophical thinking or his active pursuit of philosophy. Yet this period of his life — during which he designed his sister's mansion, trained as a primary school teacher, and taught in the Austrian system for some six years — is instrumental (and highly underestimated) in the shift in his thinking and his style. His biographers do not spend much time on this period of his life and tend to underestimate its importance.

Ray Monk (1991), Wittgenstein's biographer, devotes a chapter ("An Entirely Rural Affair") to Wittgenstein's years as a school teacher in rural Austria, yet even his otherwise brilliant account of Wittgenstein's life does not do justice to the importance of this episode in Wittgenstein's life or its importance for his later philosophy. His account of Wittgenstein's teaching service in the village schools of Trattenbach, Hassach, and Puchberg is based mainly upon the personal memoirs of surviving pupils who paint Wittgenstein as a teacher with exacting standards, little patience, and one who was given to violent outbursts against his students.

These are significant biographical details. Indeed, it is suggested by Fania Pascal (1984, pp. 37–38) that it was an episode in Wittgenstein's career as a teacher that involved hitting one of his girl pupils (and which he later denied to the principal), that "stood out as a crisis of his early manhood" and caused him to give up teaching. Rhees (1984, p. 191), commenting upon this same episode, quotes from a letter from Wittgenstein to Russell: "how can I be a logician before I'm a human being! *Far* the most important thing to settle accounts with myself!" The event is highly significant for Wittgenstein: it constituted one of the two sins to which he wished to confess (see Monk, 1991, p. 367).

Monk also notes Wittgenstein's misgivings of Glöckel's school reforms and the publication of Wittgenstein's *Wörterbuch für Volksschullen* (a spelling dictionary) in 1925, and yet Monk's account of this period is overshadowed by Ramsey's visit, the correspondence with both Russell and Ogden over the publication of the *Tractatus*, and Wittgenstein's eventual return to philosophy. He does not recognize the significance of Wittgenstein's experience as a school teacher for his later philosophy or for the question of style. Monk also refers to William Bartley's notorious use of Wittgenstein's coded remarks in his notebooks to cast aspersions on Wittgenstein's homosexuality. He ought to have given more attention, perhaps, to the substance of Bartley's (1973) claims concerning the link between Glöckel, Bühler (a developmental psychologist), and Wittgenstein, a link that tends to get ignored in the literature. Glock (1996), for instance, in his intellectual sketch mentioning the "wilderness years" makes virtually no mention of the significance of these matters.

The furor caused by Bartley's claims concerning Wittgenstein's homosexuality has clouded the issue concerning the influence of Wittgenstein's school-teaching years on his later philosophy. It is now time, with the distance of some 20 years, to raise this matter afresh and to examine critically the nature of Bartley's claims. Bartley (1973), despite his notorious and unsavory claims about Wittgenstein's sexuality, is one of the few scholars to devote any space to Wittgenstein's development during the 1920s. Bartley's (1973, p. 20) major historical claim is that there are

"Certain similarities between some themes of Glöckel's program and Bühler's theories on the one hand, and ideas which infuse the later work of Wittgenstein." He documents how Wittgenstein enrolled in the *Lehrerbildungsanstalt* in the *Kundmanngasse* in September 1919. He suggests that the Wittgenstein family in the immediate postwar years of reconstruction had turned its attention away from patronizing the arts to social welfare programs. (Margaret Stonborough was Herbert Hoover's personal representative in charge of work for the American Food Relief Commission.) Otto Glöckel was administrative head of the socialist school reform, which was directed at both the economic redevelopment of the countryside and reeducation of the peasantry. Under these circumstances, Bartley comments, Wittgenstein's decision to become a teacher of elementary school was not eccentric. Other talented Austrians also entered the school reform movement, including two philosophers associated with the Vienna Circle, Karl Popper and Edgar Zilsel. Indeed, Bartley (1973, p. 89) maintains that "The Vienna Circle itself, in its first manifesto, associated itself with the aims of the school-reform movement."

The school reform movement under Glöckel and others had attacked the old drill schools of the Hapsburgs based on passive rote learning and memorization (influenced strongly by Johann Herbart), to argue for the establishment of the *Arbeitsschule* or working school based, by contrast, on the active participation of pupils and a doctrine of learning by doing. Bartley notes that Wittgenstein was far from being an advocate of the movement; rather, he mocked and made fun of its slogans considering them vulgarizations. Bartley provides a detailed account of Wittgenstein's six years teaching at Trattenbach, Otterthal, and Puchberg: he recounts the story of Wittgenstein slapping the face of one of his girl pupils, the conspiracy against him led by Piribauer who also instituted legal proceedings, and finally the trial at Gloggnitz that acquitted Wittgenstein.

Bartley conjectures that the themes of the Austrian school reform movement and in particular the views of Karl Bühler, professor of philosophy at the University of Vienna and at the Vienna Pedagogical Institute, in large measure accounted for the profound change in Wittgenstein's philosophizing in the late 1920s. He suggests that Bühler, who was invited to Vienna by Glöckel and his colleagues in 1922, strongly influenced Wittgenstein's thinking. He bases this claim upon the striking similarities between their ideas and some historical circumstantial evidence. First, Bühler's critical variant of Gestalt psychology (said to be close to Piaget's) was opposed to psychological, epistemological, and logical atomism, and stressed, by contrast, a configurationism or contextualism in which theory-making was deemed to be a basic function of the mind. Second, Bühler's doctrine depended upon a radical linguistic conventionalism; and third, he had developed a notion of "imageless thought" that emphasized that the intentional act of representing did not require an image or model of that which it represented (Bartley, 1974, pp. 145–49).

Strikingly similar ideas, Bartley claims, figure strongly in Wittgenstein's later work and were instrumental in bringing about his change of philosophizing. Bartley documents the fact that Wittgenstein had met but did not like Bühler and hypothesizes that he had probably read Bühler's *Die Geistige Entwicklung des Kindes* that was a standard text in the new teacher training colleges.

Bartley (1973) also provides some textual evidence; he quotes Wittgenstein in *Zettel* (1981, #412) "Am I doing child psychology?" ["I am making a connexion between the concept of teaching and the concept of meaning,"(*Zettel*, p. 74e)], and mentions in this context Wittgenstein's word dictionary. He also recounts a story that Wittgenstein used to tell his pupils in Trattenbach from 1921 concerning an experiment to determine whether children who had not yet learned to speak, locked away with a woman who could not speak, could learn a primitive language or invent a new language of their own. He asks us, by way of corroboration, to consider that the *Investigations* begins with a critique of Saint Augustine's account of how a child *learns* a language and suggests that an important theme of the first part of the *Investigations* is how children learn their native tongues (Bartley, 1973, pp. 85, 149).

In a further paper, Bartley (1974, p. 324) extends this thesis concerning the influence of Bühler to include Karl Popper, who also became a school teacher in Austria during the 1920s, restating his position on Wittgenstein as one that entertained: "the possibility of construing the later thought of Wittgenstein as that of an amateur but gifted child psychologist who turned, partly as a result of his experiences in school teaching during the twenties, from an essentially associationalist psychology to a configurationalist or contextualism closer to that of the Gestaltists." Yet he climbs down from the strong claim: "Whether Wittgenstein was directly influenced by Bühler or other of the Gestalt theoreticians is uncertain. He definitely was familiar with Bühler's ideas" (Bartley, 1974, p. 325).[4]

Bartley is not alone in advancing such ideas. In fact, Stephen Toulmin (1969) had advanced similar ideas some five years earlier. Toward the end of an article considering Wittgenstein's philosophy, Toulmin (1969, p. 70) broaches the historical question concerning the sources of Wittgenstein's ideas for his later philosophical teachings: "How . . . did he [Wittgenstein] arrive at his later view of semantics, as part of 'the natural history of man'?" He answers his own question thus: "His experience as a schoolmaster in the 1920s would naturally have redirected his attention to language learning as a fruitful source of idea and illustrations" (p. 70). Toulmin goes further to mention an occasion when Wittgenstein's sister Margaret (Stonborough) brought Moritz Schlick and Wittgenstein together with Karl and Charlotte Bühler. (This is surely the source of

Bartley's reference and possibly the historical basis of his overall thesis?) Toulmin describes Bühler as one of the chief founders of development psychology (establishing a tradition in which both Vygotsky and Piaget come to stand) and a major contributor to modern linguistic theory. Further, he describes Charlotte Bühler as an original psychologist in her own right.

Further, in a footnote Toulmin (1969, p. 71 n.8) acknowledges Theodore Mischel's confirmation that the debate over "imageless thought" had "led Bühler to concentrate on precisely those topics — language as the bearer of intentionality, meaning as consciousness of rules rather than images, etc. — that Wittgenstein later put to such good use in philosophy." The issue is left unresolved by Toulmin: it may have been simply a remarkable historical coincidence.

Bartley's work has been criticized. Eugene Hargrove (1980), for instance, disputes that Wittgenstein was an active participant in the Austrian school reform movement and that this involvement significantly influenced Wittgenstein's later philosophy. It is difficult to assess the dispute as presented by Hargrove because it depends upon personal communications and on supposition. Hargrove establishes that Wittgenstein was not an active participant in the Glöckel reforms, but this was not a claim Bartley had made. Indeed, Bartley acknowledges that Wittgenstein made jokes about the movement. Hargrove (1980, p. 458) maintains that "Karl Bühler's book was not read at the teachers' college nor were his pedagogical ideas discussed there," a claim he bases upon personal communications with Franz Schiller and Hans Plass, both of whom attended the college with Wittgenstein. This claim is impossible to assess and yet it is the case that Wittgenstein attended the teachers' college in 1919 and that Bühler was not invited to Vienna until 1922. This does not mean, of course, that Wittgenstein did not read Bühler, and we must remember that the Bühlers, between them, published many books.[5] Most of Hargrove's effort goes into establishing his case against Bartley over the first claim. He disputes the textual evidence Bartley provides and yet acknowledges with Paul Englemann that it was the direct effect of Wittgenstein's contact with children rather than the school reform movement or Bühler's ideas that influenced Wittgenstein's views about language:

I believe we can see the influence of Wittgenstein's time as a teacher on almost every page of the *Investigations*, for there are very few pages in a row that do not make some reference to children. Throughout his later philosophy, Wittgenstein often supported the points he was making by citing personal observations about children. It is these observations, which he made as a school teacher and used as a pool of data later, that, as I see it, are the true influence on Wittgenstein's work, and not principles taught at the teachers college or waved in his face by the school reformers. (Hargrove, 1980, p. 461)

Hans Sluga (1996a, p. 13), most recently, has suggested that, having qualified as a primary school teacher in 1919 and taught for six years, Wittgenstein's "school experience proved an important source of philosophical ideas in later life." He suggests that it was primarily his school-teaching experience that encouraged Wittgenstein to shift from his concerns with the logic of language to the informal language of everyday life: "His attention was now drawn to the way language is learned and more generally to the whole process of enculturation. His teaching experience forms the background to the turn his philosophical thought was going to take in the 1930s" (p. 13). It was a concern that took Wittgenstein back to Mauthner's critique of language, which Sluga maintains influenced Wittgenstein to adopt a view of language not as a formal calculus based on logic, but rather one emphasizing language as a medium "designed to satisfy a multiplicity of human needs." In a footnote to these observations Sluga (p. 32 n.18) remarks: "The significance of this episode of Wittgenstein's life for his subsequent philosophizing has yet to be sufficiently explored" (and he mentions Konrad Wunsche's 1985 *Der Volksschullehrer Ludwig Wittgenstein* as making an important start).

THE STYLE OF THE *INVESTIGATIONS*:
DIALOGUE AND PEDAGOGY

Dialogue is the quintessential pedagogical form of philosophy; it defines both a style of philosophizing based upon the give and take of question and answer and a process of inquiry. It emulates the form of conversation that over time has become more disciplined in its logic. As such and within the tradition of Western philosophy dialogue has been institutionalized as a certain set of pedagogical practices and uses: teaching per se; the instructional text as dialogue; "the pedagogy of the oppressed" (Freire, 1972); the oral or written examination; the free exchange of ideas exemplifying the democratic form of life (John Dewey). Above all, dialogue has been characterized in relation to Socrates and a method based upon the logic of the dialectic.

Wittgenstein's way of doing philosophy, as we have noted, differed from traditional attempts to do philosophy: it is *aporetic* but not Socratic; it is dialogical but not in the traditional philosophical sense.[6] Wittgenstein writes: "Reading the Socratic dialogues one has the feeling; what a frightful waste of time! What's the point of these arguments that prove nothing and clarify nothing" (1980a, p. 14e). Wittgenstein is concerned that Socrates's question "What is knowledge?" (the demand for an essence) in the *Theatetus* is a demand for an exact definition where there is no exact usage of the word "knowledge" (Wittgenstein, 1958, p. 27) and that in asking the question Socrates "does not even regard it as a *preliminary* answer to enumerate cases of knowledge" (p. 20). It is not just that

Socrates's method rests upon the demand for an essence for which the dialogue seems an unnecessary and elaborate artifice, or that such a demand rules out the procedure of advancement by way of examples, or that Socrates holds the view that names signify simples and speech is the composition of names:[7] it is also the idea that Socratic dialogue is inherently unjust. He elaborates further the way in which the game of eristics takes place unfairly, without justice: "Socrates keeps reducing the sophist to silence, — but does he have *right* on his side when he does this? Well, it is true that the sophist does not know what he thinks he knows; but that is no triumph for Socrates. It can't be a case of 'You see! You don't know it!' — nor yet, triumphantly, of 'So none of us knows anything!'" (1980a, p. xx).

In so far as dialogue can be regarded as a classical pedagogical form for philosophy, Wittgenstein embraces it although not exclusively or without reservation or innovation. The *Investigations* is Wittgenstein's primary example of a dialogical work. Yet clearly it is not dialogical in the traditional sense established by Socrates. Judging by Wittgenstein's comments on Socrates, it is evident why the *Investigations* does not follow or try to emulate the Socratic form or method. Although the *Investigations* is written in the form of a dialogue, it draws upon a repertoire of dialogical strategies and gestures. Terry Eagleton (1993, p. 9) recognizes this when he writes: "[The *Investigations*] is a thoroughly dialogical work, in which the author wonders out loud, imagines an interlocutor, asks us questions which may or may not be on the level . . . forcing the reader into the work of self-demystification, genially engaging our participation by his deliberately undaunting style."

Of course, both Wittgenstein and Socrates employed a range of dialogical styles and devices. The Socratic approach, however, has tended to be construed as a single intellectual process — at the same time "both the rational path to knowledge *and* the highest form of teaching" — that assumes "that dialogue can, and should have a definite, predetermined end point" (Burbules, 1993, pp. 4, 5). This is what Burbules (1993, p. 5) calls the teleological view of dialogue, which he distinguishes from the nonteleological. The nonteleological view of dialogue is both more critical and constructivist in the sense that it does not assume "that in practice it will always lead its participants to common and indubitable conclusions; its benefits are more in edification than in finding Truth." This notion of dialogue as conversation, which emphasizes edification (or education) rather than truth, owes an intellectual debt to both Hans-Georg Gadamer (1972) and Richard Rorty (1979). It is not surprising that in such a context Burbules (1993, p. 7) should be seeking an approach to dialogue that can respond to the postmodern critique; by which he means a form of dialogue: that respects difference; that accepts the relational character of dialogue and, therefore, challenges the hierarchical power relations embedded in traditional conceptions of teacher authority; that rests upon a critical and constructivist view of knowledge, which is construed more as a process of mutual edification rather than the discovery of right answers or eternal truths; that accepts (perhaps, after Wittgenstein's private language argument) that dialogue is not first and foremost an individual performance but rather a cultural act; and, finally, "keeps the conversation open, both in the sense of open-endedness and in the sense of inviting a range of voices and styles of communication within it."

Wittgenstein's *Investigations* might be said to embody each of these features and to explicitly teach us the postmodern respect for difference; a respect for the diversity of voices, styles, and language use that characterizes a way of doing philosophy that no longer conforms to the Platonic search for essences or final truths but rather attempts to shift our thinking in a never-ending process of mutual edification. Wittgenstein, therefore, defines himself philosophically against those — like Plato, Saint Augustine, Martin Buber, the early Martin Heidegger, perhaps Gadamer, and even implicitly, Jürgen Habermas — who suggest that our being is essentially dialogical; that the essence of the self is dialogue.

Like Burbules, Bill Readings (1995a) investigates what he calls nondialectical forms of dialogue (rather than nonteleological forms) in the work of Jean-François Lyotard and in relation to the question of pedagogy. He suggests that for Lyotard the pedagogical scene is structured by a dissymetrical pragmatics such that it belongs more to the sphere of justice and ethics than of truth, and he continues in a way that throws light on the notion of nondialectical forms of dialogue — a kind of dialogue addressed by Wittgenstein in his remarks on Socrates and well exemplified in the *Investigations*:

Lyotard's dialogues are not divided monologues . . . the dialogue form is not designed to display his capacity to occupy both sides of the question; rather, it is dialogic in M. M. Bakhtin's sense. The dialogue's form is not organized dialectically, to arrive at a single conclusion that will be either the vindication and reinforcement of one position (Socrates' opponent is forced to agree with Socrates) or a synthesis of the two (as in Hans-Georg Gadamer's account of the fusion of horizons or James Joyce's "jewgreek is greekjew"). The dialogue does not thaw and resolve itself into a monologue. To put this another way, the dialogue form is not controlled solely by the sender; it is not a formal instrument in the grasp of the writing subject. (Readings, 1995, p. 196)

On the basis of Lyotard's work and the attention Lyotard pays to Emmanuel Lévinas' account of an ethics based on the Other, Readings (1995) wants to shift our thinking away from the notion of emancipation in pedagogy to that of obligation in the development of a "heteronomous politics of education."

It is no accident that we have brought together Readings, Lyotard, and Wittgenstein in this way. Lyotard makes active use of Wittgenstein. In *The Postmodern Condition* Lyotard (1984) locates the problem of the legitimation of knowledge and of education within the general context of the crisis of narratives and distinguishes between the modern and the postmodern in terms of the appeal to a metalanguage. The postmodern he defines simply as "incredulity towards metanarratives." The rule of consensus that governed Enlightenment narratives and cast truth as a product of agreement between rational minds has been rent asunder; the narrative function has been dispersed into many language elements, each with its own pragmatic valencies. In arguing this position Lyotard views himself as philosophizing "after" Wittgenstein. The later Wittgenstein, according to Lyotard, teaches us how to philosophize after the end of metaphysics when philosophy can no longer appeal to a metalanguage as a final arbiter to settle matters of truth; indeed, Lyotard interprets Wittgenstein's philosophy as a response to the question of nihilism, that is, how to philosophize after the loss of all transcendental standards.[8]

This is the philo-hermeneutical context within which we can usefully view and interpret the *Investigations* as a pedagogical form of dialogue more concerned to edify — to change our style of thinking — than to arrive at timeless truths in the manner of traditional philosophy. The *Philosophical Investigations* self-reflectively mirrors and models the multiplicity of language games and gestures it attempts to describe. Stylistically, the *Investigations* achieves the same consistency of form and content as did, albeit in a radically different way, the *Tractatus*. It functions as an exemplary pedagogical text, the aim of which is not for Wittgenstein's students to imitate his thoughts or his style of thinking but to think for themselves.

Recently Jane Heal (1995) has argued not only that the *Investigations* is a dialogue (in a precise sense) but also that, rather than defining himself against the philosophical tradition, Wittgenstein employs the dialogue form as a means to pursue in a discursively rational way traditional philosophical questions. Heal (1995, pp. 63–64) argues: "We may both recognize a rationale for Wittgenstein's [dialogical] procedure and also see that there are things to be said against it; we need not be locked into an outlook which thinks that that use of conventional expository forms is a betrayal of Wittgenstein, or a betrayal of lack of understanding of him; but equally we need not think that his particular way of writing is an unnecessary and regrettable obfuscation." We think that Heal's analysis of the dialogue form of the *Investigations* is helpful, but we believe — for reasons that must now appear obvious — that her interpretation that Wittgenstein in the *Investigations* is not defining himself against the philosophical tradition, is incorrect, if defining himself thus amounts to a denial that Wittgenstein was actively seeking a new way of doing philosophy.[9]

Nothing follows from our position concerning the use of conventional expository forms. Wittgenstein's adoption of the dialogue form, along with his adoption of and innovation with other styles — and his close and deliberate attention to the different forms of philosophy — was part of Wittgenstein's deliberate experimentation designed to shift our thinking. He certainly did not want his students to imitate him in either the forms or the contents of his thought. If his students could think differently using conventional forms then we would imagine Wittgenstein would be perfectly happy.[10] Yet it is clear that Wittgenstein adopts extra-discursive forms, in addition to conventional forms, in an experimental and innovative attempt to break down the traditional view that there is only one way to do philosophy.

In a close textual examination of sections #146–47, #208–11, and #258, Heal (1995, p. 73) argues that the *Investigations* is a deliberately crafted dialogue making use of many different kinds of speech act, in which "the other speaker is each of us, if we recognize ourselves in the words and are willing to enter the exchange." She comments that there is no consistent device that Wittgenstein uses to signal dialogue: there are no named characters in the tradition of Plato, Berkeley, or Hume. It is only from the context that we can identify the other voice; a voice that is not "the soul talking to herself" but a genuine "other" to the dialogue, that is, the reader, who understands.

Heal attempts to dismiss the interpretation of the Wittgenstein of the *Investigations* as defining himself against tradition. By this she means a view of Wittgenstein as non-argumentative and anti-philosophical and she argues that to hold this view one must also hold to a dichotomy "between arguing in a discursive rational manner and promoting insight by means other than argument" (1995, p. 76). Heal argues against holding the distinction suggesting that Wittgenstein "wishes to get us to apprehend differently the point of philosophical thinking or the spirit in which one should do it" (p. 76). The appropriateness of the dialogue form, Heal (p. 80) suggests, is intimately tied up with "The difference between one who has read a theoretical non-dialogue version of the thought and one who has pursued them via the dialogue route is closely analogous to the difference between one who realises 'All humans are mortal' and one who realises 'I, like everyone else, am mortal.'"

In other words, for Heal the question of the appropriateness of the dialogue form is tied up with the therapeutic conception of Wittgenstein's philosophy, which acts as a sort of prophylactic to relativism (and conventionalism), and at the same time can provide personal liberation and an enhanced sense of self responsibility and freedom.[11] The dialogue form, then, makes us recognize where we stand (we stand here!) and that, as it happens, "we do make such and such judgements with full sincerity" (p. 82). Heal's remarks in this context are, we think, perfectly in order. We would simply say that the appropriateness of dialogue is demanded by the pedagogical style of Wittgenstein's *Investigations*, which has as its aim to show the fly the way out of the fly-bottle. The aim of the great educator is to teach us to think for ourselves.

NOTES

This chapter was written while Michael Peters was a Visiting Fellow at the Australian National University, Research School of Social Sciences, Political Science Program. We thank Barry Hindess for his kindness and support.

1. The earliest and most significant cultural reading of Wittgenstein was given by Janik and Toulmin (1973). There have been relatively few literary readings of Wittgenstein (but see Lang, 1990 and contributors to the special edition of *New Literary History*, 1988). Most who adopt a literary approach tend to focus upon his aesthetics or want to extract a theory or distinctive approach to literature (Brill, 1995; Perloff, 1992, 1996). Brill (1995, pp. 142–43) concludes "A reliance on the philosophy of Ludwig Wittgenstein will prove to be enormously useful to the future of literary criticism and theory (metacriticism): from issues of axiological debate . . . , to investigations into the foundational grammars of critical and literary language games; from a realization of the possibility of organic certainties which need not be hegemonic not adversely limiting in their efforts, to an acceptance of the importance of useful critical discriminations." See our chapters 1 and 9.

2. The traditional analytic position is that there is not only a hard and fast distinction between form (or scheme) and content (logical and empirical statements), fact and value, but also between the philosopher and his or her works. This effectively rules out the significance of (auto)biography to philosophy. Yet Wittgenstein was fascinated with forms of philosophical writing (the meditation, the confession) that inserted the writer or thinker in the text or made the writer/thinker central. For instance, he was interested in the form of the confession as a philosophical form (and form of life) as it was practiced by both Saint Augustine and Leo Tolstoy. He also engaged in the practice of confession himself at least on one occasion, even after the loss of religious faith (see Monk, 1990). Justin Leiber (1997) presents a convincing account of Wittgenstein's *Investigations* as an unconventional biographical narrative, and in a passage that anticipates part of my reading of the *Investigations* (in the final section of the paper), writes:

But clearly nonetheless *Investigations* is straightforwardly first person narrative: The *I* is co-referential with Ludwig Wittgenstein of the title page, and then some, the narrative anchor piece, like the *I* of Descartes' *Meditations*, although Wittgenstein's *I* easily becomes we when a general human understanding is examined. But *Investigations* is also second person: you are asked questions, your answers are suggested or implied and then explained, criticized, or expanded; indeed, there is even second person narration in which you are described as going through various exercises or routines. There is no book I know that is more conversational, interactive, and narrational: you almost hear your responses . . . and then find yourself caught and turned about by his reply. You want to say, how can I be having an intense conversation with a man who died many decades ago?

3.   Note Nietzsche's (1968, #810) comment in *The Will to Power*: "Compared with music all communication by words is shameless; words dilute and brutalize; words depersonalize; words make uncommon common" and compare Nietzsche's discussion of nineteenth-century musicians (#105, #106), with Wittgenstein's aphoristic statement in *Culture and Value*.

4.   Bartley acknowledges two further papers on these matters: Stephen Toulmin's "Ludwig Wittgenstein, Karl Bühler and Psycholinguistics," Mimeo, 1968; and Bernard Kaplan's "Comments on S. Toulmin's 'Wittgenstein, Bühler and the Psychology of Language,'" Mimeo, 1969. Bartley says that both papers are forthcoming in the same issue of the *Boston Studies of Philosophy of Science* in which his paper is published, but neither Toulmin's nor Kaplan's paper appear in that issue.

5.   Bartley says Bühler's book was published in 1918, that is, one year before Wittgenstein attended teachers' college, whereas Toulmin says it was published in 1927.

6.   For a recent account of dialogue in relation to teaching, see Burbules (1993, p. 112), who uses the term to refer to "a conversational interaction directed intentionally toward teaching and learning." Interestingly, Burbules uses Wittgenstein's analysis of game and his notion of language game to explore the metaphor of dialogue. He is concerned to develop a theory and practice of dialogue that can respond to the postmodern critique.

7.   See the *Investigations* (1953, #46), where Wittgenstein asks "What lies behind the idea that names really signify simples?" and answers by reference to a statement made by Socrates in the *Theatetus* that names are simples and that the essence of language lies in the composition of names. Wittgenstein is combating a picture of the essence of human language and the (Socratic) idea behind it. He suggests "Both Russell's 'individuals' and my 'objects' (*Tractatus Logico-Philosophicus*) were such primary elements," suggesting that he and Russell stood in the same tradition of Western metaphysics that proceeded by trying to capture the essence of things.

8.   For various readings of the relations between Wittgenstein and Lyotard, especially in terms of education and the postmodern condition, see Peters (1989, 1994a, 1995a, 1995b) and Peters and Marshall (1996).

9.   The accent on "doing" philosophy — on philosophy as an activity — is important for Wittgenstein not only in terms of his philosophy of language where he suggests that "the whole, consisting of language and *actions* . . . [is] the 'language-game'" (1953, #7, emphasis added) or that "the *speaking* of language is part of an *activity*, or a form of life" (#23, emphasis added) but also, as he says elsewhere quoting Goethe, "In the beginning was the deed," suggesting that all forms of saying or speaking and writing are, in some sense, acts or performances. This observation has the intended implication concerning his own philosophizing, in oral or written forms.

10.   Indeed, it is the case that most of his first generation students, including, for instance, Rhees, Anscombe, Malcolm, Wright, Winch, and Barrett, use conventional expository philosophical and traditional discursive argument forms to do philosophy. None of these notable Wittgensteinians could we call radical innovators in terms of style; nor do we see any real attempt to emulate Wittgenstein's

own style. One might argue that, by contrast, Stanley Cavell not only addresses himself to the question of style in philosophy but also consciously experiments with the form of philosophical writing.

11.   Heal (1995, pp. 82–83) also suggests that Wittgenstein's way of proceeding can have its own pitfalls and dangers: it "can lead to the adoption of a kind of bullying tone," it may result in a lack of self-irony — a vigilance against all frivolity, and like other forms of therapy and exercises in personal growth, it may lead to the attempt to endlessly re-create feelings of release rather than to encourage us to move on to tackle genuine problems of the self.

11

Prolegomenon to a
Pedagogy of Self

On [Wittgenstein's] account the self is neither a Humean or Machian logical construct, nor a Kantian subject that is somehow both an empirical and transcendental consciousness, nor a causal construct as Nietzsche and Freud would have it. All these philosophers remain caught within the framework of objectivism.

— Sluga, 1996b, pp. 329–30

His position is best described . . . as antagonistic to certain common philosophical viewpoints. Thus, we can say he is anti-Cartesian, anti-Russelian, anti-Freudian, antiobjectivist, and antibehaviorist in his thinking about the mind, without being able to identify anything positive from which these negative conclusions might be thought to derive.

— Sluga, 1996b, p. 343

For Wittgenstein there is no such thing as a self, if we mean by that a substance referred to by "I." Wittgenstein was heavily influenced by Schopenhauer on the mystery of the "I," but he parts company with Schopenhauer because whereas Schopenhauer says that all that philosophy can do with the notion of the I is take one to the brink and that mysticism must take over, in the *Notebooks* Wittgenstein says that philosophy can and must elucidate this notion of the I (1961, pp. 79–89e). Also, Schopenhauer seems caught with the notion of an I as an eye that mirrors the world, whereas Wittgenstein says the world is my world because of language. Thus, he says (1961, p. 82e, compare 1971, 5.641), that "the philosophical I is not the human being, not the human body or the human soul with the psychological properties, but the metaphysical subject, the boundary (not a part) of the world." This leads Hans Sluga (1996b) to say that either the "I" refers to nothing or it refers to the body. The latter interpretation would align Wittgenstein with Nietzsche and with Nietzsche's emphasis on the body. Wittgenstein's insight is to say that it is not a referring term at all but is used instead in a special expressivist way in our language.

Wittgenstein says that "I" has two uses, as object and as subject (1958, p. 66). Thus, "I" or "my" refers to an object when one is talking of the body — "my arm is broken" — and "I" as subject when we speak of mental states — "I hear so and so," or "I see so and so," or "I have a toothache." The use of "I" in "I have a pain" does not denote a particular body (p. 74). Instead, like a cry of pain, but in a more sophisticated fashion associated with the behavior of language users, it expresses pain. As we saw in earlier chapters this was a move that attempts to break down a number of distinctions — between the inner and the outer, mind and body, and the subjective and the objective. Thus, I make sense of my inner states by uniting the inner subjective "I" with public language. "I am in pain" positions my feelings in the objective world through language. For example, we do not say of a body that it has a pain (1953, #286). Our psychological concepts are part of the grammar of the subject, which cannot be reduced to my body (we do not say, "my body has a pain"). Yet we must, Wittgenstein suggests, resist the temptation thereby to think that there is another object besides the body that is the real subject of the pain. The move from "the body" to "the subject who feels pain" (to "I") is a grammatical move, decided not by introspection but by the grammar of our language game — that is, by our practices of describing a living human being (see McGinn, 1997, p. 156). Wittgenstein remarks: "Only of what behaves like a human being can one say that it *has* pains" (1953, #283).

So "I am LW" can be understood as an expression of identity. It does not state criteria of identity but reasserts or reminds us of criteria of identity. This is not to remind us of the truth of some such proposition as "I am LW," but rather of who we are, as we express who we are, uniting an inner subjective state of pain or feeling with an object that can be identified by several criteria. Wittgenstein remarks that "an 'inner process' stands in need of outward criteria" (1953, #580).

This shifts the philosophical game away from questions about the self — "what is this (mysterious) 'I'?" — to questions about how I understand my self, my feelings, intentions, and so forth. I understand them, Wittgenstein says, by recourse to the public language into which I have been inducted. Further, a public language is but one side of the coin of a form of life. Thus, to a certain extent what I understand as my self depends upon these public concepts and the limits of language and, because these have been influenced heavily by the social sciences — in their theories and practices — I may be at the mercy of a mobile network of social theories, practices, and institutions. Wittgenstein of course attacked the social sciences (especially psychology) as not providing understanding of psychological terms. He states in the *Investigations* (1953, #xiv, p. 232), for instance:

The confusion and barrenness of psychology is not to be explained by calling it a "young science"; its state is not comparable with that of physics, for instance, in its beginnings. (Rather with that of certain branches of mathematics. Set theory. For in psychology there are conceptual confusion and methods of proof.)

The existence of the experimental method makes us think we have the means of solving the problems that trouble us; though problem and method pass one another by.

The self — the "I" — is not an object of any kind and it, therefore, cannot be a suitable focus for scientific theorizing. There is no causal story to tell or to be investigated because the notion of self is not a causal concept. As Sluga (1996b, p. 329) argues: "Psychology as a science of the soul [or self] is therefore impossible." Pedagogy, conceived of in its original German sense, as a psychological science of the development of the self, is also, therefore, based upon a serious conceptual mistake. Wittgenstein's assertion that "there is no such thing as the subject that thinks or entertains ideas" (1971, #3.621) or that "the thinking subject is surely an illusion" (1961, p. 80e), if understood and taken seriously, would seem to throw up fundamental objections to pedagogy conceived as a cognitive science of the thinking subject.

To understand this remark by Wittgenstein we must also understand the critique that Wittgenstein is mounting upon Descartes, a critique of the Cartesian subject. Sluga (1996b, p. 321) suggests that Wittgenstein's "enduring hostility to the idea of an individuated, substantive self" is a unifying theme of writings in the later period and that to the extent that a belief in such a self is associated with Descartes, we can call Wittgenstein's position anti-Cartesianism. If Wittgenstein's critique is a critique of the Cartesian subject (and the belief in an individuated substantive self) it is, first and foremost, an attack on Cartesian dualism (that is, that the self is comprised of the mind and the body, which are causally related) and the notion that the self, through introspection, can attain an indubitable self-knowledge that is more certain than other forms of knowledge (for example, empirical knowledge). It is also a critique of Cartesian moral theory that postulates an ethics of individual self-fulfilment as the highest good. Wittgenstein's trenchant critique is of Enlightenment humanist assumptions concerning the essence of human nature and of a picture that has held us captive — a picture that has infused our pedagogical practices and institutions that needs demystification.

Sluga (1996b, p. 327) notes that anti-Cartesianism at the time Wittgenstein was writing the *Tractatus* was already well rehearsed by such thinkers as Hume, Kant, Schopenhauer, and Nietzsche. Indeed, one might argue that the critique of the Cartesian subject is something that Wittgenstein develops out of Schopenhauer and shares with Nietzsche (with some significant differences, especially those centered around "the will"). Yet Sluga (1996b, p. 327) argues that Wittgenstein's anti-Cartesianism "is only one component in Wittgenstein's thinking about the mind and not the most original." His antiobjectivism, which underlies Wittgenstein's anti-Cartesianism, is what distinguishes Wittgenstein's position and makes it original.

Sluga's (1996b, p. 343) interpretation is instructive because he emphasizes that the difficulties with Wittgenstein lie precisely in the fact that he offers "no positive account of the nature of the self" and, accordingly, any moral insights are negative inferences in the sense that, for Wittgenstein, the "I" is not an object and the subject does not refer. Wittgenstein's position, he suggests, is "best described . . . as antagonistic to certain common philosophical viewpoints," and it proceeds from the nature of his discussions, writings, and view of what it is to do philosophy. Wittgenstein is not interested in putting forward a theory of the self. Indeed, the self is exactly that which we ought not to theorize: he sees the theoretical attitude, insofar as it is associated either with a philosophical search for essences or with the methods of science, as major impediments to our understanding. Wittgenstein's manner of proceeding can be likened to adopting different therapies so as to make the problem completely disappear (1953, #133). As he suggests in the same vein: "The philosopher's treatment of a question is like the treatment of an illness" (#255). We might paraphrase him thus: "What the philosopher or psychologist (or therapist) has to say about the self, is not a philosophy or science of the self, but something for *philosophical* treatment" (compare #254). Wittgenstein's aim is not to produce a new theory, because "The problem of the self is not resolved by advancing a theory" (Sluga, 1996b, p. 343), but rather to change our whole style of thinking or way of approaching the problem. As Sluga (pp. 342–43) argues: "We have solved the problem only when it no longer concerns us and when our attention is turned to the process of living itself. Wittgenstein expresses, thus an unwavering conviction that our deepest human problems call for practical resolution."

Interestingly, Sluga concludes his account of Wittgenstein on the self by contrasting Wittgenstein's thinking with that of Michel Foucault. It is the kind of contrast that we believe is both useful and necessary to what we call a pedagogy of self. He begins by noting that our "I"-utterances force us to modify Wittgenstein's account by adducing or defining a notion of self-image or self-conception; a temporal construct of self, one anchored in time and space, that helps us make sense of ourselves and our experiences. This notion of self "is not a real object existing with causal powers" (Sluga, 1996b, p. 348) — it is a discursive fiction that is nonetheless necessary in thinking of ourselves historically as moral agents. It is exactly this question concerning the practices of self-forma-tion as an ethical subject that Sluga maintains is the center of Foucault's inquiries. Foucault (1984, p. 208) stated "My objective has been to create a history of the different modes by which, in our culture, human beings are made subjects. My work has dealt with three modes of objectification which transform human beings into subjects." Sluga (1996b, p. 349) remarks that Wittgenstein only manages to reach moral conclusions that follow from "the negative discovery that the self is not an object. Hence, he never gets to the positive ideal of an 'esthetics of existence' that Foucault envisaged" and that Wittgenstein, morally speaking, tended toward a life of ascetic denial. He concludes:

In this respect he [Wittgenstein] remains close to Schopenhauer's ethics whereas Foucault's affirmation of a positive self-constitution links him to Nietzsche. The critique of Wittgenstein's views suggested in these observations is, in effect, that which Nietzsche directed against what he called Schopenhauer's nihilism. What is certain is that Wittgenstein saw his task as demolishing objectivist accounts of the self and that he did not address the philosophical issues arising from the process of self-formation. In this we can surely see a limitation in his thinking about the self; it is a limitation, moreover, which restricted the scope of Wittgenstein's reflections on moral issues. (Sluga, 1996b, pp. 349–50)

In accordance with Wittgenstein's remarks and mostly in agreement with Sluga's account but also on the basis of our analysis completed in chapters 3–6, we will argue for the move from the philosophy of the self to a pedagogy of the self. The term "pedagogy of self" here is meant to capture both the Wittgensteinian approach to the philosophy of the self — in particular his critique of the Cartesian subject (and the permanent critique of the tradition of the philosophy of the subject inaugurated by Descartes) — and the more positive sense in which Foucault investigates the *problematique* of ethical self-constitution. Yet we do not fully agree with Sluga's account, especially his remarks concerning Wittgenstein in relation to Foucault, for a number of reasons. First, Foucault describes his project as history (albeit in the special Nietzschean sense of genealogy) rather than philosophy. For Foucault, his project requires both philosoph-ical concepts and detailed empirical inquiry. His employment of a "concrete example" to "serve as a testing ground for analysis" (cited in Rabinow, 1997, p. xi) is different from Wittgenstein's attention to actual and particular examples. Second, we think that Wittgenstein's attitude to morality was manifested in his actions: whether ascetic or not, they showed a commitment to a philosophical form of life; they manifested themselves in a set of self-critical reflective practices and in an ethical *ethos* based on the notion of a community or culture embodying a form of life. Third, it is not the case that all we can extract from Wittgenstein is a set of negative conclusions based on the observation that the self is not an object, because in Wittgenstein's view of language, of language games, is an implicit positive view of the self as consisting in linguistic and cultural practices, as a construction of discourse. This is not simply to iterate a truism that Wittgenstein shares with structuralism, that we are not the authors of our own semantic intentions, but also to provide new resources for understanding the self in terms of the "'atomization' of the social into flexible networks of language games" (Lyotard, 1984, p. 17). In this way Wittgenstein might be viewed as someone who teaches us how to philosophize in the new millenium and how to provide a positive response to the question of nihilism: of nothingness in relation to the self, of the dissolution of culture and of self (or at least of certain essences or organic metaphors) — of the crisis of identity in (post)modernity (see chapters 2, 7, and 8). Lyotard is one example of a thinker following Wittgenstein who has pursued this line of argument:

A self does not amount to much, but no self is an island; each exists in a fabric of relations that is now more complex and mobile than ever before. Young or old, man or women, rich or poor, a person is always located at "nodal points" of specific communication circuits, however tiny these may be. Or better: one is always located at a post through which various kinds of messages pass. No one, not even the least privileged among us, is ever entirely powerless over the messages that traverse and position him at the post of sender, addressee, or referent. One's mobility in relation to these language game effects . . . is tolerable, at least within certain limits . . . ; it is even solicited by regulatory mechanisms, and in particular by self-adjustments the system undertakes in order to improve its performance. (Lyotard, 1984, p. 15)

We are, however, in agreement with Sluga that Foucault provides a positive account of self-constitution in a way that makes ethics central. The relationship of the self to itself is what for Foucault constitutes the very stuff of ethics and beginning from this premise, as Rabinow (1997: xvii) notes, "Foucault understands thought as the exercise of freedom." A Foucauldian genealogy of pedagogy reveals a shifting emphasis from "the subject of knowledge" and "the thinking subject," accompanied by an ethics of individual self-fulfilment, to "thinking as an exercise of freedom." Insofar as pedagogy of self involves a Nietzschean affirmation of self-overcoming it places an analysis of ethical self-formation at the center of investigation. Following what Rabinow calls the "ethical fourfold" based on the categories of ethical substance, mode of subjectification, ethical work, and *telos*, we might suggest that a pedagogy of self be structured through:

the way that the individual has to constitute this or that part of himself as the prime material of his moral conduct;

the way in which the individual establishes his relation to the rule and recognizes himself as obligated to put it into practice;

the work one performs to attempt to transform oneself into the ethical subject of one's behavior (what are the means by which we can change ourselves in order to become ethical subjects?); and

the place an action occupies in a pattern of conduct. It commits an individual . . . to a certain mode of being, a mode of being characteristic of the ethical subject. (cited in Rabinow, 1997, pp. xxix–xxxviii)

Such observations have immense implications for a pedagogy because they provide a critique of the traditional view of liberal education that is concerned with the development of mind, as in the Greek-inspired writings in education of Paul Hirst (e.g., 1983), and the notion of the development of the autonomous person as an aim of education. In such accounts education is based upon a philosophy of the self, upon a notion of consciousness and the mind, and a notion that the autonomous person can be developed so that (s)he is intellectually independent of the authority of others, of tradition, and of dogma. Autonomous persons can think for themselves. This was in part the Enlightenment message: that reason would be liberating. However, the notion of the self or subject and its pursuit in education becomes tenuous if we take Wittgenstein seriously, and dangerous if we take Foucault seriously (Marshall, 1996).

What then would a shift to a pedagogy of the self, a possibility implied by the Wittgensteinean and Foucauldean critique, involve? By a pedagogy of the self we mean a critical learning and teaching process that involved non-dominating and non-manipulative processes, that permitted us to become and encouraged us to view positively the critical process of perpetual self-overcoming. This would also be a critical and reflective pedagogy, but it would not operate upon humanist assumptions concerning, for example, the whole person, nor would it be child-centered because, against notions of the critical inherited directly from Kant or Marx, it would oppose the negative account of Wittgenstein that the self is not an object and it would draw the positive conclusion that what requires critique most of all in the discourses of the human sciences (and especially pedagogy) is that which treats the self as an object to be investigated philosophically or scientifically. There are two general aspects in a critical pedagogy of the self: that of a critique of institutions and their practices, including education, and that of a critical pedagogy of the self, where the self was in control of the constitution of the self and was able to become or overcome efforts to dominate or constitute the self by others and by the theories and practices of institutions based upon the controlling and technocratic aspects of the social sciences. In this sense, a critical pedagogy of self draws upon Foucault's positive insight that still links us to the Enlightenment but seeks to overcome its ideological distortions in the form of humanism, in either its liberal or Marxist guises: that "games of truth" involve an ascetic practice of self-formation of the subject, that is, as an exercise of the self on the self in order to develop or transform oneself (see "The Ethics of the Concern of the Self as a Practice of Freedom," in Rabinow, 1997). Foucault explicitly addresses the "pedagogical institution" in these very terms when he writes:

I see nothing wrong in the practice of a person who, knowing more than others in a specific game of truth, tells those others what to do, teaches them, and transmits knowledge and techniques to them. The problem in such practices where power — which is not a bad thing in itself — must inevitably come into play is knowing how to avoid the kind of domination effects where a kid is subjected to the arbitrary and unnecessary authority of a teacher, or student put under the thumb of a professor who abuses his authority. I believe that this problem must be framed in terms of rules of law, rational techniques of government and ethos, practices of the self and of freedom. ("The Ethics of the Concern of the Self as a Practice of Freedom," in Rabinow, 1997, pp. 289–99)

For Foucault the self was always not something that is given. Rather he adopted a position enunciated early by Nietzsche (1983, p. 163): "Be yourself. You are none of the things you now do, think, desire." For both Nietzsche and Foucault: "Our body is but a social structure" (Nietzsche, 1989, 21:19), and our self is contingent, and hanging because of shifting social and cultural forces (Nietzsche, 1968, p. 552). Foucault tracks out in considerable detail how the self is constituted either by technologies of domination —as in for example, *Discipline and Punish* — or by technologies of the self, where one is able to constitute one's own identity — for example, in the *History of Sexuality*, vols. II and III.

Foucault also bypasses the question "What is the self" and instead asks the question "How is the self constituted." At best Foucault sees it as a kind of logical form, not fixed or immutable, capable of change through care by the self of the self, and a concomitant reconceptualizing of the self through caring for the self. Care for the self is to be a form of exercise upon the self and not a Schopenhauerean renunciation of the self. If "I" is a self (a form) to be cared for it is not a self to be known through the human sciences, but it does involve the exercise of reason.

In both Wittgenstein and Foucault we can see a rejection of a philosophy of the self. First they do not start from a priori theories of the self, from essences, or from some stable feature discovered in human nature (for example, rationality as the defining characteristic of human being).

They do not even ask those questions that might lead to philosophical theories of the self — although the Wittgenstein of the *Tractatus* comes close. Thus, they are no longer seeking a stability or a foundation for the self in anything that might be called human nature. In relation to education this is clearly an implicit attack upon all theories in education that start from assumptions about the self and human nature

THE CARE OF THE SELF

The concept of expression and the notion of first person statements such as "I am in pain" being an expression of pain, and "I am LW" as somehow being an expression of identity, have been introduced in Chapter 4. In particular Wittgenstein was at pains to say that "I" was not a referring expression, and that "I am in pain" was not a description or report of an inner mental state or object. It is possible to communicate pain by expressions of pain, by cries, groans, or grimaces and also by more sophisticated utterances such as "I am in pain." About these latter utterances he says that they have been learned in social situations where as a child one has been in pain, that one does not know that one is in pain but that one cannot be mistaken that one is in pain, and that these utterances are not reports or descriptions of inner mental states but expressions.

These expressions of behavior are important to Wittgenstein because, in one sense, they can be seen as mediating between the inner and the outer. For Wittgenstein language is public and on the outer (if that may be said), whereas my sensation of pain, say, is on the inner and cannot be known or experienced by anyone other than myself. It is our characteristic expressive behavior — expressions of pain like a cry, and linguistic expressions such as "I am in pain" — that permits us to understand the subjective and how it is related to the objective. Linguistic expressions of pain employ concepts from a public language but their use in first person utterances cannot normally be mistaken, whereas their use in third person descriptions like "He is in pain" can be mistaken (he is acting, and so forth). The first person "I" identifies a center of consciousness, and the public concept "pain" unites that center of consciousness to the public-experienced world through language, which in turn sets the limits of that public-experienced world. The inner and the outer, the subjective and the objective, are thus connected through immediate expressions and through linguistic expressions. Hence, we see the importance of the difference between first and third person statements for Wittgenstein.

As we have seen above Wittgenstein seemed to have reached a conclusion that we never reach the "I"; in the sense of a substance, of a what it is, it remains mysterious. To make sense of our lives, however, we must to a certain extent be involved in introspection about our inner subjective feelings, attitudes, intentions, and so on. This Wittgenstein accepts — we must introspect to make sense of our lives, of those inner feelings, attitudes, intentions, and so on. He does not ask us to make sense of our lives, to test our claims about intentionality and so forth, by exploring inner mental states or structures or inner states of mind. Wittgenstein's insight here is that there may be (probably are) inner structures but that he sees this as too problematic. (Hume, too, could never catch the "I" but only perceptions, sensations, and so forth — see Chapter 3. So it is Hume who has problematized this whole psychological approach and who is, ironically, seen often as the father of modern psychology.)

We meet only an "I" speaking, promising, choosing, and so forth. What Wittgenstein does is to accede to the notion of introspection, but to avoid the problems of what the "I" is, yet make sense of our emotions, feelings, and so forth, to "insert" this notion of introspection into a public language. We make sense of our lives, feelings, and attitudes by seeing how my purported feelings, attitudes, hopes, and so forth position me within the grammar of the public language that I have learned. For example, I have this churned up feeling about my next door neighbor — but am I envious, jealous, or what? By careful analysis (introspection) of what I feel about my neighbor (friend, lover, wife, husband) and by recourse to the public criteria or grammar of envy and jealousy in our everyday language, I can make sense of my inner feelings. Sense is made by melding the inner and subjective with the outer and objective, the churned up, confused feeling with its expression from the everyday language into which one has been inducted from childhood. It is now made sense of because we now know what it is that we are feeling. In these years we learn the language of subjectivity, and in learning how we position ourselves in a form of life by how we make sense of our subjective states by describing them in the objective language, we learn how we become a self or subject.

That does not resolve the question of the "I," because it remains mysterious. Is it because we want to know what it is that is the problem? Do we feel cheated because to a certain extent Wittgenstein has ducked the question? Perhaps, in Wittgensteinean fashion, this is an example of philosophy asking the wrong type of question. Instead of seeing how "I" is used in language some philosophers, assuming that it is a referring expression, want to ask to what it refers, and seeking answers to that question can take us down a murky path of philosophical theories, which includes Descartes, Locke, Hume, Rousseau, and Schopenhauer and humanists, such as Sartre and Beauvoir. Making sense of how we use "I" and psychological expressions leaves the self in a constrained field. If I am to make sense of my life often I have to confront ideas, concepts, and theories about myself that have penetrated everyday life from the human sciences. Whether Wittgenstein is correct that there is something wrong about the human sciences, the fact is that many concepts, ideas, and theories about the self have become part of our understanding of ourselves; as examples the concept of the subconscious, class background, and more recent shifts in the notion of the citizen as a possessor of rights to a person who has responsibilities, involve theoretical notions from the social sciences that do impinge upon my understanding of myself. Am I really repressing my feelings about person X; are my responses to certain matters of taste and style explicable in terms of my class background; and am I really irresponsible and demanding of state resources because I claim them, for example, health, as a right? How am I make to make sense of these theoretical [if much diluted] descriptions of myself? If all that I can do is to get clear about these notions, then how do I change myself; how do I take care of myself if I don't like the self that I "see,"encounter, or discover in making sense of my feelings, attitudes, and so forth.

In general, Wittgenstein says that philosophy cannot change the world — in describing the world philosophy can only say how the world is, how I found it. We believe this to be unsatisfactory and the issue to be treated better in the writings of Foucault where he discusses the notion of care of the self. This notion is to be found in his later writings, that is, post-1976 and the publication of *The History of Sexuality*, Vol. I.

The problem identified so far in Wittgenstein's discussion of the mysterious "I" is that of the question, "what is the 'I' (subject or self)." Foucault is to ask a different kind of question about the "I": not what is it, but how is my identity, the subject or self, constituted. In talking about power we can note in Foucault's thought a similar avoidance of a what question as he avoids questions about the nature of power and its ownership. Instead his question is concerned with power relations or as we might normally express it, with how power is exercised. Just as questions about the nature and ownership of power take us into a juridico-discursive notion of power, so also questions about the nature of the self take us into juridical notions of the self — as the possessor of rights, the autonomous individual, and so on.

In one of the last interviews that he was to give (January 1984) Foucault was initially asked by one of his interlocuters (Foucault, 1984, p. 281): "Having followed the latest developments in your thought . . . I would like to know if your current philosophical approach is still determined by the poles of subjectivity and truth." To which Foucault immediately replied:

I have always been interested in this problem, even if I framed it somewhat differently. I have tried to find out how the human subject fits into certain games of truth. . . . This is the theme of my book *The Order of Things*, in which I attempted to see how, in scientific discourses, the human subject defines itself as a speaking, living, working individual. . . . I tried to grasp it in terms of what may be called a practice of the self . . . as an exercise of the self on the self by which one attempts to develop and transform oneself, and to attain a certain mode of being.

Clearly this is a stronger view of the self or subject than that of Wittgenstein. It is not merely a Wittgensteinean notion of making sense of the self in a world, which is more or less given, because the limits of this world are determined by language and in which the languages of the human sciences are rejected as providing understanding of the self. Instead it is an active view of the self involving practices through which one not only understands and comes to terms with oneself but where one attempts to "develop and transform oneself" in relation to "models that he finds in his culture, and are proposed, suggested, imposed upon him by his culture, his society, and his social group" (Foucault, 1984a, p. 291). These practices are nevertheless not merely invented by the subject (as, for example, the mad, the ill, the delinquent, and, perhaps, even the sexual subject was a subject that was the object of a theoretical discourse) although that subject was not merely passive. The problematic for Foucault then is how the subject or self is constituted by itself in relation to games of truth (where Foucault brackets the truth of these games).

If one is concerned with questions about how the subject is constituted then Foucault believed that one could not start with a theory of the subject and on the basis of that theory ask how certain knowledge of the subject was possible (Foucault, 1984a, p. 290). He wished to explore the relations between the subject and games of truth and the ways in which games of truth constituted the subject in certain ways, so that knowledge of the subject was in a certain sense inevitable because that knowledge had in fact constituted the subject in certain ways. Knowledge of the self was not, therefore, the possible outcome of a theory of the subject, but was instead the power effect of certain theoretical views from games of truth that contained accounts of the subject.

Foucault's interest is in the constitution of an ethical subject. This is not the Kantian ethical subject, that is, one identified by rational (or ideological) considerations, but one revealed in practices, one shown in practices. This is not the ethical person of Wittgenstein either, where nothing can be said about ethics but can only be shown because for Wittgenstein this ethical person is embedded in a form of life, where reason-giving has run out. For Foucault quite a lot can be said about this ethical person, and reflection upon the ethical status of the subject can be part of the exercise of care for the self. For Foucault ethics is not just a theory but is rather a practice and an embodiment of a style — this is what he means by ethics as an *ethos*.

We can see some fundamental principles here. First, for Foucault that aspect of ethics that is his concern is not theoretical or merely theoretical and abstract but is concerned instead primarily with practices, because "what is ethics, if not the practice of liberty, the considered practice of liberty" (Foucault, 1984a, p. 284). For Foucault "freedom is the ontological condition of ethics" and ethics as an *ethos* is reflected in how one cares for the self (p. 284). However, the expressions "how one cares for the self," "the self caring for the self," and "the relation of the self to the self" seem odd. How are we to make sense of them because how can one mysterious object, a self, be in relationship to itself, how can it take care of itself? How can care be reflexive? This is of course to return to what notions about the self. For Foucault the self or subject is not a substance (an answer to the *what* question):

It is not a substance. It is a form, and this form is not primarily or always identical to itself. You do not have the same relationship to yourself when you constitute yourself as a political subject who goes to vote or speaks at a meeting and when you are seeking to fulfil your desires in a sexual relationship. Undoubtedly there are relationships and interferences between these different forms of the subject; but we are not dealing with the same type of subject. In each case, one plays, one establishes a different type of relationship to oneself. (Foucault, 1984a, p. 290)

Saying it is a form does not really solve any problems because questions can now be asked about a form — for example, what is it and how does it enter into relationships with other forms? Some sense can be made of this notion of a form, however, if we see it as some kind of conceptualization, and concepts can enter into relationships with one another. So a form of the self is a conceptual structure (as a politician, lover, and so forth), covering the behavior, style, and practices of the self. It is, thus, an intellectual structure concerning the *ethos*, or the practice of liberty in a variety of circumstances that in turn are embedded in regimes of truth. Thus, the "I" (a form) constitutes itself in one form at one time and in another form at another time and can reconstitute a particular form (care of the self). Where forms are imposed the "I" can resist and reconstitute itself. "Care for the self" is a relationship between forms that permits refinement of a form, a resistance against imposed forms, and the constituting of multiple forms.

The self also seems to be a type of power relationship. In Foucault's earlier writing (for example, *Discipline and Punish*) one technique that he discussed was that of surveillance and how in the panopticon one must consider that one is under total and continual surveillance. However, an even stronger ideal was to be self surveillance, so that the self checked its behavior in accordance with the normalized notion of the subject constituted in institutions in accordance with certain regimes of truth. Thus, when self surveillance revealed a deviation from the norms the subject could exercise power over the self to correct such deviations. Care for the self can be seen as a later and much refined notion of this earlier notion of self surveillance.

Fundamental to care of the self is truth, because Foucault sees the problem for the Western world as being its subjugation to regimes of truth. "How did it come about that all of Western culture began to revolve around this obligation to regimes of truth?" (Foucault, 1984a, p. 295). Foucault stresses in many sources that in Western culture "Know thyself" has replaced "Care for the self" as the primary notion for understanding the self. Care for the self came to be seen as narcissistic under the domination of "Know thyself," but one can only escape from the domination of truth by playing those games of truth differently.

Here the philosopher has a unique and distinctive role, to expose the power relations, to question domination, and to permit individuals to become free. "Philosophy is that which calls into question domination at every level and in every form in which it exists, whether political, economic, sexual, institutional, or what have you. To a certain extent, this critical function of philosophy derives from the Socratic injunction 'take care of yourself,' in other words, 'Make freedom your foundation, through the mastery of yourself'" (Foucault, 1984a, p. 301).

This is a very different role for the philosopher than that which we find in Wittgenstein. If resolving philosophical puzzles is an activity yet philosophy leaves everything as it is, for the world is as I found it. This is a passive role for philosophy in society. If we consider Foucault's much more active view of philosophy and his own political activities post-1968 we can see not only that philosophy can make people freer than they ever imagined but also that the world as I found it need not be the same world as I leave it.

Bibliography

Abrams, M. H. (1981) *Glossary of Literary Terms.* New York: Holt Rhinehart & Winston.

Allison, D. (ed.). (1977) *The New Nietzsche.* New York: Delta.

Altieri, C. (1995) "Personal Style as Articulate Intentionality." In C. Van Eck, J. McAllister, & R. Van de Vall (eds.), *The Question of Style in Philosophy and the Arts,* pp. 201–19. Cambridge: Cambridge University Press.

Altieri, C. (1994) *Subjective Agency: A Theory of First-Person Expressivity and Its Social Implications.* Oxford: Blackwell.

Anscombe, G.E.M. (1981) *Metaphysics and the Philosophy of Mind, The Collected Papers of G.E.M. Anscombe,* vol. II, pp. 21–36. Oxford: Blackwell.

Aschheim, S. E. (1992) *The Nietzsche Legacy in Germany 1890–1990.* Berkeley: University of California Press.

Aspin, D. (1982) "Philosophy of Education." In L. Cohen, J. Thomas, & L. Mauion (eds.), *Educational Research and Development in Britain 1970–1980.* Windsor: NFER-Nelson.

Austin, J. (1962) *How to Do Things With Words.* J. Urmson (ed.) London: Oxford University Press.

Bachmann, I. (1971) *Malina.* Frankfurt: Suhrkamp. (English translation 1990).

Baker, G. & P.M.S. Hacker. (1983) *Wittgenstein: Understanding and Meaning. An Analytical Commentary on the Philosophical Investigations,* vol I. Oxford: Blackwell.

Baker, G. P. & P.M.S. Hacker. (1980) *Wittgenstein: Understanding and Meaning.* Oxford: Blackwell.

Barrett, C. (1988) "Wittgenstein, Leavis, and Literature," *New Literary History,* 2 (Winter): 387–401.

Barrow, Robin. (1994) "Philosophy of Education: Analytic Tradition." In T. Husen

& T. Postlethwaite (eds.), *The International Encyclopedia of Education*, 2d ed. Oxford: Pergamon.

Bartley, W. W., III. (1974) "Theory of Language and Philosophy of Science as Instruments of Educational Reform: Wittgenstein and Popper as Austrian Schoolteachers." In Robert S. Cohen & Marx W. Wartofsky (eds.), *Methodological and Historical Essays in the Natural and Social Sciences*, Boston Studies in the Philosophy of Science. Dordrecht: D. Reidel.

Bartley, W. W., III. (1973) *Wittgenstein*. Philadephia, Pa.: J. B. Lippincott.

Bataille, G. (1945) *Sur Nietzsche* (On Nietzsche). Paris: Gallimard.

Bearn, G. (1997) *Waking to Wonder: Wittgenstein's Existential Investigations*. New York: State University of New York Press.

Beauvoir, S. de. (1968) *Force of Circumstance*. Harmondsworth: Penguin.

Beauvoir, S. de. (1965) *The Prime of Life*. Harmondsworth: Penguin.

Beauvoir, S. de. (1956) *The Mandarins*. Translated by L. Friedman. Cleveland, Ohio: World Publishing.

Behler, E. (1996) "Nietzsche in the Twentieth Century." In B. Magnus & K. Higgins (eds.), *The Cambridge Companion to Nietzsche*, pp. 281–322. Cambridge: Cambridge University Press.

Bernhard, T. (1982) *Wittgenstein's Neffe: eine Freudschaft*. Frankfurt au Main: Suhrkamp.

Bernstein, C. (1990) "Wittgensteiniana," *Fiction International*, 18(2): 72–84.

Bernstein, C. (1987) *The Sophist*. Los Angeles, Calif.: Sun & Moon Press.

Bernstein, R. (1987) "One Step Forward, Two Steps Back," *Political Theory*, 15(4): 539–63.

Blanchot, M. (1987) "Reflections on Nihilism: Crossing of the Line." In Harold Bloom (ed.), *Friedrich Nietzsche*, pp. 35–42. New York: Chelsea House.

Borradori, G. (1994) *The American Philosopher*. Translated by R. Crocitto. Chicago, Ill.: University of Chicago Press.

Bouveresse, J. (1995) *Wittgenstein Reads Freud: the Myth of the Unconscious*. Translated by Carol Cosman. Princeton, N.J.: Princeton University Press.

Bouveresse, J. (1992) "'The Darkness of this Time': Wittgenstein and the Modern World." In A. P. Griffiths (ed.), *Wittgenstein: Centenary Essays*. Cambridge: Cambridge University Press.

Breazeale, D. (1979) *Philosophy and Truth: Selections from Nietzsche's Notebooks of the Early 1870s*. London: Humanities Press.

Breuer, J. & S. Freud. (1957) *Studies on Hysteria*. Translated and edited by James Strachey & Alan Tyson. New York: Basic Books.

Bridgwater, P. (1972) *Nietzsche in Anglosaxony: A Study of Nietzsche's Impact on English and American Literature*. Leicester: Leicester University Press.

Brill, S. (1995) *Wittgenstein and Critical Theory: Beyond Postmodernism and Towards Descriptive Investigations*. Athens, Ohio: Ohio University Press.

Burbules, N. (1993) *Dialogue in Teaching: Theory and Practice*. New York: Teachers College Press.

Burrows, J. (1990) "Conversational Politics: Rorty's Pragmatist Apology for Liberalism." In A. Malachowsky (ed.), *Reading Rorty*. Oxford: Blackwell.

Cacciari, M. (1996) *Posthumous People: Vienna at the Turning Point*. Stanford, Calif.: Stanford University Press.

Cage, J. (1990) *Charles Eliot Norton Lectures 1988–89*. Cambridge, Mass.: Harvard University Press.

Calinescu, M. (1987) *Five Faces of Modernity: Modernism, Avant-Garde, Decadence, Kitsch, Postmodernism*. Durham, N.C.: Duke University Press.

Capaldi, N. (1993) "Analytic Philosophy and Language." In R. Harré & R. Harris (eds.), *Linguistics and Philosophy: The Controversial Interface*. Oxford: Pergamon Press.

Cavell, S. (1995) *Philosophical Passages: Wittgenstein, Emerson, Austin and Derrida*. Oxford: Blackwell.

Cavell, S. (1994) *A Pitch of Philosophy: Autobiographical Exercises*. Cambridge, Mass.: Harvard University Press.

Cavell, S. (1988) "Declining Decline: Wittgenstein as a Philosopher of Culture," *Inquiry*, 31: 253–64.

Cavell, S. (1976) *Must We Mean What We Say?* New York: Cambridge University Press.

Cioffi, F. (ed.). (1973) *Freud*. London: MacMillan.

Coppleston F. (1965) *A History of Philosophy*, vol. 7, part II. New York: Image Books.

Danto, A. (1965) *Nietzsche as Philosopher*. New York: Macmillan.

Dasenbrock, R. W. (ed.). (1989) *Redrawing the Lines: Analytic Philosophy, Deconstruction, and Literary Theory*. Minneapolis: University of Minnesota Press.

Davenport, G. (1981) *The Geography of the Imagination: Forty Essays*. San Francisco, Calif.: North Point.

Davidson, A. (ed.). (1997) *Foucault and His Interlocutors*. Chicago, Ill.: University of Chicago Press.

Davidson, A. (1997) "Introduction." In Arnold Davidson (ed.), *Foucault and His Interlocuters*, pp. 1–17. Chicago, Ill.: University of Chicago Press.

Davies, A. (1987) *Signage*. New York: Roof.

Dearden, R. F. (1982) "Philosophy of Education, 1952–82," *British Journal of Educational Studies*, 30(1): 57–81.

Deleuze, G. (1983) *Nietzsche and Philosophy*. Translated by H. Tomlinson. New York: Columbia University Press.

Deleuze, G. (1962) *Nietzsche et Philosophie*. Paris: Presses Universitaires de France.

De Man, P. (1979) *Allegories of Reading*. New Haven, Conn.: Yale University Press.

Derrida, J. (1995) "Is There A Philosophical Language?" In E. Weber (ed.), *Points . . . Interviews, 1974–1994*. Translated by P. Kamuf & others. Stanford, Calif.: Stanford University Press.

Derrida, J. (1992) "Interview with Jacques Derrida and Letter by Barry Smith," *Cambridge Review*, October: 131–39.

Derrida, J. (1988) "Afterword: Toward an Ethic of Discussion." In G. Graff (ed.), *Limited Inc*. Evanston, Ill.: Northwestern University Press.

Derrida, J. (1983) "The Time of the Thesis: Punctuations." In A. Montefiore (ed.), *Philosophy in France Today*, pp. 34–50. Cambridge: Cambridge University Press.

Derrida, J. (1978) "Violence and Metaphysics: An Essay on the Thought of Emmanuel Levinas." In J. Derrida, *Writing and Difference*. Translated by A. Bass. Chicago, Ill.: University of Chicago Press.

Descartes, René. (1967) "Meditations on First Philosophy." In E. S. Haldane &

G.R.T. Ross (trans.), *The Philosophical Works of Descartes*. Cambridge: Cambridge University Press.

Descombes, V. (1995) Foreword to Jacques Bouveresse, *Wittgenstein Reads Freud: the Myth of the Unconscious*, pp. vii–viii. Translated by Carol Cosman. Princeton, N.J.: Princeton University Press.

Dreyfus, H. & P. Rabinow. (1983) *Michel Foucault: Beyond Structuralism and Hermeneutics*. Chicago, Ill.: University of Chicago Press.

Drury, M. O'C. (1984) "Some Notes on Conversations with Wittgenstein." In R. Rhees (ed.), *Recollections of Wittgenstein*, pp. 76–171. Oxford: Oxford University Press.

Drury, M. O'C. (1967) "A Symposium: Assessments of the Man and the Philosopher." In K. T. Fann (ed.), *Ludwig Wittgenstein: The Man and His Philosophy*. Sussex: Harvester Press.

Duffy, B. (1987) *The World as I Found It*. New York: Ticknor.

Eagleton, T. (1993) "Introduction to Wittgenstein." *Wittgenstein: The Terry Eagleton Script*. The Derek Jarman Film. London: British Film Institute.

Eagleton, T. (1987) *Saints and Scholars*. London: Verso.

Eagleton, T. (1986) *Against the Grain: Selected Essays, 1975–1985*. London: Verso.

Eagleton, T. (1982) "Wittgenstein's Friends," *New Left Review*, 135 (September–October): 64–90.

Edel, A. (1972) "Analytic Philosophy of Education at the Cross-Roads," *Educational Theory*, 22(2): 131–52.

Engelmann, P. (1967), *Letters from Ludwig Wittgenstein, With a Memoir*. B. F. McGuinness (ed.). Oxford: Blackwell.

Eribon, D. (1991) *Michel Foucault (1926–1984)*. Translated by Betsy Wing. Cambridge: Cambridge University Press.

Fann, K. T. (ed.). (1967) *Ludwig Wittgenstein: The Man and His Philosophy*. Sussex: Harvester Press.

Farrenkopf, J. (1992–93) "Nietzsche, Spengler, and the Politics of Cultural Despair," *Interpretation*, 20(2) (Winter): 165–85.

Finch, H. R. (1995) *Wittgenstein*. Rockport, Mass.: Element Books.

Fogelin, R. J. (1996) "Wittgenstein's Critique of Philosophy." In H. Sluga & D. G. Stern (eds.), *The Cambridge Companion to Wittgenstein*, pp. 34–58. Cambridge: Cambridge University Press.

Foucault, M. (1990) *The Care of the Self: The History of Sexuality*, vol. III. Harmondsworth, Penguin.

Foucault, M. (1988) "Technologies of the Self." In L. H. Martin, H. Gutman, & P. H. Hutton (eds.), *Technologies of the Self*, pp. 18–49. Amherst, Mass.: University of Massachusetts Press.

Foucault, M. (1987) *Mental Illness and Psychology*. Los Angeles: University of California Press.

Foucault, M. (1986) "Nietzsche, Freud, Marx." *Critical Texts*, 3: 1–5.

Foucault, M. (1985) *The Use of Pleasure: The History of Sexuality*, vol. II. New York: Vintage.

Foucault, M. (1984a) "The Ethics of the Concern of the Self as a Practice of Freedom." Reprinted in Paul Rabinow (ed.), (1997) *Michel Foucault, Ethics*, pp. 281–302. Translated by R. Hurley and others. London: Penguin.

Foucault, M. (1984b) "What is Enlightenment?" In Paul Rabinow (ed.), *The Foucault Reader*, pp. 32–50. New York: Pantheon.

Foucault, M. (1980a) *The History of Sexuality*, vol. I. New York: Vintage.

Foucault, Michel (1980b) "Truth and Power." In Colin Gordon (ed.), *Power/Knowledge: Selected Interviews and Other Writings*, pp. 109–33. New York: Pantheon.

Foucault, M. (1979) "Governmentality." *Ideology and Consciousness*, 7: 5–26.

Foucault, M. (1977) "Nietzsche, Genealogy, History." In D. F. Bouchard (ed.), *Language, Counter-Memory, Practice*, pp. 139–64. Ithaca, N.Y.: Cornell University Press.

Foucault, M. (1966) *Discipline and Punish*. Harmondsworth: Penguin.

Foucault, M. (1961) *Folie et Déraison: La Historie de la Folie à L'Age Classique*. Paris: Plon.

Fraser, N. (1990) "Solidarity or Singularity?" In A. Malachowsky (ed.), *Reading Rorty*, pp. 303–21. Oxford: Blackwell.

Frege, G. (1960) *Translations from the Philosophical Writings of Gottlob Frege*. Edited by P. T. Geach & Max Black. Oxford: Blackwell.

Freire, P. (1972) *Pedagogy of the Oppressed*. Harmondsworth: Penguin.

Freud, S. (1946) "The History of the Psychoanalytical Movement." *Collected Papers*, vol. 1. Translated by Joan Riviere. New York: International Psycho-Analytic Press.

Freud, S. (1932) *The Interpretation of Dreams*. Translated by A. A. Brill. London: George Allen and Unwin.

Fromm, E. (1982) *Greatness and Limitations of Freud's Thought*. London: Abacus.

Gadamer, H.-G. (1972) *Truth and Method*. New York: Crossroad.

Garrett, B. (1997) "Anscombe on I." *The Philosophical Quarterly*, 47: 507–11.

Gasking, D.A.T. & A. C. Jackson. (1967) "Wittgenstein as a Teacher." In K. T. Fann (ed.), *Ludwig Wittgenstein: The Man and His Philosophy*. Sussex: Harvester Press.

Gilroy, D. P. (1982) "The Revolutions in English Philosophy and Philosophy of Education," *Educational Analysis*, 4(1): 75–92.

Glock, H.-J. (1996) *A Wittgenstein Dictionary*. Cambridge, Mass.: Blackwell.

Gould, S. J. (1981) *The Mismeasure of Man*. New York: Norton.

Greenberg, C. (1973) "Modernist Painting." In G. Battock (ed.), *The New Art*. New York: Dutton.

Gutman H. (1988) "Rousseau's Confessions: A Technology of the Self." In L. H. Martin, H. Gutman, & P. H. Hutton (eds.), *Technologies of the Self*, pp. 99–120. Amherst: University of Massachusetts Press.

Haack, R. (1976) "Philosophies of Education," *Philosophy*, 51: 159–76.

Haber, H. (1994) *Beyond Postmodern Politics: Lyotard, Rorty, Foucault*. New York: Routledge.

Hacker, P.M.S. (1996) *Wittgenstein's Place in Twentieth-Century Analytic Philosophy*. Oxford: Blackwell.

Hacker, P.M.S. (1990) *Wittgenstein: Meaning and Mind*. Oxford: Blackwell.

Hacker, P.M.S. (1986) *Insight and Illusion*. Oxford: Clarendon Press.

Haller, R. (1988) *Questions on Wittgenstein*. London: Routledge and Kegan Paul.

Haller, R. (1981) "Wittgenstein and Austrian Philosophy." In J. C. Nyiri (ed.), *Austrian Philosophy: Studies and Texts*. Munich: Philosophia Verlag.

Hargrove, E. (1980) "Wittgenstein, Bartley, and the Glöckel School Reform,"
    History of Philosophy, 17: 453–61.
Harré, R. & G. Gillett. (1994) *The Discursive Mind*. Thousand Oaks, Calif.: Sage.
Harris, K. (1988) "Dismantling a Deconstructionist History of Philosophy of
    Education," *Educational Philosophy and Theory*, 20(1): 50–58.
Harris, K. (1982) *Teachers and Classes: A Marxist Analysis*. London: Routledge and
    Kegan Paul.
Harris, K. (1980) "Philosophers of Education: Detached Spectators or Political
    Practitioners?" *Educational Philosophy and Theory*, 12(1): 19–36.
Harris, K. (1979) *Education and Knowledge*. London: Routledge and Kegan Paul.
Heal, J. (1995) "Wittgenstein and Dialogue." In T. Smiley (ed.), *Philosophical
    Dialogues: Plato, Hume, Wittgenstein*. Dawes Hicks Lectures on Philosophy,
    Proceedings of the British Academy 85. Oxford: Oxford University Press.
Heidegger, M. (1991) *Nietzsche*. Vol. 2: *The Eternal Recurrence of the Same*. Trans-
    lated by David Farrell Krell. San Francisco, Calif.: Harper.
Heidegger, M. (1961) *Nietzsche*, 2 vols. Pfullingen: Neske.
Heller, E. (1988) *The Importance of Nietzsche*. Chicago, Ill.: University of Chicago
    Press.
Hendley, S. (1995) "Putting Ourselves Up for Question: A Postmodern Critique of
    Richard Rorty's Postmodernist Bourgeois Liberalism," *The Journal of Value
    Inquiry*, 29: 241–253.
Hollinger, D. (1995) *Postethnic America: Beyond Multiculturalism*. New York: Basic
    Books.
Hume, D. (1964) *A Treatise of Human Nature*. Oxford: Clarendon Press.
Jameson, F. (1984). Foreword to J.-F. Lyotard's *The Postmodern Condition: A Report
    on Knowedge*, pp. vii–xxi. Translated by G. Bennington & B. Massumi.
    Manchester: Manchester University Press.
Janaway, C. (1994) *Schopenhauer*. Oxford: Oxford University Press.
Janaway, C. (1989) *Self and World in Schopenhauer's Philosophy*. Oxford: Clarendon
    Press.
Janik, A. (1989) *Style, Politics and the Future of Philosophy*. Dordrecht: Kluwer.
Janik, A. (1985) *Essays on Wittgenstein and Weininger*. Amsterdam: Rudopi.
Janik, A. (1981) "Wittgenstein: An Austrian Enigma." In J. C. Nyiri (ed.), *Austrian
    Philosophy: Studies and Texts*. Munich: Philosophia Verlag.
Janik, A. & S. Toulmin. (1973) *Wittgenstein's Vienna*. London: Weidenfield &
    Nicholson.
Jarman, D. (1993). "This is Not a Film of Ludwig Wittgenstein." In *Wittgenstein:
    The Terry Eagleton Script. The Derek Jarman Film*. London: British Film
    Institute.
Johnson, W. E. (1923) *Logic*. Cambridge: Cambridge University Press.
Jung, C. G. (1973) "Sigmund Freud in His Historical Setting." In F. Cioffi (ed.),
    Freud, pp. 49–56. London: MacMillan.
Kaminsky, J. (1993) *A New History of Educational Philosophy*. Westport, Conn.:
    Greenwood Press.
Kaminsky, J. (1988a) "*The First 600 Months . . .* Revisited: A Response to Harris,"
    Educational Philosophy and Theory, 20(1): 50, 59–62.
Kaminsky, J. (1988b) "Philosophy of Education in Australasia: A Definition and a
    History," *Educational Philosophy and Theory*, 20(1): 12–26.

Kaminsky, J. (1986) "The First 600 Months of Philosophy of Education 1935–1985: A Deconstructionist History," *Educational Philosophy and Theory*, 18(2): 42–47.

Kant, I. (1987) *Critique of Judgment*. Translated by W. S. Pluhar. Indianapolis: Hackett.

Kaufmann, W. (1974) *Nietzsche: Philosopher, Psychologist, Antichrist*, 4th ed. Princeton, N.J.: Princeton University Press.

Kenny, A. (1973) *Wittgenstein*. Harmondsworth: Penguin.

Kosuth, J. (1991) *Art After Philosophy and After: Collected Writings 1966–1990*. Cambridge, Mass.: MIT Press.

Lang, B. (1995) "The Style of Method: Repression and Representation in the Genealogy of Philosophy." In C. Van Eck, J. McAllister, & R. Van de Vall (eds.), *The Question of Style in Philosophy and the Arts*, pp. 18–36. Cambridge: Cambridge University Press.

Lang, B. (1990) *The Anatomy of Philosophical Style*. Oxford: Blackwell.

Lang, B. (ed.). (1980) *Philosophical Style*. Chicago, Ill.: Nelson-Hall.

Large, D. (1993) Translator's introduction to S. Kofman, *Nietzsche and Metaphor*. London: Athlone Press.

Law, J. D. (1989) "Reading with Wittgenstein and Derrida." In R. W. Dasenbrock, (ed.), *Redrawing the Lines: Analytic Philosophy, Deconstruction, and Literary Theory*, pp. 140–68. Minneapolis: University of Minnesota Press.

Leiber, J (1997) "On What Sort of Speech Act Wittgenstein's Investigations Is and Why It Matters," *Philosophical Forum*, 27(3) (Spring): 232–67.

Le Rider, J. (1993) *Modernity and Crises of Identity: Culture and Society in Fin-de-Siècle Vienna*. Translated by R. Morris. Oxford: Polity Press.

Le Rider, J. (1990) "Between Modernism and Postmodernism: The Viennese Identity Crisis." Translated by R. Manheim. In E. Timms & R. Robertson (eds.), *Vienna 1900: From Altenberg to Wittgenstein*. Edinburgh: Edinburgh University Press.

Levi, A. W. (1967) "Wittgenstein as Dialectician." In K. T. Fann (ed.), *Wittgenstein: The Man and His Philosophy*, pp. 366–79. New York: Dell.

Lilla, M. (ed.). (1994) *New French Thought: Political Philosophy*. Princeton, N.J.: Princeton University Press.

Locke, J. (1964) *An Essay Concerning Human Understanding*. Oxford: Clarendon Press.

Löwith, K. (1995) *Martin Heidegger and European Nihilism*. Translated by Gary Steiner. Edited by Richard Wolin. New York: Columbia University Press.

Lurie, Y. (1992) "Culture as a Human Form of Life: A Romantic Reading of Wittgenstein," *International Philosophical Quarterly*, 32(2): 193–204.

Lyotard, J.-F. (1994) *Lessons on the Analytic of the Sublime: Kant's Critique of Judgment, Sections 23-29*. Stanford, Calif.: Stanford University Press.

Lyotard, J.-F. (1993) "Wittgenstein 'After'," in *Political Writings*, pp. 19–22. Translated by B. Readings & K. Geiman. Minneapolis: University of Minnesota Press.

Lyotard, J.-F. (1992) *The Postmodern Explained to Children*. Sydney: Power Press.

Lyotard, J.-F. (1989a) "Analysing Speculative Discourse as Language-Game." In A. Benjamin (ed.), *The Lyotard Reader*, pp. 265–74. Oxford: Blackwell.

Lyotard, J.-F. (1989b) "Universal History and Cultural Differences." In A. Benjamin (ed.), *The Lyotard Reader*. Oxford: Blackwell.

Lyotard, J.-F. (1988) *The Differend: Phrases in Dispute*. Translated by George ven den Abeele. Minneapolis: University of Minnesota Press.

Lyotard, J.-F. (1984) *The Postmodern Condition: A Report on Knowledge*. Translated by G. Benninton & B. Massumi. Manchester: Manchester University Press.

Lyotard, J.-F. with J. L. Thébaud (1985) *Just Gaming*. Translated by W. Godzich. Minneapolis: University of Minnesota Press.

MacCabe, C. (1993) Preface to *Wittgenstein: The Terry Eagleton Script: The Derek Jarman Film*. Worcester, Mass.: Trinity Press.

Macey, D. (1993) *The Lives of Michel Foucault*. London: Hutchinson.

Macmillan, C.J.B. (1995) "How Not to Learn: Reflections on Wittgenstein and Learning." In P. Smeyers and J. D. Marshall (eds.), *Philosophy and Education: Accepting Wittgenstein's Challenge*, pp. 37–62. Dordrecht: Kluwer.

Macmillan, C.J.B. (1985) "Rational Teaching." *Teachers College Record*, 86, 411–22.

Magnus, B. & B. Higgins (eds.). (1996) *The Cambridge Companion to Nietzsche*. Cambridge: Cambridge University Press.

Malcolm, N. (1967) "A Symposium: Assessments of the Man and the Philosopher." In K. T. Fann (ed.), *Ludwig Wittgenstein: The Man and His Philosophy*. Sussex: Harvester Press.

Maloney, K. (1985) "Philosophy of Education: Definitions of the Field, 1942–1982," *Educational Studies*, 16(3): 235–58.

Mann, T. (1973) "Freud and the Future." In F. Cioffi (ed.), *Freud*, pp. 57–76. London: MacMillan.

Margolis, J. (1995) "A Recent Biopsy of Recent Analytic Philosophy," *The Philosophical Forum*, 26(3): 161–88.

Marshall, J. D. (1996) *Michel Foucault: Personal Autonomy and Education*. Dordrecht: Kluwer.

Marshall, J. D. (1995a) "Wittgenstein and Foucault: Resolving Philosophical Puzzles." In P. Smeyers & J. D. Marshall (eds.), *Philosophy and Education: Accepting Wittgenstein's Challenge*, pp. 205–20. Dordrecht: Kluwer.

Marshall, J. (1995b) "On What We May Hope: Rorty on Dewey and Foucault," *Studies in Philosophy and Education*, 13: 307–23.

Marshall, J. (1987) *Positivism or Pragmatism: Philosophy of Education in New Zealand*. Auckland: University of Auckland, New Zealand Association for Research in Education.

Marshall, J. (1985) "Wittgenstein on Rules: Implications for Authority and Discipline in Education," *Journal of Philosophy of Education*, 19(1): 3–11.

McCaffery, S. (1987) *Evoba: The Investigations Meditations, 1976–78*. Toronto: Coach House.

McCarty, L. P. & D. C. McCarty. (1995). "Wittgenstein on the Unreasonableness of Education: Connecting Teaching and Meaning." In P. Smeyers & J. D. Marshall (eds.), *Philosophy and Education: Accepting Wittgenstein's Challenge*. Dordrecht: Kluwer.

McGinn, M. (1997) *Wittgenstein and the Philosophical Investigations*. London: Routledge.

McGrath, W. (1974) *Dionysian Art and Populist Politics in Austria*. New Haven, Conn.: Yale University Press.

McGuinness, B. (1988) *Wittgenstein A Life: Young Ludwig 1889–1921*. London: Duckworth.

McGuinness, B. (ed.). (1982) *Wittgenstein and His Times*. Oxford: Blackwell.

Merleau-Ponty, M. (1962) *The Phenomenology of Perception*. London: Routledge and Kegan Paul.

Miller, G. (1996) *Psychology: the Science of Mental Life*. London: Pelican.

Miller, J. (1993) *The Passion of Michel Foucault*. New York: Simon and Schuster.

Monk, R. (1990) *Ludwig Wittgenstein: The Duty of Genius*. London: Vintage.

Moore, G. E. (1967) "Wittgenstein's Lectures in 1930–33." In K. T. Fann (ed.), *Ludwig Wittgenstein: The Man and His Philosophy*. Sussex: Harvester Press.

Murdoch, I. (1954) *Under the Net*. London: Chatto & Windus.

Nehamas, A. (1985) *Nietzsche: Life as Literature*. Cambridge, Mass.: Harvard University Press.

New Literary History, 19 (1988) Special Issue on Wittgenstein.

Nietzsche, F. (1996) *Human, All-Too-Human: A Book for Free Spirits*. Translated by R. J. Hollingdale. Cambridge: Cambridge University Press.

Nietzsche, F. (1992) *Ecce Home*. Translated by R. J. Hollingdale. Harmondsworth: Penguin.

Nietzsche, F. (1989) *Beyond Good and Evil: Prelude to a Philosophy of the Future*. Translated by W. Kaufmann. New York: Vintage Books.

Nietzsche, F. (1983) *Untimely Meditations*. Translated by R. J. Hollingdale. Cambridge: Cambridge University Press.

Nietzsche, F. (1979) *Philosophy and Truth: Selections from Nietzsche's Notebooks of the Early 1870s*. Edited and translated by D. Breazeale. London: Humanities Press.

Nietzsche, F. (1974) *The Gay Science*. Translated by W. Kaufmann. New York: Vintage Books.

Nietzsche, F. (1968) *The Will to Power*. Translated by W. Kaufmann & R. J. Hollingdale. Edited by W. Kaufmann. New York: Vintage Books.

Nietzsche, F. (1961) *Thus Spake Zarathustra: A Book for Everyone and Noone*. Translated by R. J. Hollingdale. Harmondsworth: Penguin.

Nietzsche, F. (1956) *The Birth of Tragedy and the Genealogy of Morals*. Translated by F. Golffing. Garden City, N.Y.: Anchor Books.

Norris, C. (1984) *The Deconstructive Turn: Essays in the Rhetoric of Philosophy*. New York: Routledge.

Nyiri, J. C. (1982) "Wittgenstein's Later Work in Relation to Conservativism." In B. McGuinness (ed.), *Wittgenstein and His Times*. Oxford: Blackwell.

Palmer, M. (1981) *Notes for Echo Lake*. San Francisco, Calif.: North Point Press.

Pascal, F. (1984) "A Personal Memoir." In Rush Rhees (ed.), *Recollections of Wittgenstein*. Oxford: Oxford University Press.

Patton, P. (1995) "Post-Structuralism and the Mabo Debate: Difference, Society and Justice." In M. Wilson & A. Yeatman (eds.), *Justice and Identity*. Wellington: Bridget Williams.

Perloff, M. (1996) *Wittgenstein's Ladder: Poetic Language and the Strangeness of the Ordinary*. Chicago, Ill.: University of Chicago Press.

Perloff, M. (1992) "Toward a Wittgensteinian Poetics," *Contemporary Literature*, 33(2): 191–213.

Peters, M. (1995a) "Introduction: Lyotard, Education, and the Postmodern Condition." In M. Peters (ed.), *Education and the Postmodern Condition*. Westport, Conn.: Bergin and Garvey.

Peters, M. (1995b) "Philosophy and Education: 'After' Wittgenstein." In P. Smeyers & J. D. Marshall (eds.), *Philosophy and Education: Accepting Wittgenstein's Challenge*. Dordrecht: Kluwer.

Peters, M. (1995c) "Radical Democracy, the Politics of Difference, and Education." In B. Kanpol & P. McLaren (eds.), *Critical Multiculturalism: Uncommon Voices in a Common Struggle*. Westport, Conn.: Bergin and Garvey.

Peters, M. (1994a) "Individualism and Community: Education and the Politics of Difference," *Discourse*, 14(2): 65–78.

Peters, M. (1994b) "Review of Jean-François Lyotard's *Political Writings, Surfaces*" (E-journal), *Folio* IV: 3–13.

Peters, M. (1992) "Performance and Accountability in 'Post-Industrial Society': The Crisis of British Universities," *Studies in Higher Education*, 17(2): 123–40.

Peters, M. (1989) "Techno-Science, Rationality and the University: Lyotard on the 'Postmodern Condition,'" *Educational Theory*, 39: 93–105.

Peters, M. (1984) *The Problem of Rationality: An Historicist Approach for Philosophy of Education*. Unpublished doctoral dissertation, University of Auckland.

Peters, M. & J. Marshall. (1996) *Individualism and Community: Education and Social Policy in the Postmodern Condition*. London: Falmer Press.

Peters, M. & J. Marshall. (1995) "After the Subject: A Response to Mackenzie," *Educational Philosophy and Theory*, 27(1): 41–54.

Phillips, D. C. (1994) "Philosophy of Education: Historical Overview." In T. Husen & T. Postlethwaite (eds.), *The International Encyclopedia of Education*, 2d ed. Oxford: Pergamon.

Prado, P. W. (1991) "The Necessity of Contingency: Remarks on Linkage," Translated by R. Bearsworth, *L'Esprit Créateur: Passages, Genres, Differends: Jean-François Lyotard*. R. L. Kauffmann, guest editor, 31(1): 90–106.

Putnam, H. (1995) *Pragmatism*. Oxford: Blackwell.

Quigley, A. (1988) "Wittgenstein's Philosophizing and Literary Theorizing," *New Literary History*, 2 (Winter): 210–37.

Rabinow, P. (ed.). (1997) *Michel Foucault: Ethics, Subjectivity, Truth*. New York: New Press.

Rawls, J. (1985) "Justice as Fairness: Political not Metaphysical," *Philosophy and Public Affairs*, 14: 251–73.

Rawls, J. (1980) "Kantian Constructivism in Moral Theory," *Journal of Philosophy*, 77(9): 515–77.

Readings, B. (1995a) "From Emancipation to Obligation: Sketch for a Heteronomous Politics of Education." In M. Peters (ed.), *Education and the Postmodern Condition*. Westport, Conn.: Bergin and Garvey.

Readings, B. (1995b) "The University without Culture?" *New Literary History*, 26(3): 465–92.

Readings, B. (1993a) "For a Heteronomous Cultural Politics: The University, Culture and the State," *The Oxford Literary Review*, 15: 163–200.

Readings, B. (1993b) "Foreword: The End of the Political." In J.-F. Lyotard, *Political Writings*. Translated by B. Readings & K. P. Geiman, pp. xiii-xxvi. Minneapolis: University of Minnesota Press.

Readings, B. (1992) "Pagans, Perverts or Primitives? Experimental Justice in the Empire of Capital." In A. Benjamin (ed.), *Judging Lyotard*. London: Routledge.

Rhees, R. (1967) "A Symposium: Assessments of the Man and the Philosopher." In

K. T. Fann (ed.), *Ludwig Wittgenstein: The Man and His Philosophy*. Sussex: Harvester Press.

Rhees, R. (ed.). (1984) *Recollections of Wittgenstein*. Oxford: Oxford University Press.

Rizvi, F. (1987) "Wittgenstein on Grammar and Analytic Philosophy of Education," *Educational Philosophy and Theory*, 19(2): 33–46.

Rorty, R. (1993) "Human Rights, Rationality, and Sentimentality," *Yale Review*, 83: 1–20.

Rorty, R. (1991a) *Objectivity, Relativism, and Truth: Philosophical Papers*, vol. 1. Cambridge: Cambridge University Press.

Rorty, R. (1991b) *Essays on Heidegger and Others: Philosophical Papers*, vol. 2. Cambridge: Cambridge University Press.

Rorty, R. (1990) "The Dangers of Over-Philosophication: Reply to Arcilla and Nicholson," *Educational Theory*, 40(1): 41–44.

Rorty, R. (1989) *Contingency, Irony and Solidarity*. Cambridge: Cambridge University Press.

Rorty, R. (1983) "Postmodern Bourgeois Liberalism," *Journal of Philosophy*, 80: 583–89.

Rorty, R. (1982) *Consequences of Pragmatism*, pp. 90–109. Brighton: Harvester Press.

Rorty, R. (1980) *Philosophy and the Mirror of Nature*. Oxford: Blackwell.

Rosen, S. (1962) *Nihilism: A Philosophical Essay*. New Haven, Conn.: Yale University Press.

Rousseau, J-J. (1925) *The Confessions: Translated from the French*. London: W. Glaisher.

Russell, B. (1967) *The Problems of Philosophy*. London: George Allen and Unwin.

Russell, B. (1946) *The History of Western Philosophy*. London: George Allen and Unwin.

Ryle, G. (1949) *The Concept of Mind*. London: Hutchinson.

Schopenhauer, A. (1973) *The World as Will and Representation*. Translated by J. Kemp. 3 vols. London: Kegan, French & Hall.

Schopenhauer, A. (1948) *The World as Will and Representation*. Translated by R. B. Haldane & J. Kemp. London: Routledge and Kegan Paul.

Schopenhauer, A. (1923) *The World as Will and Idea*. Translated by R. B. Haldane & J. Kemp. London: Kegan Trench & Paul.

Schorske, C. (1980) *Fin-de-Siècle Vienna: Politics and Culture*. New York: Alfred Knopf.

Schrift, A. (1996) "Nietzsche's French Legacy." In B. Magnus & K. Higgins (eds.), *The Cambridge Companion to Nietzsche*, pp. 323–55. Cambridge: Cambridge University Press.

Schrift, A. (1995) *Nietzsche's French Legacy: A Genealogy of Poststructuralism*. London: Routledge.

Shoemaker, S. (1963) *Self Knowledge and Self Identity*. Ithaca, N.Y.: Cornell University Press.

Silliman, R. (1986) *The Age of Huts*. New York: Roof.

Sluga, H. (1996a) "Ludwig Wittgenstein: Life and Work. An Introduction." In H. Sluga & D. G. Stern (eds.), *The Cambridge Companion to Wittgenstein*, pp. 1–33. Cambridge: Cambridge University Press.

Sluga, H. (1996b) "'Whose House is That?': Wittgenstein on the Self." In H. Sluga

& D. G. Stern (eds.), *The Cambridge Companion to Wittgenstein*, pp. 320–53. Cambridge: Cambridge University Press.

Smeyers, P. & J. D. Marshall (eds.). (1995) *Philosophy and Education: Accepting Wittgenstein's Challenge*. Dordrecht: Kluwer.

Smith, B. (ed.). (1994) *European Philosophy and the American Academy*. La Salle, Ill.: The Hegeler Institute.

Smith, B. (1978) "Wittgenstein and the Background of Austrian Philosophy." In E. Leinfellner, W. Leinfellner, H. Berghel, & A. Hubner (eds.), *Wittgenstein and His Influence on Contemporary Thought*. Vienna: Verlag Holder-Pichler-Tempsky.

Staten, H. (1984) *Wittgenstein and Derrida*. Lincoln: University of Nebraska Press.

Strawson, P. (1959) *Individuals: An Essay in Descriptive Metaphysics*. London: Methuen.

Tarski, A. (1946) *An Introduction to Logic*. Oxford: Oxford University Press.

Taubeneck, S. (1991) "Translator's Afterword: Walter Kaufman and After." In E. Behler, *Confrontations: Derrida, Heidegger, Nietzsche*. Translated by S. Taubeneck. Stanford, Calif.: Stanford University Press.

Taylor, C. (1989) *Sources of the Self: the Making of Modern Identity*. Cambridge, Mass.: Harvard University Press.

Tilghman, B. R. (1991) *Wittgenstein, Ethics and Aesthetics: The View from Eternity*. London: MacMillan.

Toulmin, S. (1969) "Ludwig Wittgenstein," *Encounter*, 32(1): 58–71.

Toynton, E. (1997) "The Wittgenstein Controversy," *The Atlantic Monthly*, June, pp. 28–41.

Tuck, B. (1983) "Education and Tests of Scholastic Ability: Is There a Baby in the Bath Water?" *New Zealand Journal of Educational Studies*, 18(2): 165–71.

Van Eck, C., J. McAllister, & R. Van de Vall (eds.). (1995) *The Question of Style in Philosophy and the Arts*. Cambridge: Cambridge University Press.

Wain, K. (1995) "Richard Rorty, Education and Politics," *Educational Theory*, 45(3): 395–409.

Waismann, F. (1965) *The Principles of Linguistic Philosophy*. London: Macmillan.

Waldrop, K. (1987) *Water Marks*. Toronto: Underwhich.

Waldrop, R. (1987) *The Reproduction of Profiles*. New York: New Directions.

Walker, J. (1984) "The Evolution of the APE: Analytic Philosophy of Education in Retrospect," *Access*, 3(1): 1–16.

Weiner, D. (1992) *Genius and Talent: Schopenhauer's Influence on Wittgenstein's Early Philosophy*. London: Associated University Presses.

Wijdeveld, P. (1994) *Ludwig Wittgenstein, Architect*. Cambridge, Mass.: MIT Press.

Williams, M. (1988) "Transcendence and Return: The Overcoming of Philosophy in Nietzsche and Wittgenstein," *International Philosophical Quarterly*, 38(4): 403–19.

Winch, P (1963) *The Idea of a Social Science and Its Relation to Philosophy*. London: Routledge and Kegan Paul.

Wittgenstein, L. (1988) *Wittgenstein's Lectures on Philosophical Psychology, 1946–47*. Edited by P. T. Geach. Hemel Hempstead: Harvester Wheatsheaf.

Wittgenstein, L. (1982) *Last Writings on the Philosophy of Psychology*. Edited by G. H. von Wright and Heikki Nyman. Oxford: Blackwell.

Wittgenstein, L. (1981) *Zettel*, 2d ed. Edited by G.E.M. Anscombe and R. Rhees. Oxford: Blackwell.

Wittgenstein, L. (1980a) *Culture and Value*, 2d ed. Edited by G. H. von Wright (in collaboration with Heikki Nyman). Translated by Peter Winch. Oxford: Blackwell.

Wittgenstein, L. (1980b) *Remarks on the Philosophy of Psychology*, vols. I and II. Edited by G. H. von Wright and Heikki Nyman. Chicago, Ill.: University of Chicago Press.

Wittgenstein, L. (1979) *Remarks on Frazer's Golden Bough*. Translated by A. C. Miles. Edited by R. Rhees. Retford: Brynmill.

Wittgenstein, L. (1975) *Philosophical Remarks*. Oxford: Blackwell.

Wittgenstein, L. (1973) "Conversations on Freud." In F. Cioffi (ed.), *Freud*, pp. 76–86. London: MacMillan.

Wittgenstein, L. (1971) *Tractatus Logico-Philosophicus*. Edited by D. F. Pears & B. F. McGuinness. London: Routledge & Kegan Paul.

Wittgenstein, L. (1969) *On Certainty*. Oxford: Blackwell.

Wittgenstein, L. (1967) *Lectures and Conversations on Aesthetics, Psychology and Religious Belief*. Edited by C. Barrett. Berkeley: University of California Press.

Wittgenstein, L. (1961) *Notebooks, 1914–1916*. Oxford: Blackwell.

Wittgenstein, L. (1958) *The Blue and the Brown Books*. Oxford: Blackwell.

Wittgenstein, L. (1953) *Philosophical Investigations*. Translated by G.E.M. Anscombe. Oxford: Blackwell.

Worth, S. (1997) "Wittgenstein's Musical Understanding," *British Journal of Aesthetics*, 37(2): 158–67.

Wright, G. H. von (1993) *The Tree of Knowledge and Other Essays*. Cologne: E. J. Brill.

Wright, G. H. von (1982) "Wittgenstein in Relation to his Times." In B. McGuinness (ed.), *Wittgenstein and His Times*. Oxford: Blackwell.

Wright, G. H. von (1969) "The Wittgenstein Papers," *The Philosophical Review*, 78: 483–503.

Yeatman, A. (1994) *Postmodern Revisionings of the Political*. New York: Routledge.

Yeatman, A. (1992) "Minorities and the Politics of Difference," *Political Theory Newsletter*, 4(1): 1–10.

Zukofsky, L. (1963) *Bottom: On Shakepeare*. Austin, Texas: The Ark Press.

Zwicky, J. (1992) *Lyric Philosophy*. Toronto: University of Toronto Press.

Zwicky, J. (1986) *Wittgenstein Elegies*. Toronto: Academic Printing and Publishing.

Index

ABOUT THE AUTHORS

Michael Peters is Senior Lecturer in Education at the University of Auckland.

James Marshall is Dean and Professor of Education, University of Auckland.

ISBN 0-89789-480-4

HARDCOVER BAR CODE